1000 Days Instant Pot Cookbook

Easy, Healthy and Fast Instant Pot Recipes with 1000 Days Meal Plan for Your Electric Pressure cooker

By Robert Randolph

Legal & Disclaimer

The information and contents herein are not designed to replace or take the place of any form of medical or professional advice and are not meant to replace the need for independent medical, financial, legal or other professional advice or services, as may be required. The content and information in this book have been provided for educational and entertainment purposes only.

The content and information in this book have been compiled from reliable sources and are accurate to the author's best knowledge, information, and belief. The author cannot guarantee this book's accuracy and validity and cannot be held liable for any errors and/or omissions. Further, changes will be periodically made to this book when needed. It is recommended that you consult with a health professional who is familiar with your personal medical history before using any of the suggested remedies, techniques, or information in this book.

Upon using the contents in this book, you agree to hold harmless the author from and against any damages, costs, and expenses, including any legal fees potentially resulting from the application of the information provided You agree to accept all risks associated with using the information presented inside this book.

Table of Content

Introduction

Nowadays, we never have enough time doing many things. We are always in a hurry to leave our office or finish our everyday work at home. Being at home or office, the time is always an asset in this modern lifestyle. We also cannot neglect the need for consuming wholesome foods as a well-balanced nutrition is very important to stay healthy.

Instant Pot takes care of both your everyday nutritional needs and time crunch by making food in minutes. You can imagine Instant Pot as a cooking robot, which makes delicious meals for you in minutes. Instant pot frees a lot of your time by doing almost all cooking work so that you can spend more time with your family.

The Instant Pot is a variation of the electric pressure cooker that enables you to prepare healthy and flavorful meals in a fraction of the time conventional cooking methods would take. A pressure cooker is a device that uses water or another cooking liquid inside a sealed vessel to cook food under pressure at a faster rate than it would cook normally. Electric pressure cooking turns tough, inexpensive cuts of meat into delectable dishes and it takes the guesswork out of preparing multi-serving meals like soups, stews, and more. You only need to add the ingredients and press a button!

This cookbook will make it an easy ride for you to cook your delicious breakfast, meat, poultry, seafood, vegetarian, soup, desserts, rice and pasta recipes. There are detailed instructions for every recipe that ensures your cooking is perfected. With this book, you will be able to prepare your meals and conveniently carry out other activities for the day.

Some of the core functional buttons

Depending on the model of the Pot that you are using, you will have the option to tinker with a multitude of different functions, controlled by a plethora of buttons.

If you are a new user, these buttons might seem a little bit confusing at first! Therefore, I have outlined the functions of the buttons that are typically found in the Pot.

- **Sauté:** You should go for this button if you want to sauté your vegetables or produces inside your inner pot while keeping the lid open. It is possible to adjust the level of brownness you desire by pressing the modify button as well. As a small tip here, you can very quickly push the Sauté Button followed by the Adjust Button two times to simmer your food.
- **Keep Warm/Cancel:** Using this button, you will be able to turn your pressure cooker off. Alternatively, you can use the adjust button to keep maintaining a warm temperature ranging from 145 degree Celsius (on average) to 167 (at more) degree Celsius depending on what you need.
- **Manual:** This is pretty much an all-rounder button which gives a higher level of flexibility to the user. Using this button followed by the + or – buttons, you will be able to set the exact duration of cooking time which you require.
- **Soup:** This mode will set the cooker to a high-pressure mode giving 30 minutes of cooking time (at normal); 40 minutes (at more); 20 minutes (at less)
- **Meat/Stew:** This mode will set the cooker to a high-pressure mode giving 35 minutes of cooking time (at normal); 45 minutes (at more); 20 minutes (at less)
- **Bean/Chili:** This mode will set the cooker to a high-pressure mode giving 30 minutes of cooking time (at normal); 40 minutes (at more); 25 minutes (at less)
- **Poultry:** This mode will set the cooker to a high-pressure mode giving 15 minutes of cooking time (at normal); 30 minutes (at more); 5 minutes (at less)
- **Rice:** This is a fully automated mode which cooks rice on low pressure. It will adjust the timer all by itself depending on the amount of water/rice present in the inner cooking pot.
- **Multi-Grain:** This mode will set the cooker to a high-pressure mode giving 40 minutes of cooking time (at normal); 45 minutes (at more); 20 minutes (at less)
- **Porridge:** This mode will set the cooker to a high-pressure mode giving 20 minutes of cooking time (at normal); 30 minutes (at more); 15 minutes (at less)
- **Steam:** This will set your pressure cooker to high pressure with 10 minutes cooking time at normal. 15 minutes cook time at more and 3 minutes cook time at less. It is advisable to use this mode with a steamer basket or rack for best results.
- **Slow Cooker:** This button will normally set the cooker at 4-hour mode. However, you change the temperature by keeping it at 190-201 degree Fahrenheit (at low); 194-205 degree Fahrenheit (at normal); 199-210 degree Fahrenheit (at high);
- **Pressure:** This button allows you to alter between high and low-pressure settings.

- **Yogurt:** This setting should be used when you are in the mood for making yogurt in individual pots or jars
- **Timer:** This button will allow you to either decrease or increase the time by using the timer button and pressing the + or – buttons.

The benefits of Instant pot

There are some fantastic advantages that you will enjoy while using your Instant Pot! Below are just some of the more notable ones.

- **Multi-functionality:** Let me start with the most obvious one first. Yes, the Instant Pot is an extremely versatile and multi-functional appliance! Just this one device is enough to replace your Slow Cooker, Rice Cooker, Steamer and even Sauté pan! This makes the Instant Pot a fantastic appliance for small kitchens or families.
- **Save time and energy:** Thanks to the pressure cooking process of the Instant Pot, foods are cooked almost 70% faster than other traditional cooking methods. This process uses much less water while cooking! Since the exterior of the pot is insulated, it dramatically minimizes energy and heat loss, which altogether contributes to the lower energy required to boil, cook or steam meals!
- **Preserves nutrients:** Unlike the other cooking methods out there, the Instant Pot requires to have enough water to produce the steam required for the meal, instead of requiring the produces to be submerged completely. This helps to prevent the vitamins and all essential minerals from the vegetables and other produce to wash away.
- **Kills of harmful Micro-Organism:** Pressure cooker allows the internal temperature to reach extremely high levels where most bacteria and viruses are killed off. Even the tough to kill ones that are found on raw maize or corns.
- **Sturdy construction:** The Stainless Steel construction of the Instant Pot makes it a device that is built to last! And unlike plastic, the stainless steel does not compromise the flavor of the dishes as well, so you can rest easy knowing that all the flavor profiles of your meal will be preserved correctly.
- **Mess-free and clean cooking:** The Instant Pot has a perfect sealing mechanism that prevents any unpleasant odor or debris from escaping and spreading across your kitchen. Thus, you can enjoy a clean and whole hearty cooking experience with the pot.

- **Sturdy construction:** The Stainless Steel construction of the Instant Pot makes it a device that is built to last! And unlike plastic, the stainless steel does not compromise the flavor of the dishes as well, so you can rest easy knowing that all the flavor profiles of your meal will be preserved correctly.

Keep the IP Clean

Throughout everyday usage, your pot is bound to accumulate some dirt and debris! To ensure that it stays good for a long time, cleaning this debris is important!

Therefore, I have provided a brief outline of you can keep your pot clean and enhance its longevity.

The IP can be a little bit tricky to clean unless you take your time and learn how to do it properly. You should give the pot a quick wipe-down before you use it for the first time and wash any removable parts. After cooking, the cleaning process is very different – here's what you should do:

1. Unplug the Instant Pot before you do any cleaning.
2. Remove the inner pot and clean it well with hot water and dish soap.
3. Take the silicone sealing ring out of the lid and clean it well – wipe down the inside of the lid with a damp cloth as well just to remove condensation.
4. Check the small parts in the plastic housing such as the steam release valve and the anti-block shield for food particles.
5. Wipe down the inside of the inner housing with a damp cloth to remove condensation and any sticky residue left behind by spills.
6. Use a damp cloth to wipe around the edges of the inner housing, getting into all of the recesses where liquid and food particles could collect.
7. Let everything air dry and then reassemble the Instant Pot for storage.

Cleaning your Instant Pot shouldn't take you very long, so make sure you take the time to do it after each use – this is the best way to keep your Instant Pot clean and in good repair for as long as possible. If the stainless-steel inner pot becomes discolored over time, you can renew the finish by wiping it with vinegar.

Instant Pot Breakfast Recipes

INSTANT POT BREAKFAST RECIPES

1. Wild West Style Omelet Quiche

(Servings:4, Cooking Time: 10 minutes)

Ingredients:

- 6 large eggs, well beaten
- 8 ounces Canadian Bacon, chopped
- 1/2 cup half and half
- 1/8 teaspoon salt
- 1/8 teaspoon ground black pepper
- 1/2 to 3/4 cup diced peppers, red, green and/or orange
- 3-4 organic spring onions, sliced in thin coins, reserving tops for garnish
- 3/4 cup shredded cheese

Directions for Cooking:

1. Lightly grease with cooking spray a soufflé dish that fits inside the Instant Pot.
2. Add 1 ½ cups of water in pot and place trivet.
3. In mixing bowl, whisk well eggs and milk. Season with pepper and salt.
4. In prepared soufflé dish, evenly spread bacon, peppers, and cheese.
5. Pour egg mixture over bacon mixture and mix well.
6. Cover top of dish with foil and place on a trivet.
7. Close Instant Pot, press manual, choose high pressure, and set time to 10 minutes.
8. Once done cooking, do a quick pressure release (QPR).
9. Carefully remove dish out of the Instant Pot, remove foil, and garnish with green onions.
10. Serve and enjoy.

Nutrition information:
Calories per serving: 365; Carbohydrates: 6.0g; Protein: 29.0g; Fat: 24.0g; Sugar: 2.0g; Sodium: 1151mg

---

2. Mini Frittata from Leftover Meat

(Servings:4, Cooking Time: 5 minutes)

Ingredients:

- 5 eggs
- ½ cup almond milk
- ¼ tsp salt
- ¼ tsp pepper
- 2 ½ tbsp shredded cheddar cheese
- 1 cup diced leftover meat
- 2 tbsp green onions, sliced

Directions for Cooking:

1. Lightly grease with cooking spray a soufflé dish that fits inside the Instant Pot.
2. Add 1 ½ cups of water in pot and place trivet.
3. In mixing bowl, whisk well eggs and milk. Season with pepper and salt.
4. In prepared soufflé dish, evenly spread bacon, peppers, and cheese.
5. Pour egg mixture over bacon mixture and mix well.
6. Cover top of dish with foil and place on a trivet.
7. Close Instant Pot, press manual, choose high pressure, and set time to 10 minutes.
8. Once done cooking, do a quick pressure release (QPR).
9. Carefully remove dish out of the Instant Pot, remove foil, and garnish with green onions.
10. Serve and enjoy.

Nutrition information:
Calories per serving: 168; Carbohydrates: 3.7g; Protein: 17.8g; Fat: 8.6g; Sugar: 3.1g; Sodium: 292.5mg

---

3. No-Crust Quiche with Spinach & Tomato

(Servings: 6, Cooking Time:30 minutes)

Ingredients:

- 12 large eggs
- 3 cups fresh baby spinach, roughly chopped
- 1 cup diced seeded tomato
- 3 large green onions, sliced
- 4 tomato slices for topping the quiche
- 1/2 cup milk
- 1/2 teaspoon salt
- 1/4 teaspoon fresh ground black pepper
- 1/4 cup shredded Parmesan cheese

Directions for Cooking:

1. Lightly grease with cooking spray a 1.5-quart round baking dish that fits in your Instant Pot.
2. Add 1 ½ cup of water in pot and place trivet.
3. Meanwhile, in a large mixing bowl whisk eggs. Stir in milk, salt, and pepper. Whisk thoroughly.
4. Evenly spread in layers in a prepared dish the tomato, spinach, and then green onions. Pour egg mixture over the veggies. Add the tomato slice for topping on top of the eggs, carefully. Sprinkle with cheese
5. Cover dish with foil, place on a trivet inside the pot.
6. Cover Instant Pot, press manual button, choose high pressure, and set time to 20 minutes.
7. Allow for 10-minutes natural pressure release and then do a quick release.
8. Remove from pot, serve and enjoy.

Nutrition information:

Calories per serving: 233; Carbohydrates: 14.1g; Protein: 18.4g; Fat: 11.9g; Sugar: 6.1g; Sodium: 482mg

---

4. Breakfast Egg Casserole Mexican Style

(Servings: 8, Cooking Time:26 minutes)

Ingredients:

- 8 large eggs, well-beaten
- 1-pound mild ground sausage
- 1/2 large red onion, chopped
- 1 red bell pepper, chopped
- 1 can black beans, rinsed
- 1/2 cup green onions
- 1/2 cup flour
- 1 cup Cotija cheese
- 1 cup mozzarella cheese
- sour cream, cilantro to garnish (optional)

Directions for Cooking:

1. Press the sauté button on Instant Pot and wait for it to get hot.
2. Once hot, add onion and sausage. Sauté for 6 minutes or until sausage is cooked. Press the cancel button.
3. Transfer cooked sausage into a round casserole dish that fits inside your Instant Pot and evenly spread. Add cheeses, beans and chopped veggies on top of sausage in an even layer.
4. Add 1 ½ cups of water in Instant Pot and place trivet.

---

5. Meanwhile, in a large bowl, whisk eggs. Add flour and whisk until thoroughly combined. Pour into dish. Cover dish with foil and place in pot.
6. Close Instant Pot, press pressure cook button, choose high settings and set time to 20 minutes.
7. Once done cooking, do a QPR.
8. Remove dish, slice into suggested servings, and enjoy.

Nutrition information:
Calories per serving: 334; Carbohydrates: 14.9g; Protein: 25.2g; Fat: 18.9g; Sugar: 1.7g; Sodium: 675.7mg

---

5. Peppers, Cheese & Sausage Frittata

(Servings: 3, Cooking Time:15 minutes)

Ingredients:

- ¼ cup cheddar cheese, shredded
- ¼ tsp salt
- ¼ tsp white pepper
- ½ cup bell pepper, chopped
- ½ tsp Italian seasoning
- 1 ½ tsp heavy cream
- 1 cup Italian sausage, cooked
- 4 eggs

Directions for Cooking:

1. Lightly grease a 7-inch round pan with cooking spray. Add 1 ½ cups of water in Instant Pot and place trivet.
2. In a medium bowl whisk well salt, white pepper, Italian seasoning, heavy cream, and eggs.
3. In prepared pan, evenly spread in layers the sausage, bell pepper, and then followed by the cheese.
4. Pour in egg mixture. Cover pan with foil and place on a trivet.
5. Close Instant Pot, press manual button, choose high settings, and set time to 15 minutes.
6. Once done cooking, do a QPR.
7. Serve and enjoy.

Nutrition information:
Calories per serving: 237; Carbohydrates: 2.9g; Protein: 15.6g; Fat: 17.8g; Sugar: 1.0g; Sodium: 717mg

---

6. Decadent Eggs in Ramekins

(Servings:3, Cooking Time:2 minutes)

Ingredients:

- 1 Tablespoon chives
- 3 eggs
- 3 Tablespoons cream
- 3 tsp Butter, room temp
- sea salt and freshly ground pepper

Directions for Cooking:

1. Ready 3 pieces of ramekins and add a teaspoon of butter in each one. With a pastry brush, brush insides of the ramekin with the butter.
2. Add a tablespoon of cream in each ramekin.
3. Crack an egg in each of the ramekin. Season eggs with pepper and salt. And then evenly divide chives on each of the egg.
4. Close Instant Pot, press pressure cook button, choose low settings, and set time to 2 minutes.
5. Once done cooking, do a QPR.
6. Serve and enjoy.

Nutrition information:

Calories per serving: 116; Carbohydrates: 0.9g; Protein: 6.1g; Fat: 9.7g; Sugar: 0.7g; Sodium: 141.3mg

---

7. Hash Brown and Egg Casserole

(Servings: 4, Cooking Time: 30 minutes)

Ingredients:

- 6 eggs
- 2 cups frozen hash browns
- ¼ cup unsweetened almond milk
- ½ cup fat free shredded cheddar cheese
- 1 tsp sea salt
- 1 tsp pepper
- ½ onion, diced
- ½ green pepper, diced
- ½ red pepper, diced
- 1 stalk green onion, sliced for garnish

Directions for Cooking:

1. Press sauté button and lightly grease pot with cooking spray. When hot, sauté red pepper, green pepper, and onion for 6 minutes or until tender.
2. Press cancel button and stir in frozen hash browns and stir to separate and soften.
3. In a round casserole dish that fits inside the Instant pot, lightly grease insides with cooking spray.
4. Transfer hash brown mixture into prepared dish.
5. Add 1 ½ cup of water in Instant Pot and place trivet.
6. In a mixing bowl, whisk well pepper, salt, ¼ cup cheese, milk, and eggs. Pour over hash brown mixture. Stir a bit
7. Close Instant Pot, press manual button, choose high settings, and set time to 20 minutes.
8. Once done cooking, do a QPR.
9. Remove dish inside pot and sprinkle remaining cheese and the green onions.
10. Serve and enjoy.

Nutrition information:

Calories per serving: 267; Carbohydrates: 32.9g; Protein: 17.4g; Fat: 7.6g; Sugar: 9.4g; Sodium: 970mg

---

8. Walnut-Banana Oats

(Servings: 4, Cooking Time:10 minutes)

Ingredients:

- ¼ tsp cinnamon for topping
- ½ medium banana, peeled and sliced for topping
- 1 cup steel cut oats
- 1 cup unsweetened almond milk
- 1 large ripe banana, mashed
- 1 teaspoon ground cinnamon
- 1 teaspoon pure vanilla extract
- 1/4 cup walnuts, chopped fine
- 2 cups water
- 2 tablespoons chia seeds
- 2 tablespoons ground flaxseeds (flaxseed meal)
- 2 tablespoons pure maple syrup
- 2 tbsp chopped and toasted walnuts for topping
- Pinch salt

Directions for Cooking:

1. Except for topping ingredients, add everything in Instant Pot and mix well.
2. Close Instant Pot, press manual button, choose high settings, and set time to 10 minutes.
3. Once done cooking, do a QPR.
4. Scoop into bowls and top with cinnamon, banana, and walnuts.
5. Serve and enjoy.

Nutrition information:

Calories per serving: 332; Carbohydrates: 48.0g; Protein: 11.0g; Fat: 12.0g; Sugar: 11.0g; Sodium: 78mg

---

9. Creamy Oats with Peaches

(Servings: 8, Cooking Time:10 minutes)

Ingredients:

- 1 teaspoon ground cinnamon
- 1 teaspoon salt
- 1/3 cup sugar
- 3 1/2 cups milk
- 3 1/2 cups water
- 4 cups Old Fashioned Oats
- 4 peaches

Nutrition information:

Calories per serving: 243; Carbohydrates: 51.9g; Protein: 12.2g; Fat: 7.0g; Sugar: 20.6g; Sodium: 341mg

Directions for Cooking:

1. Wash and peel peaches. Chop and then save ¼ for topping.
2. In Instant pot, add all ingredients as well as ¾ of the chopped peaches. Mix well.
3. Close Instant Pot, press multigrain button, and set time to 6 minutes.
4. Once done cooking, do a QPR.
5. Serve and enjoy with a sprinkling of fresh chopped peaches.

---

10. Eggs & Ham Brekky Casserole

(Servings: 6, Cooking Time:25 minutes)

Ingredients:

- 1 cup chopped ham
- 1 cup milk
- 1 teaspoon pepper
- 1 teaspoon salt
- 1/2 onion, diced
- 10 large eggs
- 2 cups shredded cheddar cheese
- 4 medium red potatoes, peeled and diced

Directions for Cooking:

1. Add 2 cups of water in Instant Pot and place trivet.
2. In a heatproof bowl that fits inside your Instant Pot, crack eggs and whisk well.
3. Season with pepper and salt. Whisk thoroughly.
4. Stir in onions, ham, cheese, and milk. Mix thoroughly.
5. Add diced potatoes. Cover bowl securely with foil. Place bowl inside pot.
6. Close Instant Pot, press manual button, choose high settings, and set time to 25 minutes.
7. Once done cooking, do a QPR.
8. Serve and enjoy.

Nutrition information:

Calories per serving: 452; Carbohydrates: 28.0g; Protein: 28.3g; Fat: 25.1g; Sugar: 4.7g; Sodium: 1083mg

---

11. Smoked Salmon & Eggs in Ramekins

(Servings: 4, Cooking Time:4minutes)

Ingredients:

- 4 Eggs
- 4 Slices of smoked salmon
- 4 Slices of Cheese
- 4 Fresh Basil leaves for garnish
- Olive Oil

Directions for Cooking:

1. Add a cup of water in Instant pot and place trivet on bottom.
2. Lightly grease each ramekin with a drop of olive oil each. Spread well.
3. Crack an egg in each ramekin. Place a slice of cheese, a slice of smoked salmon, and basil leaf in each ramekin.
4. Cover each ramekin with foil and place on trivet.
5. Close Instant Pot, press manual button, choose low settings, and set time to 4 minutes.
6. Once done cooking, do a QPR.
7. Serve and enjoy.

Nutrition information:

Calories per serving: 241; Carbohydrates: 0.9g; Protein: 17.5g; Fat: 18.3g; Sugar: 0.2g; Sodium: 433mg

---

12. Nutty-Strawberry Oatmeal

(Servings: 2, Cooking Time:10 minutes)

Ingredients:

- 1 ½ Cups Water
- 1 cup chopped strawberries, for topping
- 1 Cup Freshly Squeezed Orange Juice
- 1 Cup Steel Cut Oats
- 1 Tbsp Chopped Dried Apricots
- 1 Tbsp Dried Cranberries
- 1 Tbsp Raisins
- 1/4 Tsp Ground Cinnamon
- 1/8 Tsp Salt
- 2 Tbsp Butter
- 2 Tbsp Pure Maple Syrup
- 3 Tbsp Chopped Pecans, for topping

Directions for Cooking:

1. Lightly grease Instant Pot insert with cooking spray and then add all ingredients except for topping ingredients. Mix well.
2. Close Instant Pot, press manual button, choose high settings, and set time to 10 minutes.
3. Once done cooking, do a QPR.
4. Transfer to two bowl and evenly divide toppings on bowl.
5. Serve and enjoy.

Nutrition information:

Calories per serving: 422; Carbohydrates: 72.4g; Protein: 11.1g; Fat: 19.2g; Sugar: 30.0g; Sodium: 270mg

---

13. Vanilla-Latte Oatmeal

(Servings: 4, Cooking Time:20 minutes)

Ingredients:

- 1 cup milk
- 1 cup steel cut oats
- 1 teaspoon espresso powder
- 1/4 teaspoon salt
- 2 1/2 cups water
- 2 tablespoons sugar
- 2 teaspoon vanilla extract
- finely grated chocolate
- freshly whipped cream

Directions for Cooking:

1. Mix well salt, espresso powder, sugar, oats, milk, and water in Instant Pot.
2. Close Instant Pot, press manual button, choose high settings, and set time to 10 minutes.
3. Once done cooking, do a natural release for 10-minutes and then do a QPR.
4. Uncover pot and stir in vanilla extract. Spoon into 4 bowls.
5. Garnish with grated chocolate and whipped cream.
6. Serve and enjoy.

Nutrition information:

Calories per serving: 166; Carbohydrates: 27.6g; Protein: 6.5g; Fat: 6.8g; Sugar: 11.4g; Sodium: 177mg

---

14. Egg & Bacon Breakfast Risotto

(Servings: 2, Cooking Time:10 minutes)

Ingredients:

- 1 1/2 cups Chicken Broth
- 1/3 cup Chopped Onion
- 2 Eggs
- 2 tablespoons Grated Parmesan Cheese
- 3 slices Center Cut Bacon, chopped
- 3 tablespoons Dry White Wine
- 3/4 cup Arborio Rice
- Chives, for garnish
- Salt and Pepper, to taste

Directions for Cooking:

1. Press sauté button and cook bacon to a crisp, around 8 minutes.
2. Stir in onion and sauté for 3 minutes.
3. Add rice and sauté for a minute.
4. Pour in wine and deglaze pot. Continue sautéing until wine is completely absorbed by rice, around 5 minutes.
5. Stir in chicken broth.
6. Close Instant Pot, press manual button, choose high settings, and set time to 5 minutes.
7. Meanwhile, cook eggs sunny side up to desired doneness.
8. Once done cooking, do a QPR. Stir in pepper, salt, and parmesan.
9. Divide risotto evenly on to two plates, add egg, and sprinkle with chives.
10. Serve and enjoy.

Nutrition information:

Calories per serving: 292; Carbohydrates: 16.0g; Protein: 12.0g; Fat: 11.0g; Sugar: 1.0g; Sodium: 959mg

---

15. Breakfast Quinoa with Cinnamon-Apple

(Servings: 4, Cooking Time:9 minutes)

Ingredients:

- 1 ½ cups Water
- 1 Chopped Apple
- 1 cup Quinoa
- 1/2 tsp Vanilla
- 1/4 cup Gentle Sweet
- 1/4 tsp Mineral Salt
- 2 tbsp Cinnamon

Directions for Cooking:

1. Mix all ingredients in Instant Pot. Thoroughly combine.
2. Close Instant Pot, press manual button, choose high settings, and set time to 1 minute.
3. Once done cooking, do a natural release for 8-minutes and then do a QPR.
4. Serve and enjoy.

Nutrition information:

Calories per serving: 192; Carbohydrates: 37.0g; Protein: 6.3g; Fat: 2.7g; Sugar: 4.9g; Sodium: 150mg

---

16. Strawberry-Cheesecake Flavored Breakfast Quinoa

(Servings: 3, Cooking Time:11 minutes)

Ingredients:

- 1 1/2 cups uncooked quinoa
- 1/2 cup vanilla Greek yogurt
- 1/2 teaspoon vanilla
- 1/4 teaspoon sweet spice mix such as pumpkin pie spice
- 2 1/4 cups water
- 2 cups sliced strawberries
- 2 tablespoons raw honey

Directions for Cooking:

1. In Instant Pot, add all ingredients and mix well.
2. Close Instant Pot, press manual button, choose high settings, and set time to 1 minute.
3. Once done cooking, do a natural release for 10-minutes and then do a QPR.
4. Serve and enjoy.

Nutrition information:
Calories per serving: 405; Carbohydrates: 74.7g; Protein: 15.6g; Fat: 5.6g; Sugar: 17.2g; Sodium: 20mg

---

17. Cornmeal-Porridge Jamaican Style Brekky

(Servings: 4, Cooking Time:20 minutes)

Ingredients:

- 1 cup milk
- 1 cup yellow cornmeal, fine
- 1 tsp vanilla extract
- 1/2 cup sweetened condensed milk
- 1/2 tsp nutmeg, ground
- 2 sticks cinnamon
- 3 pimento berries
- 4 cups water separated

Directions for Cooking:

1. In a mixing bowl, whisk well cornmeal and a cup of water.
2. Add 1 cup milk and 3 cups water in Instant Pot. Stir in cornmeal mixture and mix well.
3. Stir in cinnamon sticks, berries, vanilla, and nutmeg. Mix well.
4. Close Instant Pot, press porridge button, and set time to 6 minutes.
5. Once done cooking, do a natural release all the way until it's safe to open pot.
6. Stir in condensed milk.
7. Serve and enjoy.

Nutrition information:
Calories per serving: 225; Carbohydrates: 42.0g; Protein: 6.1g; Fat: 3.9g; Sugar: 5.8g; Sodium: 49mg

---

18. Tradit onal Pancake in Instant Pot

(Servings:2, Cooking Time:40minutes)

Ingredients:

- 1 1/2 cups milk
- 2 1/2 tsp baking powder
- 2 cups all-purpose flour
- 2 large eggs
- 2 tbsp granulated white sugar
- 2 tbsp maple syrup

Directions for Cooking:

1. In a large mixing bowl, whisk well eggs. Stir in milk, baking powder, and white sugar. Mix thoroughly.
2. Add flour and mix well.
3. Grease Instant Pot with cooking spray on bottom and sides. Pour batter in pot.
4. Close Instant Pot, press multigrain button, choose low settings, do not seal vent and set time to 40 minutes.
5. Once done cooking, open pot no need to release pressure as there is no pressure.
6. Serve with syrup and enjoy.

Nutrition information:
Calories per serving: 746.5; Carbohydrates: 133.5g; Protein: 25.0g; Fat: 12.0g; Sugar: 34.4g; Sodium: 160.5mg

---

19. Oat, Millet & Apple Porridge

(Servings: 8, Cooking Time:35 minutes)

Ingredients:

- ¼ tsp salt
- ½ cup rolled oats
- ½ tsp ground ginger
- ¾ cup dry millet
- 1 tsp ground cinnamon
- 2 apples, cored and diced
- 3 cups water

Directions for Cooking:

1. Press brown button on Instant Pot and toast millet until fragrant and browned, around 5 to 10 minutes. Stir frequently.
2. Press cancel button and stir in remaining ingredients and mix well.
3. Close Instant Pot, press manual button, choose high settings, and set time to 10 minutes.
4. Once done cooking, allow for a 15-minute natural release and then do a QPR.
5. Serve and enjoy.

Nutrition information:
Calories per serving: 110; Carbohydrates: 24.2g; Protein: 3.2g; Fat: 1.3g; Sugar: 24.2g; Sodium: 76mg

---

20. Hashed Sweet Potato

(Servings: 4, Cooking Time:20 minutes)

Ingredients:

- 6 large eggs
- 1 tablespoon Italian seasoning
- 1⁄2 teaspoon sea salt
- 1⁄2 teaspoon ground black pepper
- 1⁄2-pound ground pork sausage
- 1 large sweet potato, peeled and cubed
- 1 small onion, peeled and diced
- 2 cloves garlic, minced
- 1 medium green bell pepper, seeded and diced
- 2 cups water

Nutrition information:

Calories per serving: 546; Carbohydrates: 17.7g; Protein: 32.2g; Fat: 38.2g; Sugar: 7.2g; Sodium: 1785mg

Directions for Cooking:

1. Lightly grease a heatproof glass dish that fits in Instant Pot.
2. Add water in pot and place trivet.
3. In a medium mixing bowl, whisk well eggs. Season with pepper, salt, and Italian seasoning.
4. Add bell pepper, garlic, onion, sweet potato, and sausage in bowl and mix well. Pour into prepared dish and cover dish with foil.
5. Place on trivet in Pot.
6. Close Instant Pot, press manual button, choose high settings, and set time to 10 minutes.
7. Once done cooking, allow for a 10-minute natural release and then do a QPR.
8. Serve and enjoy.

---

21. Cheesy Eggs in Instant Pot

(Servings: 4, Cooking Time:35 minutes)

Ingredients:

- ¼ cup milk
- ½ teaspoon pepper
- 1 cup shredded cheddar cheese, divided
- 1 stalk green onions, chopped
- 1 teaspoon kosher salt
- 2 cups frozen hash browns
- 6 eggs
- 6 slices bacon, chopped

Directions for Cooking:

1. Press sauté button and sauté bacon until crisped, around 8 minutes.
2. Stir in hash browns and cook for 2 to 3 minutes until no longer frozen.
3. With cooking spray, lightly grease a round heatproof dish that fits in Instant Pot and whisk eggs. Stir in pepper, salt, ½ cup shredded cheese, and milk. Mix well.
4. Add hash browns and bacon into dish and mix well. Cover dish with foil.
5. Press cancel button, add water, and place trivet on bottom of Instant Pot. Add dish on top of trivet.
6. Close Instant Pot, press pressure cook button, choose high settings, and set time to 20 minutes.
7. Once done cooking, do a QPR.
8. Remove foil, sprinkle remaining cheese and chopped onions. Cover and let it sit in pot for 5 minutes more.
9. Serve and enjoy.

Nutrition information:

Calories per serving: 567; Carbohydrates: 22.4g; Protein: 28.0g; Fat: 40.5g; Sugar: 2.5g; Sodium: 1131mg

---

22. Simple Breakfast Hash

(Servings: 4, Cooking Time:10 minutes)

Ingredients:

- 6 eggs, beaten
- 1 cup shredded American cheese
- 1 cup chopped breakfast ham
- 6 small potatoes, shredded

Directions for Cooking:

1. Lightly grease Instant Pot insert with cooking spray and press sauté button.
2. In processor, shred the potatoes and squeeze excess moisture. Add to pot and cook for 5 minutes.
3. Whisk eggs in a bowl.
4. Shred meat and cheese in processor.
5. After 5 minutes, breakup the shredded potatoes and add ¼ cup of water. Mix well.
6. Stir in shredded meat and cheese. Mix well.
7. Pour in whisked eggs and lightly combine.
8. Close Instant Pot, press manual button, choose high settings, and set time to 1 minute.
9. Once done cooking, do a QPR.
10. Serve and enjoy.

Nutrition information:

Calories per serving: 502; Carbohydrates: 43.8g; Protein: 25.8g; Fat: 24.8g; Sugar: 6.3g; Sodium: 1864mg

---

23. Spinach, Sausage & Sweet Potato Hash

(Servings: 4, Cooking Time:15 minutes)

Ingredients:

- 3 large sweet potatoes, peeled and cut into 1-inch pieces
- 1 tablespoon olive oil, divided
- 1/2 teaspoon Kosher salt
- 12-ounces Italian sausage
- 1 small onion, finely chopped
- 2 cloves garlic, minced or put through a garlic press
- 1/2 teaspoon ground sage
- 1/4 teaspoon freshly ground black pepper
- 11-ounces baby spinach
- 4 large eggs, optional

Directions for Cooking:

1. Preheat oven to 425°F.

On a baking pan, add sweet potatoes and drizzle with salt and 2 teaspoons olive oil. Roast for 30 minutes or until fork tender.

1. Midway through roasting time, stir potatoes. Once done roasting turn oven off and set sweet potatoes aside.
2. Press sauté button on Instant Pot and heat remaining oil. Sauté sausage and crumble to pieces. Cook for 10 minutes.
3. Stir in pepper, sage, garlic, and onions. Sauté for three minutes.
4. Stir in spinach and sweet potatoes and mix well.
5. Break eggs on top of the mixture.
6. Close Instant Pot, press pressure cook button, choose low settings, and set time to 1 minute.
7. Once done cooking, do a QPR.
8. Serve and enjoy.

Nutrition information:

Calories per serving: 508; Carbohydrates: 29.2g; Protein: 26.6g; Fat: 31.9g; Sugar: 8.5g; Sodium: 1481mg

---

24. Potato Hash with Spanish Chorizo

(Servings: 4, Cooking Time: 22 minutes)

Ingredients:

- Instant Pot Duo
- 6 Large Potatoes, peeled and diced
- 1 Chorizo Sausage, sliced thinly
- 4 Slices Bacon, sliced into chunks
- 1 Large Onion, peeled and diced
- 250 g Soft Cheese
- 2 Tbsp Greek Yoghurt
- 1 Tbsp Garlic Puree
- 1 Tbsp Olive Oil
- 200 ml Vegetable Stock
- 3 Tbsp Rosemary
- 3 Tbsp Basil
- Salt & Pepper

Directions for Cooking:

1. Press sauté button and heat oil. Once hot sauté garlic and onion for 5 minutes or until onions are soft.
2. Add sausages and potatoes. Sauté for 3 minutes.
3. Add bacon and cook for 3 minutes more.
4. Stir in stock. Mix well and then press cancel button.
5. Close Instant Pot, press soup button, and set time to 10 minutes.
6. Meanwhile, in a large shallow dish mix well soft cheese, yoghurt, rosemary, basil, salt, and pepper. Mix well and set aside.
7. Once done cooking, do a QPR.
8. Transfer pot mixture into shallow dish and toss well to coat in cheese mixture.
9. Serve and enjoy.

Nutrition information:
Calories per serving: 749; Carbohydrates: 99.0g; Protein: 29.6g; Fat: 27.2g; Sugar: 7.2g; Sodium: 1936mg

---

25. French Toast Casserole

(Servings: 4, Cooking Time: 30 minutes)

Ingredients:

- 3 eggs
- 1 cup half and half cream
- 1/2 cup milk
- 1 Tbsp cinnamon
- 1 tsp vanilla
- 1 loaf of French bread cubed
- 1/2 cup blueberries - more to taste

Directions for Cooking:

1. Lightly spray Instant Pot insert with cooking spray the bottom and sides.
2. Add cubed bread evenly in pot.
3. In a bowl, whisk well eggs, vanilla, cinnamon, cream, and milk. Pour over bread cubes. Toss bread to coat and soak up the milk mixture.
4. Sprinkle blueberries on top.
5. Close Instant Pot, press pressure cook button, choose high settings, and set time to 15 minutes.
6. Once done cooking, allow a complete natural release.
7. Serve and enjoy.

Nutrition information:
Calories per serving: 159; Carbohydrates: 20.0g; Protein: 7.7g; Fat: 5.4g; Sugar: 11.8g; Sodium: 162mg

---

26. Ranch Dressed Bacon-Potato Brekky

(Servings: 6, Cooking Time: 15 minutes)

Ingredients:

- 2-lb red potatoes, scrubbed and cubed into 1-inch pieces
- 3 bacon strips, sliced into small pieces
- 2 tsp dried parsley
- 1 tsp kosher salt
- 1 tsp garlic powder
- 4-oz. cheddar cheese, shredded
- 1/3 cup Ranch dressing, liquid

Directions for Cooking:

1. Press sauté button and cook bacon until crisped, around 8 minutes.
2. Stir in salt, garlic powder, dried parsley, and potatoes.
3. Stir in 1/3 cup of water.
4. Close Instant Pot, press manual button, choose high settings, and set time to 7 minutes.
5. Once done cooking, do a QPR.
6. Stir in cheese and ranch dressing.
7. Serve and enjoy.

Nutrition information:

Calories per serving: 248; Carbohydrates: 33.5g; Protein: 7.3g; Fat: 9.7g; Sugar: 3.2g; Sodium: 820mg

---

27. Banana Bread for Breakfast

(Servings: 16, Cooking Time:1 hour and 10 minutes)

Ingredients:

- 1 1/2 cup Steel Cut Oats
- 2 Ripe Bananas
- 4 Eggs
- 1/3 cup Raw Organic Honey
- 2 tsp Pure Vanilla Extract
- 1/2 tsp Baking Soda
- Pinch of Sea Salt
- 1/4 cup +2 tbsp Mini Dairy Free Chocolate Chips

Directions for Cooking:

1. In a high-powered blender, add all ingredients except for chocolate chips and blend on high until smooth and creamy.
2. Fold in ¼ cup chocolate chips and pour batter in a 7-inch springform pan. Sprinkle remaining chocolate chips on top of batter, Cover securely with foil.
3. Add 1 ½ cups of water in Instant pot and place trivet. Place pan on top of trivet.
4. Close Instant Pot, press manual button, choose high settings, and set time to 60 minutes.
5. Once done cooking, do a natural release for 10-minutes and then do a QPR.
6. Serve and enjoy.

Nutrition information:

Calories per serving: 87; Carbohydrates: 16.7g; Protein: 3.2g; Fat: 2.5g; Sugar: 9.0g; Sodium: 66mg

---

28. Slow Cooked Cinnamon-Oats

(Servings: 8, Cooking Time:4 hours)

Ingredients:

- 2 cups steel-cut oats
- 8 cups milk
- 2 tbsp butter
- 1/2 cup light brown sugar
- 1 tsp vanilla extract
- 1/2 tsp ground cinnamon
- 1/4 tsp ground nutmeg
- 1 tsp salt
- 1-pint blueberries
- 1 1/2 cups chopped, roasted, and unsalted cashews

Directions for Cooking:

1. Except for cashews and blueberries, mix all ingredients in Instant Pot insert.
2. Close Instant Pot, press slow cook button, keep vent on release position, choose low settings, and set time to 4 hours.
3. Once done cooking, open pot and stir in blueberries and cashews.
4. Serve and enjoy.

Nutrition information:
Calories per serving: 543; Carbohydrates: 53.0g; Protein: 19.0g; Fat: 31.0g; Sugar: 28.0g; Sodium: 405mg

---

29. Another Breakfast Burrito Recipe

(Servings:10, Cooking Time:35 minutes)

Ingredients:

- 1 cup diced ham (or protein of your choice)
- 1/2 cup shredded cheese
- 1/4 cup milk
- 1/4 cup sour cream
- 1/4 tsp salt
- 1/8 tsp pepper
- 10 tortilla
- 2 1/2 cups O'Brien hash browns
- 6 eggs

Directions for Cooking:

1. Add a cup of water in Instant pot and place trivet.
2. Lightly grease a heatproof dish that fits inside Instant Pot and evenly spread ham, followed by hash brown.
3. Whisk well salt, pepper, shredded cheese, sour cream, milk and eggs in a medium bowl. Pour over hash browns. Cover dish with foil securely.
4. Place dish on trivet in Instant Pot.
5. Close Instant Pot, press manual button, choose high settings, and set time to 25 minutes.
6. Once done cooking, do a QPR.
7. Remove foil and stir egg mixture.
8. Close Instant Pot, press manual button, choose high settings, and set time to 10 minutes.
9. Once done cooking, do a QPR.
10. Evenly divide into 6 tortilla and roll like a burrito.
11. Serve and enjoy.

Nutrition information:
Calories per serving: 276; Carbohydrates: 23.0g; Protein: 11.5g; Fat: 15.8g; Sugar: 1.1g; Sodium: 314mg

---

30. Easy-Cheesy Breakfast Egg Casserole

(Servings:4, Cooking Time:22 minutes)

Ingredients:

- 8 eggs
- Pinch salt and pepper
- 1/2 cup sausage, diced
- 1/2 cup diced bell pepper
- 1/2 cup diced onion
- 1/4 cup milk
- 1/4 tsp garlic salt
- 1/2-3/4 c cheese

Directions for Cooking:

1. Grease well a pan that fits inside your Instant Pot. As 1 ½ cups water in Instant Pot insert and place trivet.
2. Evenly spread layer sausage, bell pepper, onion, and cheese.
3. In a bowl whisk well eggs, salt and pepper. Stir in milk and then pour over sausage.
4. Cover top of dish securely with foil and place on trivet inside the Instant Pot.
5. Close Instant Pot, press pressure cook button, choose high settings, and set time to 12 minutes.
6. Once done cooking, do a natural release for 10 minutes and then do a QPR.
7. Serve and enjoy.

Nutrition information:
Calories per serving: 343; Carbohydrates: 12.0g; Protein: 20.0g; Fat: 23.0g; Sugar: 2.0g; Sodium: 474mg

---

31. Broccoli and Egg Casserole

(Servings: 6, Cooking Time:4 hours)

Ingredients:

- 1/2 teaspoon salt
- 1/3 cup all-purpose flour
- 1/4 cup butter, melted
- 2 cups shredded cheddar cheese
- 3 cups cottage cheese
- 3 cups frozen, chopped broccoli, thawed and drained
- 3 tablespoons finely chopped onion
- 6 eggs, lightly beaten
- Additional shredded cheddar cheese, optional

Directions for Cooking:

1. Lightly grease bottom and sides of Instant Pot Insert.
2. Evenly layer and spread broccoli and chopped onion in insert.
3. In a bowl, whisk eggs, melted butter, and salt. Stir in cottage cheese, cheddar cheese, and flour. Pour over broccoli.
4. Close Instant Pot, press slow cook button, choose high settings, and set time to 1 hour.
5. Once done, open pot and stir.
6. Close Instant Pot, press slow cook button, choose low settings and set time to 3 hours.
7. Once done cooking, open pot, serve and enjoy.

Nutrition information:
Calories per serving: 435; Carbohydrates: 13.0g; Protein: 29.0g; Fat: 30.0g; Sugar: 4.0g; Sodium: 730mg

---

32. Scotch Eggs in Pressure Cooker

(Servings: 4, Cooking Time: 25minutes)

Ingredients:

- 4 large eggs
- 1-lb country style ground sausage
- 1 tablespoon vegetable oil

Directions for Cooking:

1. Add a cup of water in Instant Pot, place eggs in a steamer basket and place inside pot.
2. Close Instant Pot, press pressure cook button, choose high settings, and set time to 6 minutes.
3. Once done cooking, do a 6-minute natural release and then do a QPR.
4. Remove eggs and place in an ice water bath. When cool enough to handle, peel eggs.
5. Evenly divide ground sausage into four parts. Use one part of sausage to cover one peeled egg. Repeat process to remaining eggs.
6. Discard water in Instant Pot. Press sauté button and once all water has evaporated, add vegetable oil. Sauté Scotch eggs for two minutes on fours ides. Transfer Scotch Eggs to a plate.
7. Add a cup of water in Instant Pot and place trivet. Place Scotch Eggs on trivet.
8. Close Instant Pot, press pressure cook button, choose high settings, and set time to six minutes.
9. Once done cooking, do a QPR.
10. Serve and enjoy.

Nutrition information:

Calories per serving: 491; Carbohydrates: 5.2g; Protein: 28.0g; Fat: 39.1g; Sugar: 1.2g; Sodium: 1440mg

---

33. Buckwheat Porridge in Instant Pot

(Servings: 4, Cooking Time:26 minutes)

Ingredients:

- 1 cup raw buckwheat groats
- 3 cups rice milk
- 1 banana sliced
- 1/4 cup raisins
- 1 tsp ground cinnamon
- 1/2 tsp vanilla

Directions for Cooking:

1. Rinse groats and place inside Instant Pot insert.
2. Stir in vanilla, cinnamon, raisins, banana, and milk.
3. Close Instant Pot, press pressure cook button, choose high settings, and set time to 6 minutes.
4. Once done cooking, do a 20-minute natural release and then do a QPR.
5. Serve and enjoy.

Nutrition information:

Calories per serving: 281; Carbohydrates: 53.3g; Protein: 9.4g; Fat: 3.5g; Sugar: 11.7g; Sodium: 547mg

---

34. Maple-Cranberry Oatmeal

(Servings: 9, Cooking Time:5 hours)

Ingredients:

- 8 cups water
- 2 cups steel-cut oats
- 2/3 cup dried cranberries, chopped
- 1/2 cup maple syrup
- 1 tbsp cinnamon
- 1/2 tsp salt
- 3 cups slivered almonds, toasted

Directions for Cooking:

1. Except for the almonds, mix all ingredients in Instant Pot.
2. Close Instant Pot, press slow cook button, choose low settings, and set time to 5 hours.
3. Once done cooking, open pot and stir in almonds.
4. Serve and enjoy.

Nutrition information:
Calories per serving: 287; Carbohydrates: 35.4g; Protein: 10.1g; Fat: 16.8g; Sugar: 14.5g; Sodium: 137mg

---

35. Pepper, Ham & Broccoli Frittata

(Servings: 4, Cooking Time:30 minutes)

Ingredients:

- 8 ounces ham cubed
- 1 cup sweet peppers sliced
- 2 cups frozen broccoli
- 4 eggs
- 1 cup half and half
- 1 cup shredded cheddar cheese
- 1 tsp salt
- 2 teaspoons ground pepper

Directions for Cooking:

1. Grease well a heatproof dish that fits inside your Instant Pot, add 2 cups of water in Instant Pot followed by a trivet.
2. Evenly spread and layer sweet peppers, cubed ham, and broccoli.
3. Whisk well pepper, salt, half and half, and eggs. Stir in cheese. Pour over mixture in Instant Pot. Cover securely with foil and place on trivet in Instant Pot.
4. Close Instant Pot, press pressure cook button, choose high settings, and set time to 20 minutes.
5. Once done cooking, do a 10-minute natural release and then do a QPR.
6. Remove dish from pot and flip on a plate after letting it cool for at least 10 minutes.
7. Serve and enjoy.

Nutrition information:
Calories per serving: 373; Carbohydrates: 14.4g; Protein: 29.7g; Fat: 22.3g; Sugar: 6.8g; Sodium: 1670mg

---

36. Carrot Cake Flavored Oatmeal

(Servings: 8, Cooking Time:20 minutes)

Ingredients:

- 4-1/2 cups water
- 1 can (20 ounces) crushed pineapple, undrained
- 2 cups shredded carrots
- 1 cup steel-cut oats
- 1 cup raisins
- 2 teaspoons ground cinnamon
- 1 teaspoon pumpkin pie spice

Directions for Cooking:

1. Grease Instant Pot insert.
2. Add all ingredients in pot and mix well.
3. Close Instant Pot, press manual button, choose high settings, and set time to 10 minutes.
4. Once done cooking, do a 10-minute natural release and then do a QPR.
5. Serve and enjoy.

Nutrition information:

Calories per serving: 91; Carbohydrates: 23.1g; Protein: 2.7g; Fat: 0.9g; Sugar: 13.3g; Sodium: 22mg

---

37. Cheese and Bacon Quiche

(Servings: 6, Cooking Time:4 hours)

Ingredients:

- 1 box refrigerated pie crusts
- 2 cups shredded Monterrey Jack cheese
- 1 cup cooked bacon
- 6 eggs
- 1 cup milk
- 1/4 teaspoon salt
- 1/4 teaspoon freshly ground pepper

Directions for Cooking:

1. Grease Instant Pot insert on bottom and sides. Press pie crust on bottom and up to 2-inches up on the sides of the pot. Overlap seams by ¼-inch.
2. Close Instant Pot, press slow cook button, choose high settings, and set time to 1 hour and 30 minutes.
3. Meanwhile, whisk eggs, milk, salt and pepper. And set aside
4. Once done cooking, open pot, pour in egg mixture, and top with cheese.
5. Close Instant Pot, press slow cook button, choose low settings and set time to 2 hours and 30 minutes.
6. Once done cooking, open pot.
7. Serve and enjoy.

Nutrition information:

Calories per serving: 524; Carbohydrates: 22.0g; Protein: 25.0g; Fat: 37.0g; Sugar: 2.0g; Sodium: 912mg

---

38. 6-Ingredient Breakfast Granola

(Servings: 4, Cooking Time:2 hours and 30 minutes)

Ingredients:

- 1 ½ cups old-fashioned oats
- 2 cups crisp brown rice cereal
- 2 large egg whites, room temperature
- ¼ cup honey
- ¼ cup chopped cashews
- ¼ cup pecan halves

Directions for Cooking:

1. Line a rimmed baking pan with foil and coat lightly with cooking spray you Instant Pot insert.
2. Toss well to mix in a large bowl the oats and rice cereal.
3. In another bowl, whisk well eggs. Stir in honey and mix well. Pour over bowl of cashews and mix well using a spatula. Transfer to Instant Pot.
4. Close Instant Pot, press slow cook button, do not seal vent, choose high settings, and set time to 2 hours and 30 minutes.
5. Once done cooking, open pot, and spread on prepared pan.
6. Once cooled completely, mix in cashews and pecan halves. Toss well to coat.
7. Serve and enjoy.

Nutrition information:

Calories per serving: 361; Carbohydrates: 69.3g; Protein: 12.4g; Fat: 11.0g; Sugar: 19.0g; Sodium: 33mg

---

39. Simple Cinnamon French Toast

(Servings: 6, Cooking Time:2 hours and 30 minutes)

Ingredients:

- 1 loaf of crusty bread, cut into 1inch cubes
- 1/3 cup golden raisins
- 4 eggs
- 2 cups milk
- 1/4 cup pure maple syrup
- 1 teaspoon vanilla extract
- 1 teaspoon ground cinnamon

Directions for Cooking:

1. Grease well Instant Pot insert on bottom and sides.
2. Evenly spread sliced bread in Pot.
3. Sprinkle raisins over the bread.
4. Whisk well cinnamon, vanilla, maple syrup, milk, and eggs in a medium bowl.
5. Pour mixture over the bread in Pot.
6. With a fork, press down on the bread to soak the liquid.
7. Close Instant Pot, press slow cook button, choose high settings, and set time to 2 hours and 30 minutes.
8. Once done cooking, open pot.
9. Serve and enjoy.

Nutrition information:

Calories per serving: 323; Carbohydrates: 51.0g; Protein: 13.0g; Fat: 7.0g; Sugar: 21.0g; Sodium: 403mg

---

40. Coconut-Rice Pudding in Instant Pot

(Servings: 5, Cooking Time:4 hours and 30 minutes)

Ingredients:

- 1 cup brown basmati rice
- 3 cups milk
- 1 13.5-ounce can light coconut milk
- 1/4 cup pure maple syrup
- 1 teaspoon vanilla extract
- 1/2 cup raisins

Directions for Cooking:

1. Place rice on a sieve and wash. Drain water completely and place rice in Instant Pot.
2. Stir in vanilla extract, maple syrup, coconut milk, and milk. Mix well.
3. Close Instant Pot, press slow cook button, choose low settings, and set time to 4 hours and 30 minutes.
4. Once done cooking, open pot and stir in raisins.
5. Serve and enjoy.

Nutrition information:

Calories per serving: 373; Carbohydrates: 59.0g; Protein: 8.0g; Fat: 11.0g; Sugar: 27.0g; Sodium: 85mg

---

41. An Extra-Ordinary Breakfast Casserole

(Servings: 12, Cooking Time: 8 hours)

Ingredients:

- 1 package (30 ounces) frozen shredded hash brown potatoes
- 1-pound Jones No Sugar Pork Sausage Roll, cooked and drained
- 1 medium onion, chopped
- 1 can (4 ounces) chopped green chilies
- 1-1/2 cups shredded cheddar cheese
- 12 large eggs
- 1 cup 2% milk
- 1/2 teaspoon salt
- 1/2 teaspoon pepper

Directions for Cooking:

1. Grease well the sides and bottom of Instant Pot and evenly spread in layers half of the potato, onion, chilies, and then followed by cheese. Repeat layering for the remaining half of the ingredients.
2. Whisk well pepper, salt, milk, and eggs in a large bowl. Pour into pot of potatoes.
3. Close Instant Pot, press slow cook button, choose low settings, and set time to 8 hours.
4. Once done cooking, do a QPR.
5. Serve and enjoy.

Nutrition information:

Calories per serving: 397; Carbohydrates: 23.6g; Protein: 17.7g; Fat: 26.4g; Sugar: 2.3g; Sodium: 578mg

---

42. Cornbread for Breakfast

(Servings: 8, Cooking Time:2 hours)

Ingredients:

- 2 tablespoons unsalted butter
- 1 1/2 cup cornmeal
- 1 1/2 cup all-purpose flour
- 2 tablespoons sugar
- 1 tablespoon baking powder
- 1 teaspoon kosher salt
- 1 teaspoon chili power
- 2 cups buttermilk
- 2 large eggs

Directions for Cooking:

1. Press sauté button and melt butter in Instant Pot. Once melted, press cancel and coat sides and bottom of Instant pot with the melted butter.
2. In a bowl whisk well, eggs and buttermilk. Stir in salt, chili powder, and baking powder and mix thoroughly.
3. Whisk in sugar, flour, and cornmeal. Mix thoroughly and then pour into greased pot.
4. Close Instant Pot, press slow cook button, choose high settings, and set time to 2 hours.
5. Once done cooking, open pot.
6. Serve and enjoy.

Nutrition information:

Calories per serving: 275; Carbohydrates: 48.0g; Protein: 8.0g; Fat: 5.0g; Sugar: 7.0; Sodium: 315mg

---

43. Delicata and Apple Porridge

(Servings: 3, Cooking Time:20 minutes)

Ingredients:

- 4 small or 2 large apples unpeeled, flesh cut from the cores
- 1 delicata squash washed and whole
- 1/2 cup bone broth with little fat, or water instead
- 3 Tablespoons slippery elm
- 3 Tablespoons gelatin
- 2 Tablespoons maple syrup
- 1/2 teaspoon cinnamon
- 1/8 teaspoon cloves
- 1/8 teaspoon ginger
- pinch sea salt

Directions for Cooking:

1. Place delicata squash and apple chunks in Instant Pot. Add bone broth, cinnamon, cloves, ginger, and salt.
2. Close Instant Pot, press manual button, choose high settings, and set time to 8 minutes.
3. Once done cooking, allow for a 10-minute natural release and then do a QPR.
4. Remove squash and let it cool enough to handle. Slice in half, scoop and discard.
5. Transfer pot content in a blender and scoop out squash meat and add to blender. Add maple syrup, gelatin, and slippery elm in blender and blend until smooth and creamy.
6. Serve and enjoy either hot or cold.

Nutrition information:

Calories per serving: 228; Carbohydrates: 59.0g; Protein: 2.0g; Fat: 0.7g; Sugar: 46.6g; Sodium: 71mg

44. Ham, Tomatoes, and Spinach Frittata

(Servings: 8, Cooking Time:5 hours)

Ingredients:

- 8 eggs, beaten
- 2 cloves garlic
- 2 cups spinach, chopped
- 1 cup ham, diced
- 1 small onion, chopped
- ½ cup canned coconut milk
- 1 teaspoon coconut oil
- 1 teaspoon sea salt
- ½ teaspoon pepper

Directions for Cooking:

1. Press sauté button and heat coconut oil in Instant Pot.
2. Once hot stir in garlic and onion and sauté for 5 minutes.
3. Stir in ham and cook while you whisk pepper, salt, coconut milk, and eggs in a medium bowl. Press cancel button.
4. Stir in spinach and sauté for a minute. Pour egg mixture and mix well.
5. Close Instant Pot, press slow cook button, choose low settings, and set time to 5 hours.
6. Once done cooking, open pot.
7. Serve and enjoy.

Nutrition information:

Calories per serving: 152; Carbohydrates: 3.0g; Protein: 11.0g; Fat: 11.0g; Sugar: 0.6g; Sodium: 364mg

---

45. Breakfast Fajita Casserole

(Servings: 2, Cooking Time:10 minutes)

Ingredients:

- 1/2 cup onion (sliced)
- 1 1/2 cup sliced bell peppers (green, red, and orange)
- 1 tbsp olive oil
- 4 eggs
- A sprinkle of salt and pepper
- For optional garnish: cilantro, avocado, and limes
- 2 whole wheat bread, toasted

Directions for Cooking:

1. Press sauté and heat olive oil.
2. Sauté bell peppers, onions, and garlic for 5 minutes. Press cancel button.
3. Transfer veggies into a heatproof dish that fits inside Instant pot and crack eggs on top. Securely cover dish with foil.
4. Add a cup of water in Instant Pot, place trivet, and place casserole dish on trivet.
5. Close Instant Pot, press pressure cook button, choose high settings, and set time to 2 minutes.
6. Once done cooking, do a QPR.
7. Serve and enjoy with sliced limes, cilantro, avocados and toasted bread.

Nutrition information:

Calories per serving: 478; Carbohydrates: 49.1g; Protein: 19.8g; Fat: 24.4g; Sugar: 6.4g; Sodium: 418mg

---

46. Slow Cooked Oats the Irish Way

(Servings: 8, Cooking Time:3 hours)

Ingredients:

- Cooking spray
- 4 cups vanilla soy milk
- 1 ¾ cups steel-cut oats
- ½ cup dried cherries or raisins
- ½ cup plus 3 tablespoons pure maple syrup
- ½ teaspoon salt
- ¼ teaspoon ground allspice
- 4 cups water, plus more as needed
- ½ cup blueberries, for garnish
- 1/3 cup chopped pecans, for garnish

Directions for Cooking:

1. Grease Instant Pot insert on sides and bottom with cooking spray.
2. In pot, add and thoroughly mix oats, cherries, salt, allspice, ½ cup maple syrup, and water.
3. Close Instant Pot, press slow cook button, choose high settings, and set time to 3 hours.
4. Once done cooking, open pot and stir in remaining maple syrup, pecans, and blueberries.
5. Serve and enjoy.

Nutrition information:

Calories per serving: 231; Carbohydrates: 45.1g; Protein: 7.4g; Fat: 6.3g; Sugar: 26.8g; Sodium: 210mg

---

47. Meat Lovers No-Crust Quiche

(Servings: 4, Cooking Time: 40 minutes)

Ingredients:

- 6 large eggs, well beaten
- 1/2 cup milk
- 1/4 teaspoon salt
- 1/8 teaspoon ground black pepper
- 4 slices bacon, cooked and crumbled
- 1 cup cooked ground sausage
- 1/2 cup diced ham
- 2 large green onions, chopped
- 1 cup shredded cheese

Directions for Cooking:

1. Lightly grease a soufflé dish that fits inside your Instant Pot.
2. Add a cup of water and trivet in pot.
3. Whisk well pepper, salt, milk and eggs in a large mixing bowl.
4. In prepared soufflé dish, evenly spread bacon, sausage, ham, cheese, and green onions. Pour egg mixture over and cover securely with foil. Place on top of trivet in pot.
5. Close Instant Pot, press pressure cook button, choose high settings, and set time to 30 minutes.
6. Once done cooking, do a 10-minute natural release and then do a QPR.
7. Serve and enjoy.

Nutrition information:

Calories per serving: 460; Carbohydrates: 10.0g; Protein: 29.5g; Fat: 33.4g; Sugar: 5.4g; Sodium: 784mg

---

48. Quiche the Mexican Way

(Servings: 8, Cooking Time:4 hours)

Ingredients:

- 4 green onions, chopped
- Refrigerated pie crust
- 6 eggs, whisked
- 1 cup salsa
- 1/4 teaspoon freshly ground pepper
- 1/4 teaspoon chili powder
- 2 cups shredded cheddar cheese
- 1 cup cooked cannellini beans
- 1 refrigerated pie crust

Directions for Cooking:

1. Grease bottom and sides of Instant Pot and press pie crust halves in bottom and overlap seams by at least ¼-inch.
2. Close Instant Pot, press slow cook button, choose high settings, and set time to 1 hour and 30 minutes.
3. Once done cooking, open pot.
4. Spread beans and onions evenly on top of crust. Pour salsa on top.
5. In a bowl, whisk eggs and pour over salsa. Gently toss around.
6. Top with chili powder and cheese.
7. Close Instant Pot, press slow cook button, choose low settings, and time for 2 hours and 30 minutes.
8. Open pot, serve and enjoy.

Nutrition information:

Calories per serving: 436; Carbohydrates: 26.4g; Protein: 17.3g; Fat: 29.3g; Sugar: 3.4g; Sodium: 788mg

---

49. Zucchini-Choco Breakfast Cake

(Servings:12, Cooking Time:25 minutes)

Ingredients:

- 2 organic or pastured eggs
- 3/4 cup evaporated cane juice
- 1/2 cup coconut oil
- 2 teaspoons vanilla extract
- 1 tablespoon butter melted
- 3 tablespoons cocoa powder
- 1 cup sprouted einkorn flour learn how to sprout your grains
- 1/2 teaspoon baking soda
- 1/4 teaspoon sea salt
- 3/4 teaspoon ground cinnamon
- 1 cups zucchini or squash grated
- 1/3 cup chocolate chips
- 1 cup water

Directions for Cooking:

1. In blender, blend vanilla extract, coconut oil, sweetener, and eggs.
2. Add melted butter and cocoa. Blend well.
3. Add cinnamon, sea salt, baking soda, and flour. Blend well.
4. Remove blender from stand and fold in chocolate chips and grated zucchini.
5. Grease a baking dish that fits inside the Instant Pot and pour in batter. Cover top securely with foil.
6. Add a cup of water in Instant pot, place a trivet, and put dish with batter on top of trivet.
7. Close Instant Pot, press pressure cook button, choose low settings, and set time to 10 minutes.
8. Once done cooking, do a 15-minute natural release and then do a QPR.
9. Serve and enjoy.

Nutrition information:

Calories per serving: 163; Carbohydrates: 12.7g; Protein: 2.51g; Fat: 11.8g; Sugar: 3.2g; Sodium: 122mg

---

50. Creamy potato Hash Breakfast Casserole

(Servings: 8, Cooking Time: 3 hours)

Ingredients:

- 6 potatoes, shredded
- 1 can cream of chicken soup
- 1 stick butter, melted
- 1/2 cup chopped onion
- 2 cups grated Cheddar cheese

Directions for Cooking:

1. Lightly grease sides and bottom of Instant Pot.
2. Add potatoes in pot and season with pepper and salt.
3. Mix well melted butter, cream of chicken soup, and onions in a bowl. Pour over potatoes.
4. Sprinkle cheese on top.
5. Close Instant Pot, press slow cook button, choose low settings, and set time to 3 hours.
6. Once done cooking, open pot.
7. Serve and enjoy.

Nutrition information:

Calories per serving: 379; Carbohydrates: 32.0g; Protein: 11.0g; Fat: 23.0g; Sugar: 2.0g; Sodium: 451mg

---

51. Nutella-Raspberry Breakfast Porridge

(Servings: 6, Cooking Time: 17 minutes)

Ingredients:

- 1 sliver butter (or 1/2 tsp of your favorite oil if you're vegan)
- 1 cup quinoa
- 1 can coconut milk
- 1/3 cup milk of your choice
- 1 tbsp cocoa powder the darkest you can find
- 1/2 tsp hazelnut extract
- 1-2 tbsp maple syrup depending on your preferred level of sweetness
- 1 ½ cups raspberry

Directions for Cooking:

1. Press sauté button and melt butter. Once melted add quinoa and sauté until toasted, around 10 minutes.
2. Add the remaining ingredients except for the raspberry and mix well.
3. Press cancel button.
4. Close Instant Pot, press manual button, choose high settings, and set time to 2 minutes.
5. Once done cooking, do a 5-minute natural release and then do a QPR.
6. Serve and enjoy with ¼ cup of raspberry per serving.

Nutrition information:

Calories per serving: 249; Carbohydrates: 23.0g; Protein: 5.0g; Fat: 15.0g; Sugar: 2.0g; Sodium: 16mg

---

Instant Pot Meat Recipes

52. Instant Pot Pork Carnitas

(Servings: 12, Cooking time: 90 minutes)

Ingredients:

- 6 pounds pork butt roast
- 1 ½ tablespoons salt
- 1 tablespoon dried oregano
- 2 teaspoons ground cumin
- 1 teaspoon black pepper
- ½ teaspoon chili powder
- ½ teaspoon ground paprika
- 2 tablespoons olive oil
- 1 cup orange juice
- ¼ cup water
- 1 onion, chopped
- 4 cloves of garlic, minced

Directions for Cooking:

1. Season the pork butt roast with salt, oregano, cumin, black pepper, chili powder, and paprika. Allow to marinate in the fridge for at least 3 hours.
2. Press the Sauté button on the Instant Pot and heat the oil. Place the pork butt roast and allow to sear on all sides for 5 minutes.
3. Add the rest of the ingredients.
4. Close Instant Pot, press Manual button, choose high settings, and set time to 90 minutes.
5. Once done cooking, do a QPR.
6. Remove meat from the pressure cooker and shred the meat.
7. Serve with sauce and enjoy.

Nutrition information:

Calories per serving:190; Carbohydrates: 2.4g; Protein: 11.8g; Fat: 14.5g; Sugar: 0.5g; Sodium: 471mg

---

53. Instant Korean Ribs

(Servings: 4, Cooking time: 35 minutes)

Ingredients:

- 2 pounds baby back ribs
- 1 Asian pear, peeled and grated
- 1 bulb garlic, minced
- 1 onion, minced
- ½ teaspoon grated garlic
- 1 teaspoon ground black pepper
- ½ cup soy sauce
- 2 tablespoons honey
- 2 tablespoons brown sugar
- 2 tablespoons rice vinegar
- 2 tablespoons sesame oil

Directions for Cooking:

1. Place all ingredients in the Instant Pot and mix all ingredients.
2. Close Instant Pot, press the Manual button, choose high settings, and set time to 35 minutes.
3. Once done cooking, do a QPR.
4. Serve and enjoy.

Nutrition information:

Calories per serving: 722; Carbohydrates: 25.6g; Protein: 47.7g; Fat: 48.3g; Sugar: 20g; Sodium: 619mg

---

54. Pork Tenderloin in Garlic Herb Rub

(Servings: 4, Cooking time: 20 minutes)

Ingredients:

- 1 cup chicken broth
- 1 tablespoon balsamic vinegar
- 2 pounds pork tenderloin
- 1 teaspoon garlic powder
- 1 teaspoon dried parsley
- ½ teaspoon salt
- ¼ teaspoon onion powder
- ¼ teaspoon black pepper
- 3 tablespoons honey
- 1 tablespoon ketchup
- 1 tablespoon cornstarch + 1 tablespoon water

Nutrition information:

Calories per serving: 478; Carbohydrates: 16.1g; Protein: 72.6g; Fat: 12.3g; Sugar: 3.2g; Sodium: 708mg

Directions for Cooking:

1. Pour chicken broth and balsamic vinegar in the Instant Pot. Place a trivet on top. Season the pork tenderloin with garlic powder, dried parsley, salt, onion powder, and black pepper.
2. Arrange in the trivet. Close Instant Pot, press Steam button, choose high settings, and set time to 20 minutes.
3. Once done cooking, do a QPR.
4. Remove the cooked pork and set aside. Remove the trivet as well.
5. Press the Sauté button and to the chicken broth, stir in honey, ketchup and cornstarch slurry.
6. Allow to simmer until the sauce thickens.
7. Pour over the steamed pork chops.
8. Serve and enjoy.

---

55. Hearty Pork Black Bean Nachos

(Servings: 10, Cooking time: 40 minutes)

Ingredients:

- 4-oz beef jerky, chopped
- 3 pounds pork spare ribs, cut into 2-rib sections
- 4 cans black beans, rinsed and drained
- 1 cup chopped onion
- 4 teaspoons minced garlic
- 1 teaspoon crushed red pepper flakes
- 4 cups beef broth
- Salt and pepper to taste
- Tortilla chips
- 6 strips of bacon, cooked and crumbled

Directions for Cooking:

1. Dump the beef jerky ribs, black bins, onions, garlic, red pepper flakes, and beef broth. Season with salt and pepper to taste.
2. Close Instant Pot, press the Manual button, choose high settings, and set time to 20 minutes.
3. Once done cooking, do a QPR.
4. Remove and discard the bones.
5. Serve with tortilla chips and crumbled bacon.
6. Enjoy.

Nutrition information:

Calories per serving:469; Carbohydrates: 27g; Protein:33 g; Fat: 24g; Sugar: 3g; Sodium: 1055mg

---

56. Instant Pot Gumbo

(Servings: 6, Cooking time: 15 minutes)

Ingredients:

- 1 tablespoon olive oil
- 1 onion, diced
- 6 cloves of garlic, minced
- 2 ribs celery, diced
- 1 ¾ pounds bone-in chicken thighs
- ½ pound Andouille sausage, cut into ¼" slices
- 1-pound fresh okra, chopped into ½" thick
- 1 bell pepper, diced
- 4 cups chicken stock
- 1 tablespoon Worcestershire sauce
- 1 tablespoon fish sauce
- 3 bay leaves
- 1 teaspoon cayenne pepper
- 1 teaspoon smoked paprika
- A pinch of thyme
- Salt to taste

Directions for Cooking:

1. Press the Sauté button on the Instant Pot and heat the oil. Sauté the onion and garlic until fragrant. Add the celery and cook for another minute.
2. Stir in the chicken and sausages and continue cooking for three more minutes.
3. Pour in the rest of the ingredients. Close Instant Pot, press the Manual button, choose high settings, and set time to 10 minutes.
4. Once done cooking, do a QPR.
5. Serve and enjoy.

Nutrition information:

Calories per serving: 662; Carbohydrates: 38.3g; Protein: 37.9g; Fat: 41.2g; Sugar: 5g; Sodium: 1911mg

---

57. Barbecue Pulled Pork

(Servings: 8, Cooking time: 1 hour and 40 minutes)

Ingredients:

- 2 teaspoons hot paprika
- 3 tablespoons light brown sugar
- 1 teaspoon mustard powder
- ½ teaspoon ground cumin
- Salt and pepper to taste
- 4 pounds pork shoulder
- 2 teaspoons vegetable oil
- ½ cup apple cider vinegar
- 3 tablespoons tomato paste

Directions for Cooking:

1. Place all ingredients in the Instant Pot and mix all ingredients.
2. Close Instant Pot, press the Manual button, choose high settings, and set time to 1 hour and 40 minutes.
3. Once done cooking, do a QPR.
4. Shred the meat using fork and serve.

Nutrition information:

Calories per serving: 637; Carbohydrates: 5g; Protein: 57.3g; Fat: 41.4g; Sugar: 3.7g; Sodium: 144mg

---

58. Spare Ribs and Black Bean Sauce

(Servings: 4, Cooking time: 35 minutes)

Ingredients:

- 1-pound pork spare ribs, cut into large cubes
- 1 tablespoon black bean sauce
- 1 tablespoon soy sauce
- 1 tablespoon Shaoxing wine
- 1 tablespoon grated ginger
- 3 cloves of garlic, minced
- 1 teaspoon sesame oil
- 1 teaspoon sugar
- 1 tablespoon oil
- 1 tablespoon cornstarch + 2 tablespoon water
- Chopped green onions for garnish

Directions for Cooking:

1. In a mixing bowl, combine the pork spare ribs, black bean sauce, soy sauce, Shaoxing wine, grated ginger, garlic, sesame oil, and sugar. Allow to marinate in the fridge for at least 2 hours.
2. Press the Sauté button on the Instant Pot. Heat the oil and sear the pork on all sides for 3 minutes. Put in the sauce and add water if needed.
3. Close Instant Pot, press the Manual button, choose high settings, and set time to 35 minutes.
4. Once done cooking, do a QPR.
5. Press the Sauté button again and stir in cornstarch slurry. Allow to simmer until the sauce thickens.
6. Garnish with green onions.
7. Serve and enjoy.

Nutrition information:

Calories per serving: 242; Carbohydrates: 9.2g; Protein: 25.9g; Fat: 10.9g; Sugar: 5.6g; Sodium: 538mg

---

59. Instant Pot Mesquite Ribs

(Servings: 8, Cooking time: 40 minutes)

Ingredients

- 1 cup water
- 2 tablespoons cider vinegar
- 1 tablespoon soy sauce
- 4 pounds baby back ribs
- 2 tablespoons mesquite seasoning
- ¾ cup barbecue sauce, divided

Directions for Cooking:

1. Mix all ingredients in the Instant Pot. Make sure that you only put half of the barbecue sauce. Reserve it for later.
2. Close Instant Pot, press the Manual button, choose high settings, and set time to 35 minutes.
3. Once done cooking, do a QPR.
4. Press the Sauté button and pour in the remaining amount of barbecue sauce.
5. Allow to simmer for 5 minutes.
6. Serve and enjoy.

Nutrition information:

Calories per serving: 329; Carbohydrates: 10g; Protein: 23g; Fat: 21g; Sugar: 8g; Sodium: 678mg

---

60. Ginger Pork Shogayaki

(Servings: 2， Cooking time: 55 minutes)

Ingredients

- 1-pound pork shoulder
- 2 tablespoons ginger root, grated
- 1 clove of garlic, minced
- 1 onion, chopped
- 1 tablespoon soy sauce
- ½ tablespoon white miso paste
- 2 tablespoons Japanese cooking sake
- 2 tablespoons mirin
- ¼ cup water
- 1 tablespoon peanut oil
- ½ head romaine lettuce

Directions for Cooking:

1. Place the pork shoulder, ginger root, garlic, onion soy sauce, miso paste, sake, mirin, and water in the Instant Pot. Give a good stir.
2. Close Instant Pot, press the Manual button, choose high settings, and set time to 55 minutes.
3. Once done cooking, do a QPR.
4. Before serving drizzle with peanut oil.
5. Serve with lettuce and enjoy.

Nutrition information:

Calories per serving: 772; Carbohydrates: 16.4g; Protein: 60.5g; Fat: 48.9g; Sugar: 3.7g; Sodium: 433mg

---

61. Instant Pot Hoisin Meatballs

(Servings: 6, Cooking time: 10 minutes)

Ingredients:

- 1 cup beef broth
- 3 tablespoons hoisin sauce
- 2 tablespoons soy sauce
- 1 large egg, beaten
- 4 green onions, chopped
- ¼ cup chopped onion
- ¼ cup fresh cilantro, minced
- 2 cloves of garlic, minced
- Salt and pepper to taste
- 1-pound ground beef
- 1-pound ground pork
- ¼ cup sesame seeds

Directions for Cooking:

1. In a mixing bowl, combine all ingredients and form 12 balls using your hands.
2. Place inside the fridge to set.
3. Carefully place the meatballs inside the Instant Pot.
4. Close Instant Pot, press the Manual button, choose high settings, and set time to 10 minutes.
5. Once done cooking, do a QPR.
6. Serve and enjoy.

Nutrition information:

Calories per serving:78; Carbohydrates: 1g; Protein: 6g; Fat: 5g; Sugar: 1; Sodium: 156mg

---

62. Beer-Braised Pulled Ham

(Servings: 16, Cooking time: 25 minutes)

Ingredients:

- 2 bottles of beer
- ¾ cup Dijon mustard
- ½ teaspoon ground pepper
- 1 fully cooked ham, bone-in
- 4 fresh rosemary sprigs
- 16 pretzel hamburger buns, split
- Dill pickle slices

Nutrition information:

Calories per serving: 378; Carbohydrates: 40g; Protein: 25g; Fat: 9g; Sugar: 4g; Sodium: 1246mg

Directions for Cooking:

1. Put the beer, mustard, pepper, ham, and rosemary sprigs in the Instant Pot.
2. Close Instant Pot, press the Manual button, choose high settings, and set time to 25 minutes.
3. Once done cooking, do a QPR.
4. Slice the ham and put in between hamburger buns. Garnish with pickle slices.
5. Serve and enjoy.

---

63. Sweet Balsamic Pork

(Servings: 3, Cooking time: 45 minutes)

Ingredients

- 1 ½ pound pork tenderloin cut into four pieces
- 3 cloves of garlic, minced
- ¼ cup brown sugar
- ¼ cup balsamic vinegar
- 1 tablespoon olive oil
- ¼ cup water
- 1 tablespoon soy sauce
- 1 tablespoon chopped rosemary
- 1 tablespoon cornstarch + 2 tablespoons water

Directions for Cooking:

1. In a mixing bowl, combine the pork tenderloin, garlic, brown sugar, and balsamic vinegar. Allow to marinate in the fridge for at least 2 hours.
2. Press the Sauté button on the Instant Pot. Heat the oil and sauté the marinate pork mixture for 5 minutes. Do not include the marinade.
3. Add the marinade, water, soy sauce, and rosemary.
4. Close Instant Pot, press Manual button, choose high settings, and set time to 30 minutes.
5. Once done cooking, do a QPR.
6. Once the lid is open, press the Sauté button and pour in the cornstarch slurry. Allow to simmer until the sauce thickens.
7. Serve and enjoy.

Nutrition information:

Calories per serving: 498; Carbohydrates: 24.1g; Protein: 61.7g; Fat: 15.3g; Sugar: 22.2g; Sodium: 1294mg

---

64. Chinese Pork Bone Soup

(Servings: 4, Cooking time: 1 hour and 20 minutes)

Ingredients:

- 2 ½ pounds pork bones
- 2 large carrots, roughly chopped
- 2 corn on the cob, chopped
- 1 thumb-size ginger, sliced
- 2 dried dates
- 4 cups water
- Salt to taste

Directions for Cooking:

1. Place all ingredients in the Instant Pot.
2. Close Instant Pot, press the Manual button, choose high settings, and set time to 1 hour and 20 minutes.
3. Once done cooking, do a QPR.
4. Serve and enjoy.

Nutrition information:

Calories per serving:62; Carbohydrates: 14g; Protein:1 g; Fat: 7g; Sugar:6g; Sodium: 28mg

---

65. Shrimp Pork Dumplings (Humai)

(Servings: 4, Cooking time: 10 minutes)

Ingredients:

- ½ pound tiger prawns or shrimps, finely chopped
- 2 tablespoons cornstarch
- ¼ teaspoon salt
- ¼ teaspoon oil
- ½ pound ground pork
- 2 tablespoons chicken stock
- 1 tablespoon Shaoxing wine
- 2 teaspoons soy sauce
- 1 teaspoon fish sauce
- 1 teaspoon sesame oil
- ½ teaspoon white pepper
- ½ teaspoon sugar
- 20 wonton wrappers

Directions for Cooking:

1. Place a trivet in the Instant Pot and add a cup of water.
2. In a mixing bowl, combine all ingredients except for the wonton wrappers.
3. Use your hands to mix everything.
4. Place a tablespoon of the mixture on the center of the wonton wrappers. Fold the wanton wrappers and pinch the edges to close.
5. Place gently on the trivet.
6. Close Instant Pot, press the Steam button, choose high settings, and set time to 10 minutes.
7. Once done cooking, do a QPR.
8. Serve and enjoy.

Nutrition information:

Calories per serving:793; Carbohydrates: 97.6g; Protein: 45.3g; Fat: 22.3g; Sugar: 1g; Sodium: 1302mg

---

66. Instant Pot Korean Beef

(Servings: 10, Cooking time: 25 minutes)

Ingredients:

- ½ cup beef broth
- 1/3 cup soy sauce
- 1/3 cup brown sugar
- 4 cloves of garlic, minced
- 1 tablespoon sesame oil
- 1 tablespoon rice wine
- 1 tablespoon grated ginger
- 1 teaspoon Sriracha sauce
- ½ teaspoon onion powder
- ½ teaspoon white pepper
- 3 ½ pounds boneless beef chuck roast, cut into chunks
- 2 tablespoons cornstarch + 3 tablespoons water
- 1 teaspoon sesame seeds
- 2 green onion, chopped

Nutrition information:

Calories per serving: 370; Carbohydrates: 12.8g; Protein: 43.4g; Fat: 16.6g; Sugar: 3.2g; Sodium: 278mg

Directions for Cooking:

1. Place the soy sauce, brown sugar, garlic, sesame oil, rice wine, ginger, Sriracha sauce, onion powder, white pepper, and beef in the Instant Pot. Stir to combine.
2. Close Instant Pot, press the Manual button, choose high settings, and set time to 20 minutes.
3. Once done cooking, do a QPR.
4. Open the lid and press the Sauté button. Pour in the cornstarch slurry and allow to simmer for 5 minutes until the sauce thickens.
5. Garnish with sesame seeds and green onions.
6. Serve and enjoy.

---

67. Italian Beef Dinner

(Servings: 6, Cooking time: 45 minutes)

Ingredients:

- 3 pounds beef chuck roast, cut into cubes
- 3 pounds red potatoes, scrubbed and peeled
- 3 cups carrots, roughly chopped
- ¼ cup water
- 1 can tomato sauce
- 1 teaspoon Italian herb seasoning mix

Directions for Cooking:

1. Place all ingredients in the Instant Pot and give a good stir.
2. Close Instant Pot, press the Manual button, choose high settings, and set time to 45 minutes.
3. Once done cooking, do a QPR.
4. Serve and enjoy.

Nutrition information:

Calories per serving: 457; Carbohydrates: 34g; Protein: 36g; Fat: 19g; Sugar: 6g; Sodium: 480mg

---

68. Instant Pot Mongolian Beef

(Servings: 3, Cooking time: 20 minutes)

Ingredients:

- 1 ½ pounds flank steak, sliced thinly
- 1 tablespoon cornstarch
- 1 tablespoon olive oil
- 10 cloves of garlic, minced
- 1 tablespoon grated ginger
- ½ cup brown sugar
- ½ cup soy sauce
- 1 cup water
- 1 tablespoon rice wine
- 1 teaspoon red pepper flakes
- 2 tablespoons cornstarch + 3 tablespoons water

Nutrition information:

Calories per serving: 654; Carbohydrates: 55.3g; Protein: 52.9g; Fat: 24.2g; Sugar: 44g; Sodium: 778mg

Directions for Cooking:

1. In a bowl, dust the flank steak with cornstarch. Set aside.Press the Sauté button on the Instant Pot and heat the oil.
2. Stir-fry the beef for 3 minutes then add garlic and ginger until fragrant.
3. Stir in the sugar, soy sauce, water rice wine, and red pepper flakes. Season with salt and pepper to taste.
4. Close Instant Pot, press the Manual button, choose high settings, and set time to 16 minutes.
5. Once done cooking, do a QPR.
6. Open the lid and press the Sauté button. Pour in the cornstarch slurry and allow to simmer until the sauce thickens.
7. Serve and enjoy.

---

69. Instant Pot Barbacoa Beef

(Servings: 7, Cooking time: 1 hour and 25 minutes)

Ingredients:

- 1 tablespoon olive oil
- 4 cloves of garlic, minced
- 1 small onion, chopped
- ¼ teaspoon ground cloves
- 1 tablespoon ground cumin
- 1 tablespoon Mexican oregano
- 3 pounds beef chuck roast, cut into chunks
- 2 teaspoons salt
- 1 teaspoon black pepper
- 2/3 cup water
- 2 chipotles in adobo sauce
- 1 can green chilies
- ¼ cup fresh lime juice
- 2 tablespoons apple cider vinegar
- 3 bay leaves

Directions for Cooking:

1. Press the Sauté button on the Instant Pot and heat the oil. Sauté the garlic, onion, cloves, cumin, and oregano until fragrant. Stir in the beef and sauté for 3 minutes. Season with salt and pepper to taste.
2. Close Instant Pot, press the Manual button, choose high settings, and set time to 1 hour and 25 minutes.
3. Once done cooking, do a QPR.
4. Serve and enjoy.

Nutrition information:

Calories per serving: 388; Carbohydrates: 3.4g; Protein: 52.3g; Fat: 18.6g; Sugar: 1.1g; Sodium: 823mg

---

70. Instant Pot Beef Tips

(Servings: 4, Cooking time: 15 minutes)

Ingredients:

- 3 tablespoons olive oil
- 1-pound beef sirloin steak, cut into cubes
- Salt and pepper to taste
- 1/3 cup dry red wine
- ½ pounds baby Portobello mushrooms, sliced
- 1 onion, sliced
- 2 cups beef broth
- 1 tablespoon Worcestershire sauce

Nutrition information:

Calories per serving: 378; Carbohydrates: 15.1g; Protein: 26.3g; Fat: 23.2g; Sugar: 2.3g; Sodium: 270mg;

Directions for Cooking:

1. Press the Sauté button and heat the oil.
2. Stir in the beef cubes and season with salt and pepper to taste. Continue stirring for 3 minutes to brown the beef.
3. Add the rest of the ingredients.
4. Close Instant Pot, press the Manual button, choose high settings, and set time to 12 minutes.
5. Once done cooking, do a QPR.
6. Serve and enjoy.

---

71. Sesame Beef Asparagus Salad

(Servings:6, Cooking time: 15 minutes)

Ingredients:

- 1-pound beef round steak, sliced
- 3 tablespoons soy sauce
- 2 tablespoons sesame oil
- 1 tablespoon rice vinegar
- ½ teaspoon ginger root, grated
- 4 cups steamed asparagus, cut into 2-inch pieces
- Sesame seeds for garnish
- 1 head lettuce leaves, washed and torn
- 1 carrot, peeled and julienned
- 1 radish, peeled and julienned

Nutrition information:

Calories per serving: 211; Carbohydrates: 12.5g; Protein: 20.9g; Fat: 9.4g; Sugar: 7.6g; Sodium: 201mg

Directions for Cooking:

1. In the Instant Pot, place the steak slices, soy sauce, sesame oil, rice vinegar, and ginger root.
2. Close Instant Pot, press the Manual button, choose high settings, and set time to 15 minutes.
3. Once done cooking, do a QPR.
4. Open the lid and take the beef slices out. Allow to cool before making the salad.
5. In a salad mix the rest of the ingredients. Give a toss.
6. Serve and enjoy.

---

72. Persian Beef Stew

(Servings: 3, Cooking time: 50 minutes)

Ingredients:

- 2 tablespoons vegetable oil
- 2 onions, chopped
- 2 cloves of garlic, minced
- 1 ½ pounds beef stew meat, cut into chunks
- 1 tablespoon ground cumin
- ½ teaspoon saffron threads
- ½ teaspoon turmeric
- ¼ teaspoon ground cinnamon
- ¼ teaspoon ground allspice
- Salt and pepper to taste
- ¼ cup tomato paste
- 1 can split peas, rinsed and drained
- 3 cups bone broth
- 1 can crushed tomatoes
- 4 tablespoon lemon juice, freshly squeezed

Directions for Cooking:

1. Press the Sauté button on the Instant Pot. Heat the oil and sauté the onion and garlic until fragrant. Add cumin, saffron, turmeric, cinnamon, and allspice. Stir in the beef and brown for 3 minutes. Season with salt and pepper to taste.
2. Pour in the rest of the ingredients.
3. Close Instant Pot, press the Manual button, choose high settings, and set time to 50 minutes.
4. Once done cooking, do a QPR.
5. Serve and enjoy.

Nutrition information:

Calories per serving: 472; Carbohydrates: 36g; Protein: 49g; Fat: 14g; Sugar: 7g; Sodium: 197mg

---

73. Instant Pot Beef Curry

(Servings: 4, Cooking time: 30 minutes)

Ingredients:

- 2 tablespoons coconut oil
- 1 onion, chopped
- 5 cloves of garlic, minced
- 1-pound beef stew meat, cut into chunks
- 3 large potatoes, peeled and cubed
- 6 carrots, roughly chopped
- 1 cup coconut milk
- ½ cup bone broth
- 1 ½ tablespoon curry powder
- Salt and pepper to taste
- ¼ teaspoon paprika

Directions for Cooking:

1. Press the Sauté button on the Instant Pot and heat the oil. Sauté the onion and garlic until fragrant.
2. Stir in the beef and brown on all sides for 5 minutes. Add the rest of the ingredients.
3. Close Instant Pot, press the Manual button, choose high settings, and set time to 30 minutes.
4. Once done cooking, do a QPR.
5. Serve and enjoy.

Nutrition information:

Calories per serving:363; Carbohydrates: 12g; Protein: 27g; Fat: 23g; Sugar: 4g; Sodium:565 mg

---

74. Instant Pot Beef Stew Bourguignon

(Servings: 4, Cooking time: 50 minutes)

Ingredients:

- 1-pound steak flank, cut into large strips
- ½ pound bacon tips
- 1 onion, sliced
- 2 cloves of garlic, minced
- 5 carrots, cut into sticks
- Salt and pepper to taste
- 2 tablespoons dried thyme
- 2 tablespoons parsley
- 1 cup red wine
- ½ cup beef broth
- 2 large sweet potatoes, peeled and cubed
- 1 tablespoon maple syrup

Directions for Cooking:

1. Press the Sauté button on the Instant Pot and add the steak and bacon. Allow the meat and bacon to render their fat before stirring in the onions and garlic.
2. Stir in the carrots and the rest of the ingredients.
3. Close Instant Pot, press the Manual button, choose high settings, and set time to 50 minutes.
4. Once done cooking, do a QPR.
5. Serve and enjoy.

Nutrition information:

Calories per serving:489; Carbohydrates:37.8 g; Protein: 33.5g; Fat: 22.7g; Sugar: 13g; Sodium: 1023mg

---

75. Instant Pot Shredded Beef

(Servings: 6, Cooking time: 1 hour and 10 minutes)

Ingredients:

- 3 pounds beef chuck roast
- 2 tablespoons olive oil
- 1 chipotle in adobo sauce, chopped
- 1 tablespoon adobo sauce
- 2 teaspoons dried cumin
- 2 teaspoons dried oregano
- Salt and pepper to taste
- ½ teaspoon chili powder
- 1 onion, peeled and quartered
- 1 green bell pepper, chopped
- 1 cup water

Directions for Cooking:

1. Place all ingredients in the Instant Pot. Give a good stir.
2. Close Instant Pot, press the Manual button, choose high settings, and set time to 1 hour and 20 minutes.
3. Once done cooking, do a QPR.
4. Take the beef out and shred using forks.
5. Serve with chopped cilantro and enjoy.

Nutrition information:

Calories per serving: 473; Carbohydrates: 3.9g; Protein: 61.2g; Fat: 23.9g; Sugar: 1.7g; Sodium: 213mg;

---

76. Instant Pot Salisbury Steak with Mushroom Gravy

(Servings: 6, Cooking time: 15 minutes)

Ingredients:

- 1 ½ pounds ground beef
- 3 tablespoons whole milk
- 1 tablespoon Worcestershire sauce
- 1 clove of garlic, minced
- 1/3 cup panko bread crumbs
- A pinch of salt and pepper to taste
- 1 tablespoon ghee or butter
- 8 ounces baby Portobella mushrooms, sliced
- 1 onion, sliced
- 2 cups beef broth
- 1 tablespoon tomato paste
- 1 tablespoon Dijon mustard
- 2 tablespoons parsley, minced
- 3 tablespoons cornstarch + 3 tablespoons water

Nutrition information:

Calories per serving: 367; Carbohydrates: 11.6g; Protein: 30.1g; Fat: 20.7g; Sugar: 2.7g; Sodium: 208mg

Directions for Cooking:

1. In a mixing bowl, combine the first seven ingredients. Mix until well combined and form patties using the mixture. Place in the fridge and allow to set for at least 2 hours.
2. Press the Sauté button on the Instant Pot. Gently place the patties and allow to brown for 3 minutes on each side.
3. Put in the mushrooms, onion, beef broth, tomato paste, and mustard on top.
4. Close Instant Pot, press the Manual button, choose high settings, and set time to 15 minutes.
5. Once done cooking, do a QPR.
6. Once the lid is open, stir in the parsley and the cornstarch slurry. Allow to simmer until the sauce thickens.
7. Serve and enjoy.

---

77. Chili Lime Steak Bowl

(Servings: 4, Cooking time: 15 minutes)

Ingredients:

- 2 pounds beef steak, cut into cubes
- 1 tablespoon water
- 1 teaspoon minced garlic
- 1 tablespoon chili powder
- 2 teaspoons lime juice
- Salt and pepper to taste
- 2 avocados, diced
- 1 cup tomato, diced
- 1 cup chopped cilantro

Nutrition information:

Calories per serving: 498; Carbohydrates: 12.6g; Protein: 50.3g; Fat: 27.6g; Sugar: 2.4g; Sodium: 201mg;

Directions for Cooking:

1. Place the beef steak slices, water, garlic, chili powder, and lime juice in the Instant Pot. Season with salt and pepper to taste.
2. Close Instant Pot, press the Manual button, choose high settings, and set time to 15 minutes.
3. Once done cooking, do a QPR.
4. Assemble the steak bowl by putting in a bowl the meat and garnishing with fresh avocado, tomatoes, and cilantro on top.
5. Serve and enjoy.

---

78. Instant Pot Meatloaf

(Servings: 6, Cooking time: 30 minutes)

Ingredients:

- 2 pounds ground beef
- 2 ½ cups bread crumbs
- 1 cup parmesan cheese
- 4 large eggs, beaten
- 1 tablespoon minced garlic
- 1 teaspoon steak seasoning
- Salt and pepper to taste
- 5 teaspoons brown sugar
- 2/3 cup ketchup
- 1 tablespoon mustard
- 2 teaspoons Worcestershire sauce

Nutrition information:

Calories per serving:581; Carbohydrates: 23.2g; Protein: 46.6g; Fat: 32.7g; Sugar: 10g; Sodium: 682mg

Directions for Cooking:

1. Place a trivet in the Instant Pot and pour a cup of beef broth.
2. In a mixing bowl, mix together the beef, bread crumbs, cheese, eggs, garlic, and steak seasoning. Season with salt and pepper to taste.
3. Pour meat mixture in a heat-proof pan and place on top of the trivet.
4. Close Instant Pot, press the Steam cook button, choose high settings, and set time to 30 minutes.
5. While waiting for the meatloaf to cook, combine in a saucepan the sugar, ketchup, mustard, and Worcestershire sauce. Mix until the sauce becomes thick.
6. Once done cooking, do a QPR.
7. Remove the meatloaf from the Instant Pot and allow to cool.
8. Serve with sauce and enjoy.

---

79. Simple Instant Pot Beef Stew

(Servings: 6, Cooking time: 60 minutes)

Ingredients:

- 2 pounds beef stew meat
- 4 cups water
- 5 potatoes, peeled and chopped
- 1 cup carrot, chopped
- 1 onion, chopped
- 4 stalks of celery
- Salt and pepper to taste

Nutrition information:

Calories per serving: 554; Carbohydrates:58.2g; Protein: 60.9g; Fat: 7.8g; Sugar: 5g; Sodium: 599mg

Directions for Cooking:

1. Place all ingredients in the Instant Pot.
2. Close Instant Pot, press pressure cook button, choose high settings, and set time to 60 minutes.
3. Once done cooking, do a QPR.
4. Serve and enjoy.

---

80. Instant Pot Beef Burritos

（Servings: 6，Cooking time: 15 minutes ）

Ingredients:

- 2 tablespoons vegetable oil
- 1 onion, diced
- 3 cloves of garlic, minced
- 1-pound lean ground beef
- 1 tablespoon chili powder
- 2 teaspoons cumin powder
- 1 Salt and pepper to taste
- 1/4 cup beef broth
- 1 can black beans, rinsed and drained
- 1 can corn kernels, rinsed and drained
- 1 cup diced tomatoes
- 6 flour tortillas

Nutrition information:

Calories per serving: 381; Carbohydrates: 18g; Protein: 17g; Fat: 8g; Sugar: 2g; Sodium: 318

Directions for Cooking:

1. Press the Sauté button on the Instant Pot and heat the oil. Sauté the onions and garlic until fragrant.
2. Stir in the ground beef until brown and add the chili powder and cumin powder. Season with salt and pepper to taste.
3. Pour in the broth, black beans, corn, and tomatoes.
4. Close Instant Pot, press the Manual button, choose high settings, and set time to 15 minutes.
5. Once done cooking, do a QPR.
6. Once the lid is open, ladle onto flour tortillas.
7. Serve and enjoy.

---

81. Instant Pot Picadillo

(Servings: 3, Cooking time: 20 minutes)

Ingredients:

- 1 ½ pounds lean ground beef
- ½ onion, chopped
- 2 cloves of garlic, minced
- 1 tomato, chopped
- Salt and pepper to taste
- ½ red bell pepper, chopped
- 2 tablespoons cilantro
- ½ can tomato sauce
- 1 teaspoon ground cumin
- 2 bay leaves
- 2 tablespoons capers

Nutrition information:

Calories per serving: 516; Carbohydrates: 6.7g; Protein: 61.9g; Fat: 25.5g; Sugar: 0.9g; Sodium: 572mg;

Directions for Cooking:

1. Press the Sauté button on the Instant Pot and stir in the lean ground beef. Stir until the fat has lightly rendered. Stir in the onions and garlic until fragrant.
2. Add the tomatoes and season with salt and pepper. Stir in the rest of the ingredients.
3. Close Instant Pot, press the Manual button, choose high settings, and set time to 20 minutes.
4. Once done cooking, do a QPR.
5. Serve and enjoy.

---

82. Tex Mex Beef Stew

(Servings: 6, Cooking time: 28 minutes)

Ingredients:

- 1 tablespoon chili powder
- 2 teaspoons cumin powder
- 1 teaspoon ground coriander
- ¼ teaspoon smoked paprika
- 2 pounds beef stew meat
- Salt and pepper to taste
- 1 tablespoon olive oil
- 1 onion, chopped
- 4 cloves of garlic, minced
- 1 can diced tomatoes
- 1 tablespoon apple cider vinegar
- 1 cup chopped cilantro
- 1 cup shredded cheddar cheese

Nutrition information:

Calories per serving: 434; Carbohydrates:5.8 g; Protein: 60.6g; Fat: 17.7g; Sugar: 2.4g; Sodium: 775mg

Directions for Cooking:

1. In a mixing bowl, combine the chili powder, cumin, coriander, paprika and beef stew meat. Allow to marinate in the fridge for 2 hours.
2. Press the Sauté button on the Instant Pot and heat the oil. Sauté the onion and garlic until fragrant. Add the marinated beef and allow to brown for 3 minutes.
3. Stir in the tomatoes and apple cider vinegar. Adjust the seasoning and water.
4. Close Instant Pot, press the Manual cook button, choose high settings, and set time to 25 minutes.
5. Once done cooking, do a QPR.
6. Before serving, garnish with cilantro and cheddar cheese.
7. Serve and enjoy.

---

83. Instant Pot Beef Tips

(Servings: 4, Cooking time: 20 minutes)

Ingredients:

- 4 tablespoons olive oil
- 2 pounds sirloin beef tips
- ¼ cup diced onions
- 3 tablespoons flour
- ½ teaspoon garlic salt
- ½ teaspoon black pepper
- 1 cup beef broth
- ½ cup red wine
- 1 can cream of mushroom soup

Nutrition information:

Calories per serving: 563; Carbohydrates: 14.2g; Protein: 49.9g; Fat: 32.4g; Sugar: 3.9g; Sodium: 221mg

Directions for Cooking:

1. Press the Sauté button on the Instant Pot and heat the oil. Add the sirloin beef tips and onions. Stir until meat is lightly brown.
2. Add the rest of the ingredients.
3. Close Instant Pot, press the Manual cook button, choose high settings, and set time to 20 minutes.
4. Once done cooking, do a QPR.
5. Serve and enjoy.

---

84. Instant Pot Mediterranean Beef

(Servings: 4, Cooking time: 60 minutes)

Ingredients:

- 3 tablespoons all-purpose flour
- ½ dried oregano
- Salt and pepper to taste
- 2 pounds beef chuck roast
- 2 tablespoon olive oil
- 1 onion, chopped
- 4 shallots, chopped
- ½ cup beef broth
- ¼ cup red wine
- ¼ cup balsamic vinegar
- ½ cup Medjool dates, pitted and chopped

Nutrition information:

Calories per serving: 555; Carbohydrates: 17.4g; Protein: 62.2g; Fat: 26.1g; Sugar: 3.8g; Sodium: 230mg

Directions for Cooking:

1. In a mixing bowl, rub all-purpose flour, oregano, salt and pepper on the beef chuck roast.
2. Press the Sauté button on the Instant Pot and heat the oil.
3. Place the roast and brown on all sides for at least 5 minutes.
4. Add the onion and shallots and stir until fragrant.
5. Stir in the rest of the ingredients.
6. Close Instant Pot, press the Manual cook button, choose high settings, and set time to 1 hour.
7. Once done cooking, do a QPR.
8. Serve and enjoy.

---

85. Instant Pot Taco Meat

(Servings: 4, Cooking time: 13 minutes)

Ingredients:

- 2 pounds ground beef
- 2 onions, diced
- 3 bell peppers (any color), diced
- 2 packets of taco seasoning
- 1 cup water

Nutrition information:

Calories per serving:612; Carbohydrates: 8.3; Protein: 58.6g; Fat: 36.8g; Sugar: 2.6g; Sodium: 158mg;

Directions for Cooking:

1. Press the Sauté button on the Instant Pot and stir in the beef and ground onions.
2. Allow to brown for 3 minutes while stirring constantly.
3. Add the rest of the ingredients.
4. Close Instant Pot, press the Manual cook button, choose high settings, and set time to 10 minutes.
5. Once done cooking, do a QPR.
6. Serve and enjoy.

---

86. Beef Cheesy Potatoes

(Servings: 6, Cooking time: 25 minutes)

Ingredients:

- 1 ½ pounds ground beef
- 6 large potatoes, peeled and chopped
- 2 cups cheddar cheese, shredded
- ¾ cup chicken broth
- 1 tablespoon Italian seasoning mix
- Salt and pepper to taste

Nutrition information:

Calories per serving: 806; Carbohydrates: 66.8g; Protein: 53.4g; Fat: 35.6g; Sugar: 3.5g; Sodium: 609mg;

Directions for Cooking:

1. Press the Sauté button on the Instant Pot and stir in the beef. Brown the meat until some of the oil has rendered.
2. Add the rest of the ingredients.
3. Close Instant Pot, press the Manual button, choose high settings, and set time to 20 minutes.
4. Once done cooking, do a QPR.
5. Serve and enjoy.

---

87. Sweet Potato Chili Recipe

(Servings: 5, Cooking time: 25 minutes)

Ingredients:

- 1 teaspoon olive oil
- 1 onion, diced
- 3 cloves of garlic, minced
- ½ pound ground pork
- 1-pound ground beef
- 1 large sweet potato, peeled and cut into ½" pieces
- 3 celery stalks, sliced
- 3 ½ cups crushed tomatoes
- 1 tablespoon Worcestershire sauce
- 1 teaspoon cumin
- 1 teaspoon chili powder
- Salt and pepper to taste

Nutrition information:

Calories per serving:447; Carbohydrates: 16.4g; Protein: 36.9g; Fat: 25.9g; Sugar: 4.1g; Sodium: 172mg;

Directions for Cooking:

1. Press the Sauté button on the Instant Pot and heat the olive oil. Sauté the onion and garlic until fragrant.
2. Stir in the pork and beef and allow to brown for 5 minutes.
3. Add the rest of the ingredients.
4. Close Instant Pot, press the Manual button, choose high settings, and set time to 20 minutes.
5. Once done cooking, do a QPR.
6. Serve and enjoy.

---

88. Instant Pot Stuffed Peppers

(Servings: 8, Cooking time: 25 minutes)

Ingredients:

- ½ pound ground beef
- 1/3 cup diced onions
- 1 ½ cup spaghetti sauce
- ½ teaspoon garlic salt
- 2 cups cooked rice
- 8 bell peppers, cut the top and remove the seeds
- 1 cup mozzarella cheese, shredded

Directions for Cooking:

1. Press the Sauté button on the Instant Pot and Add the beef and onions. Stir constantly.
2. Stir in the spaghetti sauce and season with garlic salt.
3. Close Instant Pot, press the Manual cook button, choose high settings, and set time to 10 minutes.
4. Once done cooking, do a QPR.
5. Transfer into a bowl and add the cooked rice. Stir to combine. Pack the mixture into hollow bell peppers and top with mozzarella cheese.
6. Place a trivet in the Instant Pot and pour water. Place the stuffed bell peppers on the trivet and close the lid. Press the Steam button and cook for 10 minutes.
7. Serve and enjoy.

Nutrition information:

Calories per serving: 265; Carbohydrates: 32g; Protein: 12g; Fat: 9; Sugar: 10g; Sodium: 930mg

---

89. Braised Brisket

(Servings: 4, Cooking time: 60 minutes)

Ingredients:

- 2 pounds beef brisket, cut into 4 pieces
- Salt and pepper to taste
- 2 cups sliced onion
- ½ cup water
- 2 tablespoons tomato paste
- 2 tablespoons Worcestershire sauce
- 2 teaspoons liquid smoke

Directions for Cooking:

1. Put all ingredients in the Instant Pot. Mix all ingredients to combine everything.
2. Close Instant Pot, press pressure cook button, choose high settings, and set time to 60 minutes.
3. Once done cooking, do a QPR.
4. Serve and enjoy.

Nutrition information:

Calories per serving: 490; Carbohydrates: 9.9g; Protein: 34.5g; Fat: 33.9g; Sugar: 4.8g; Sodium: 385mg

---

90. Instant Pot Corned Beef and Cabbages

(Servings: 5, Cooking time: 60 minutes)

Ingredients:

- 6 cloves of garlic, chopped
- 1 onion, quartered
- 2 ½ pounds corned beef brisket, cut in large slices
- 12-oz. beer
- 2 cups water
- 3 carrots, roughly chopped
- 2 potatoes, chopped
- 1 head cabbage, cut into four pieces

Nutrition information:

Calories per serving:758; Carbohydrates: 45.8g; Protein: 43.1g; Fat: 44.7g; Sugar: 8.7g; Sodium: 940mg;

Directions for Cooking:

1. In the Instant Pot, place the garlic, onion, corned beef brisket, beer, and water. Season with salt and pepper to taste.
2. Close Instant Pot, press the Manual button, choose high settings, and set time to 50 minutes.
3. Once done cooking, do a QPR.
4. Open the lid and take out the meat. Shred the meat using fork and place it back into the Instant Pot.
5. Stir in the vegetables.
6. Close the lid and seal the vent and press the Manual button. Cook for another 10 minutes. Do QPR.
7. Serve and enjoy.

---

91. Instant Pot Guinness Beef Stew Recipe

(Servings: 8, Cooking time: 40 minutes)

Ingredients:

- 2 tablespoons olive oil
- 1 tablespoon butter
- 1 cup bacon, chopped
- 1 cup shallots, chopped
- 1 ½ pounds braising steak, cubed
- Salt and pepper to taste
- 1 cup button mushrooms, sliced
- 1 cup wild mushrooms, sliced
- 2 carrots, peeled and sliced
- 2 tablespoons tomato paste
- 1 tablespoon Worcestershire sauce
- 1 tablespoon soy sauce
- 1 ½ cups Guinness beer

Directions for Cooking:

1. Press the Sauté button on the Instant Pot and heat the olive oil and butter. Stir in the bacon and shallots until fragrant.
2. Stir in the steak and season with salt and pepper to taste.
3. Add the rest of the ingredients.
4. Close Instant Pot, press the Manual button, choose high settings, and set time to 35 minutes.
5. Once done cooking, do a QPR.
6. Serve and enjoy.

Nutrition information:

Calories per serving: 503; Carbohydrates: 10g; Protein: 33g; Fat: 36g; Sugar: 4g; Sodium: 433mg

---

92. Easy Instant Pot Beef

(Servings: 4, Cooking time: 35 minutes)

Ingredients:

- 1 tablespoon butter
- 1-pound beef chunks
- Salt and pepper to taste
- 1 cup onions, chopped
- 1 tablespoon garlic, minced
- 2 carrots, sliced diagonally
- ½ cup chopped celery
- ¾ cup mushrooms, halved
- 3 potatoes, peeled and quartered
- 2 tablespoons Worcestershire sauce
- 2 tablespoons tomato paste
- 1 cup chicken broth
- 2 tablespoons all-purpose flour + 2 tablespoons water

Nutrition information:

Calories per serving: 565; Carbohydrates: 61.3g; Protein:43.9g; Fat: 13.1g; Sugar: 6.4g; Sodium: 682mg;

Directions for Cooking:

1. Turn on the Sauté button on the Instant Pot and melt the butter. Brown the beef chunks and season with salt and pepper to taste. Add the onions and garlic until fragrant.
2. Stir in the carrots, celery, mushrooms and potatoes.
3. Add the Worcestershire sauce, tomato paste, and chicken broth. Season with more salt and pepper to taste.
4. Close Instant Pot, press the Manual cook button, choose high settings, and set time to 30 minutes.
5. Once done cooking, do a QPR.
6. Open the lid and press the Sauté button. Stir in the all-purpose flour and allow to simmer until the sauce thickens.
7. Serve and enjoy.

---

93. Instant Pot Ghormeh Sabzi

(Servings: 5, Cooking time: 55 minutes)

Ingredients:

- 1 tablespoon olive oil
- 1 ½ pounds lamb meat, cubed
- 1 onion, chopped
- 4 bunches parsley, chopped
- 1 bunch cilantro, chopped
- 4 leeks, chopped
- 1 tablespoon dried fenugreek, sliced
- 4 tablespoons lemon juice, freshly squeezed
- 1 tablespoon turmeric
- 1 cup dark red kidney beans, rinsed and drained
- 1 cup water
- Salt and pepper to taste

Directions for Cooking:

1. Turn the Instant Pot and press the Sauté button. Heat the olive oil and brown the lamb meat.
2. Add the onion, parsley, cilantro, leeks, fenugreek, lemon juice, and turmeric.
3. Stir in kidney beans and water. Season with salt and pepper to taste.
4. Close Instant Pot, press the Manual button, choose high settings, and set time to 50 minutes.
5. Once done cooking, do a QPR.
6. Serve and enjoy.

Nutrition information:

Calories per serving:530; Carbohydrates: 27g; Protein: 26g; Fat: 35.2g; Sugar: 5g; Sodium: 186mg;

---

94. BBQ Instant Pot Ribs

(Servings: 3, Cooking time: 45 minutes)

Ingredients:

- 1 rack baby back ribs
- ¼ cup commercial BBQ sauce
- Salt and pepper to taste
- 1 tablespoon liquid smoke

Nutrition information:

Calories per serving: 1163; Carbohydrates: 3.9g; Protein:103.2g; Fat: 81.9g; Sugar:0.4g; Sodium: 461mg;

Directions for Cooking:

1. Place all ingredients in the Instant Pot. Give a good stir.
2. Close Instant Pot, press the Manual button, choose high settings, and set time to 45 minutes.
3. Once done cooking, do a QPR.
4. Serve and enjoy.

---

95. Instant Pot Adovado

(Servings: 10, Cooking time: 1 hour and 25 minutes)

Ingredients:

- 1 tablespoon canola oil
- 4 pounds pork shoulder, cut into cubes
- 1 onion, diced
- 6 cloves of garlic, minced
- 2 chipotle peppers in adobo sauce
- 1 tablespoon apple cider vinegar
- ½ teaspoon dried oregano
- ¼ teaspoon ground cumin
- 2 cups chicken broth
- 8 dried Mexican chilies, chopped
- Salt and pepper to taste

Directions for Cooking:

1. Press the Sauté button on the Instant Pot. Heat the canola oil and sear the pork shoulders on all sides.
2. Add the onion and garlic and sauté until fragrant.
3. Stir in the rest of the ingredients.
4. Close Instant Pot, press the Manual button, choose high settings, and set time to 1 hour and 25 minutes.
5. Once done cooking, do a QPR.
6. Serve and enjoy.

Nutrition information:

Calories per serving:217; Carbohydrates: 4.1g; Protein: 21.3g; Fat: 12.6g; Sugar: 0.9g; Sodium: 288mg

---

96. Asian Pot Roast

(Servings: 6, Cooking time: 50 minutes)

Ingredients:

- 3 pounds beef pot roast
- 1 tablespoon Chinese five-spice powder
- ¼ cup soy sauce
- ¼ cup black bean sauce
- 2-star anise
- 3 bay leaves
- 1 cup water
- 1 onion, diced
- 3 cloves of garlic, minced
- Sesame seeds for garnish

Directions for Cooking:

1. Place all ingredients in the Instant Pot except for the sesame seeds.
2. Close Instant Pot, press pressure cook button, choose high settings, and set time to 50 minutes.
3. Once done cooking, do a QPR.
4. Garnish with sesame seeds.
5. Serve and enjoy.

Nutrition information:

Calories per serving:352; Carbohydrates: 6.5; Protein: 51.9g; Fat: 13.3g; Sugar: 3.1g; Sodium: 419mg;

---

97. Apple Bacon BBQ Pulled Pork

(Servings: 10, Cooking time: 40 minutes)

Ingredients:

- 4 slices of bacon, chopped
- 1 ½ cup onion, chopped
- 1 medium apple, chopped
- 1 ½ cup ketchup
- 3 tablespoon brown sugar
- 1/3 cup Worcestershire sauce
- 3 tablespoon apple cider vinegar
- 2 teaspoon salt
- 2-pounds pork tenderloin

Directions for Cooking:

1. Press the sauté button on the Instant Pot and drop the chopped bacons. Cook until the bacon has rendered its fat. Set aside.
2. Sauté the onions and apples for a minute. Add the ketchup, brown sugar, Worcestershire sauce, and apple cider vinegar. Season with salt.
3. Add the pork tenderloin.
4. Close the lid and press the manual button. Cook on high for 35 minutes.
5. Do natural pressure release.
6. Remove the pork from the pot and shred using a fork.
7. Garnish with crispy bacon.

Nutrition information:

Calories per serving: 244; Carbohydrates: 19.0g; Protein: 25.7g; Fat: 7.4g; Sugar: 14.3g; Sodium: 983mg

---

98. Balsamic-Honey Pork Roast

(Servings: 8, Cooking time: 35 minutes)

Ingredients

- 2-pound pork roast, bones and fat removed
- ½ teaspoon garlic powder
- Salt and pepper to taste
- 1/3 cup balsamic vinegar
- 1/3 cup vegetable broth
- ¼ cup liquid aminos
- 1 tablespoon raw honey
- 1 ½ cup water

Directions for Cooking:

1. Place the pork roast in the Instant Pot and sprinkle with garlic powder, salt, and pepper. Rub the spices on the pork.
2. Add the rest of the ingredients.
3. Close the lid and select the manual button. Cook on high for 35 minutes.
4. Do QPR.
5. Serve and enjoy.

Nutrition information:

Calories per serving: 256; Carbohydrates: 5.2g; Protein: 30.4g; Fat: 11.8g; Sugar: 4.3g; Sodium: 80mg

---

99. Apple Barbecue Ribs

(Servings: 6, Cooking time: 35 minutes)

Ingredients:

- 4 cups apple juice
- ½ cup apple cider vinegar
- 1 tablespoon salt
- 3-pounds rack of ribs
- ½ tablespoon garlic powder
- ½ tablespoon black pepper
- 1 cup Southern apple cider barbecue sauce
- ½ cup water

Nutrition information:

Calories per serving:477; Carbohydrates: 29.8g; Protein: 52.9g; Fat: 14.9g; Sugar: 24.2g; Sodium: 1600mg

Directions for Cooking:

1. Place all ingredients in the pot.
2. Make sure that the pork is coated with the sauce.
3. Close the lid and press the manual button. Adjust the cooking time by pressing the "+" "-" button to 25 minutes.
4. Do quick release. Remove the ribs from the pot and set it on a baking pan. Cover the baking pan with aluminum foil and place the ribs in the oven. Cook for 10 minutes at 400°F.
5. Serve and enjoy.

---

100. Pork Tenderloin Green Chili

(Servings: 6, Cooking time: 25 minutes)

Ingredients:

- 2 cups kale, chopped
- 2 15-ounce cannellini beans, drained
- 2 cups chicken broth
- 1 4 ounce diced green chilies, drained
- 1 cup salsa verde
- 1 cup chopped green bell pepper
- 2 cups onion, chopped
- 1 tablespoon chili powder
- 1 tablespoon garlic, minced
- 1 teaspoon ground cumin
- 1 dried bay leaf
- ½ teaspoon dried oregano
- 12-ounces pork tenderloin, boneless and fat trimmed
- ½ cup cilantro, chopped

Directions for Cooking:

1. In a blender, mix together kale, half of the cannellini beans and broth. Blend until smooth.
2. Transfer this mixture into the slow cooker and add the rest of the ingredients except the cilantro.
3. Close the lid and press the manual button. Cook on high for 25 minutes.
4. Do quick pressure release to open the lid.
5. Remove the bay leaf and transfer the pork in another bowl. Shred with fork.
6. Garnish with cilantro.

Nutrition information:

Calories per serving: 287; Carbohydrates: 16.3g; Protein: 35.5g; Fat: 9.0g; Sugar: 4.8g; Sodium: 723mg

---

101. Teriyaki Pork Tenderloin

(Servings: 6, Cooking time: 25 minutes)

Ingredients:

- 2 tablespoon olive oil
- 2-pounds pork tenderloin, cut into strips
- 4 cloves of garlic, minced
- ½ large onion, chopped
- 3 red chili pepper, chopped
- ¼ teaspoon black pepper
- ½ cup teriyaki sauce
- 1 cup chicken broth
- ¼ cup brown sugar

Nutrition information:

Calories per serving: 393; Carbohydrates: 16.9g; Protein: 50.3g; Fat: 12.7g; Sugar: 14.0g; Sodium: 683mg

Directions for Cooking:

1. Press the sauté button on the Instant Pot.
2. Heat the oil and add the tenderloins. Stir constantly for 5 minutes or until they become brown.
3. Add in garlic, onion, red chili pepper and black pepper.
4. Add the remaining ingredients.
5. Close the lid and press the stew button. Adjust the cooking time to 20 minutes.
6. Do natural pressure release.
7. Serve with rice.

---

102. Southwestern Pork Chops

(Servings: 4, Cooking time: 20 minutes)

Ingredients:

- 4 4-ounces lean pork loin chop, boneless and fat trimmed
- 1 tbsp vegetable oil
- 1/3 cup salsa
- 2 tablespoon lime juice
- 1 cup water
- ¼ cup fresh cilantro

Nutrition information:

Calories per serving: 274; Carbohydrates: 2.1g; Protein: 29.4g; Fat: 16.0g; Sugar: 1.0g; Sodium: 215mg

Directions for Cooking:

1. Flatten the pork chops with your hand.
2. Add oil to the Instant Pot set at the sauté setting. Place the pork chops and cook for one minute on each side.
3. Pour the salsa and lime juice over the pork chops.
4. Add in the water.
5. Close the lid and press the stew setting. Press the "+" "-" button and adjust the time to 15 minutes.
6. Do natural pressure release.
7. Sprinkle with cilantro on top.

---

103. Tropical Beef with Peppers and Pineapple

(Servings: 4, Cooking time: 20 minutes)

Ingredients:

- 1 tablespoon olive oil
- 1 large onion, chopped
- 2-pounds round steak, cut into chunks
- ½ teaspoon salt
- 1/8 teaspoon pepper
- 1 can pineapple chunks
- 2 large green peppers, chopped
- 1 can mild green chilies
- 1 can diced tomatoes
- 1 ½ tablespoon Greek seasoning
- 1 cup water
- 2 tablespoon cornstarch + 1 tablespoon water

Nutrition information:

Calories per serving: 583; Carbohydrates: 23.5g; Protein: 71.0g; Fat: 21.2g; Sugar: 17.6g; Sodium: 785mg

Directions for Cooking:

1. Press the Sauté button and heat the oil. Sauté the onion until tender. Keep on stirring to avoid the onions from burning.
2. Season the round steak with salt and pepper. Add to the pot and brown for another five minutes.
3. Add the pineapples, green pepper, chilies and diced tomatoes. Season with Greek seasoning. Add water.
4. Close the lid and press the stew button for 15 minutes.
5. Meanwhile, mix together the cornstarch and water in a bowl.
6. Do a quick release to open the lid. Add the cornstarch slurry and press the sauté button. Simmer until the sauce thickens.
7. Enjoy.

---

104. Herb-Crusted Beef

(Servings: 6, Cooking time: 35 minutes)

Ingredients:

- 1-pound lean beef roast
- ½ teaspoon black pepper, ground
- 1 ½ teaspoon salt
- ¼ cup Dijon mustard
- 1 ½ teaspoon prepared horseradish
- 2 tablespoon low-calorie mayonnaise
- 2 cloves of garlic, minced
- 1 ½ cup water
- 1/3 cup fresh parsley, chopped
- 2 tablespoon thyme, chopped
- 2 tablespoon dill, chopped

Directions for Cooking:

1. Mix all ingredients in the Instant Pot.
2. Close the lid and press the manual button. Cook on high for 35 minutes.
3. Do natural pressure release.
4. Check if the meat is done and tender.
5. Serve and enjoy.

Nutrition information:

Calories per serving: 166; Carbohydrates: 3.2g; Protein: 11.4g; Fat: 8.0g; Sugar: 0.4g; Sodium: 770mg

---

105. Caribbean Pineapple Filet Mignon

(Servings: 1, Cooking time: 35 minutes)

Ingredients:

- 1 filet mignon
- ½ cup pineapple, chopped
- 1-piece bacon
- ¼ teaspoon jalapeno pepper
- 2 tablespoon red onions, chopped
- 2 cloves of garlic, minced
- 2 tablespoon coconut aminos or soy sauce
- 3 tablespoon honey
- ½ of a lime, juiced
- 1 tablespoon apple cider vinegar
- ¼ teaspoon ground ginger
- 1 teaspoon thyme
- ¼ teaspoon cinnamon
- 1/8 teaspoon ground cloves
- 1/8 teaspoon ground nutmeg
- Salt and pepper to taste

Directions for Cooking:

1. Place all ingredients in the Instant Pot and mix well.
2. Close the lid and press the manual button. Cook on high for 35 minutes.
3. Do natural pressure release to open the lid.
4. Serve and enjoy.

Nutrition information:

Calories per serving: 656; Carbohydrates: 85.4g; Protein: 45.5g; Fat: 18.4g; Sugar: 75.1g; Sodium: 1263mg

---

Instant Pot Poultry Recipes

106. Chinese Take-out General Tso's Chicken

(Servings: 6, Cooking time: 15 minutes)

Ingredients:

- 3 pounds chicken breasts, cut into chunks
- 1 cup potato starch
- 2 eggs, beaten
- 2 tablespoons peanut oil
- 2 tablespoons sesame seeds
- 1 tablespoon grated ginger root
- 1 tablespoon garlic, minced
- ½ cup chicken stock
- ¼ cup rice vinegar
- ¼ cup brown sugar
- ¼ cup Shaoxing wine
- ¼ cup soy sauce
- 1 teaspoon pure sesame oil
- 2 teaspoon sambal oelek

Directions for Cooking:

1. In a plastic bag, place the chicken and potato starch. Dip the chicken into the egg mixture then set aside.
2. Press the Sauté button on the Instant Pot and add oil. Place the dredged chicken pieces and sear until the chicken becomes lightly brown and puffy. Stir in the sesame seeds.
3. Stir in the rest of the ingredients and give a good stir.
4. Close Instant Pot, press the button, choose high settings, and set time to 10 minutes.
5. Once done cooking, do a QPR.
6. Serve with rice and enjoy.

Nutrition information:
Calories per serving: 549; Carbohydrates: 18.2g; Protein: 52.7g; Fat: 33.3g; Sugar: 11g; Sodium: 373mg

---

107. Best Instant Pot Chicken Breast

(Servings: 4, Cooking time: 10 minutes)

Ingredients:

- 1 teaspoon dried Italian herb mix
- ½ teaspoon paprika
- ½ teaspoon ground coriander
- ½ teaspoon ground ginger
- ½ teaspoon ground garlic powder
- Salt and pepper to taste
- 2 pounds chicken breast
- 2 tablespoons olive oil
- 1 cup chicken stock

Directions for Cooking:

1. In a mixing bowl, combine the Italian herb mix, paprika, coriander, ginger, garlic, salt and pepper. Sprinkle over the chicken breasts.
2. Press the Sauté button on the Instant Pot and heat the oil. Sauté the chicken breasts for 3 minutes on each side until lightly brown. Set aside.
3. Place a trivet or a steamer in the Instant Pot and pour the chicken stock. Place the chicken back on the steamer.
4. Close Instant Pot, press the Steam button, choose high settings, and set time to 5 minutes.
5. Once done cooking, do natural pressure release.
6. Serve and enjoy.

Nutrition information:
Calories per serving:282; Carbohydrates: 2g; Protein: 35g; Fat: 13g; Sugar: 0.3g; Sodium: 202mg

108. Hawaiian Chicken Instant Pot

(Servings: 9, Cooking time: 15 minutes)

Ingredients:

- 2 tablespoons coconut oil
- 4 ½ pounds boneless chicken thighs
- 2 cups chopped onion
- 4 cloves of garlic, minced
- 2 cups red bell pepper, chopped
- 1 cup pineapple chunks
- 1 ¼ cup pineapple juice
- ¾ cup soy sauce
- 2 tablespoons apple cider vinegar
- 1 cup dark brown sugar
- 2 tablespoons cornstarch + 3 tablespoons water

Nutrition information:

Calories per serving:703; Carbohydrates: 32.1g; Protein: 52.9g; Fat: 40.1g; Sugar: 12.4g; Sodium: 1293mg

Directions for Cooking:

1. Press the Sauté button on the Instant Pot and heat the oil.
2. Stir in the chicken, onion, and garlic. Continue stirring until the chicken turns lightly golden.
3. Add the bell pepper, pineapple chunks, pineapple juice, soy sauce, apple cider vinegar, and dark sugar.
4. Close Instant Pot, press the Manual button, choose high settings, and set time to 10 minutes.
5. Once done cooking, do a QPR.
6. Open the lid and press the Sauté button. Pour the cornstarch slurry and stir until the sauce thickens.
7. Serve and enjoy.

---

109. Honey Bourbon Chicken

(Servings: 9, Cooking time: 15 minutes)

Ingredients:

- 1 tablespoon oil
- ¾ cup onion, chopped
- 3 cloves of garlic, minced
- 2 pounds chicken, cut into bite-sized pieces
- 3 tablespoons tomato paste
- ½ cup honey
- 1/3 cup soy sauce
- ¼ cup water
- ½ teaspoon smoked paprika
- ½ teaspoon pepper
- 2 tablespoons cornstarch + 3 tablespoons water

Nutrition information:

Calories per serving:326; Carbohydrates: 20.4; Protein: 19.1g; Fat: 18.4g; Sugar: 8.2g; Sodium: 289mg

Directions for Cooking:

1. Press the Sauté button on the Instant Pot and heat the oil. Sauté the onion and garlic until fragrant.
2. Stir in the chicken until lightly golden. Add the tomato paste, honey, soy sauce, water, paprika, and pepper.
3. Close Instant Pot, press the Manual button, choose high settings, and set time to 10 minutes.
4. Once done cooking, do a QPR.
5. Open the lid and press the Sauté button. Stir in the cornstarch slurry and allow to simmer until the sauce thickens.
6. Serve and enjoy.

---

110. Creamy Tuscan Garlic Chicken

(Servings: 4, Cooking time: 15 minutes)

Ingredients:

- 2 tablespoons olive oil
- 2 pounds skinless chicken breasts, halved and pounded
- 4 cloves of garlic, minced
- 1 tablespoon Italian seasoning
- 1 teaspoon salt
- 3/4 cup chicken stock
- ¾ cup heavy cream
- ¾ cup parmesan cheese
- ½ cup sun-dried tomato

Directions for Cooking:

1. Press the Sauté button on the Instant Pot and sear the chicken breasts on all sides.
2. Stir in the garlic, Italian seasoning, and salt.
3. Pour in the chicken stock and the rest of the ingredients.
4. Close Instant Pot, press the Manual button, choose high settings, and set time to 10 minutes.
5. Once done cooking, do a QPR.
6. Serve and enjoy.

Nutrition information:

Calories per serving: 533; Carbohydrates: 10.8g; Protein: 59.9g; Fat: 26.5g; Sugar: 4g; Sodium: 1267mg

---

111. Chili Lime Chicken Thighs

(Servings: 4, Cooking time: 20 minutes)

Ingredients:

- 2 tablespoons olive oil
- 3 cloves of garlic, minced
- 1 teaspoon cumin
- 1 teaspoon chili powder
- 4 chicken thighs
- Juice from 1 lime
- 1 cup chicken stock
- Salt and pepper to taste
- 2 tablespoons cornstarch + 3 tablespoons water
- ¼ cup fresh cilantro, chopped

Directions for Cooking:

1. Press the Sauté button on the Instant Pot and heat the oil. Sauté the garlic, cumin, and chili powder until fragrant.
2. Stir in the chicken thighs and continue stirring until all sides are lightly golden.
3. Add the lime juice and chicken stock. Season with salt and pepper to taste.
4. Close Instant Pot, press the Manual button, choose high settings, and set time to 10 minutes.
5. Once done cooking, do a QPR.
6. Open the lid and stir in the cornstarch slurry and cilantro. Allow to simmer until the sauce thickens.
7. Serve and enjoy.

Nutrition information:

Calories per serving: 523; Carbohydrates: 5.9g; Protein: 34.2g; Fat: 39.7g; Sugar: 1.8g; Sodium: 264mg

---

112. One Pot Peruvian Chicken

(Servings: 9 , Cooking time: 20 minutes)

Ingredients:

- 3 pounds chicken
- 3 tablespoons paprika
- 2 tablespoons ground cumin
- 1 ½ tablespoons minced garlic
- 2 tablespoons lime juice
- 4 tablespoons canola oil
- Salt and pepper to taste
- ¼ cup chopped cilantro
- ½ cup water
- 5 jalapenos, chopped
- 1 tablespoon lime juice

Directions for Cooking:

1. Place all ingredients in the Instant Pot. Mix all ingredients until well-combined.
2. Close Instant Pot, press the Manual button, choose high settings, and set time to 20 minutes.
3. Once done cooking, do a QPR.
4. Serve and enjoy.

Nutrition information:

Calories per serving: 397; Carbohydrates: 3.2g; Protein: 28.9g; Fat: 29.6g; Sugar: 0.6g; Sodium: 111mg

---

113. Chicken Cacciatore

(Servings: 4 , Cooking time: 15 minutes)

Ingredients:

- 1 tablespoon oil
- 1 ¼ pounds chicken thighs, cut into large chunks
- 1 onion, diced
- 3 teaspoons garlic, minced
- 1 tablespoon Italian seasoning
- 2 bell peppers, cut into strips
- 1 can crushed tomatoes
- Salt and pepper to taste

Nutrition information:

Calories per serving: 199; Carbohydrates: 6g; Protein: 28g; Fat: 6g; Sugar: 3g; Sodium: 711mg

Directions for Cooking:

1. Press the Sauté button on the Instant Pot and stir in the chicken, onion, and garlic until fragrant.
2. Add the Italian seasoning and the rest of the ingredients.
3. Close Instant Pot, press the Manual button, choose high settings, and set time to 10 minutes.
4. Once done cooking, do a QPR.
5. Serve and enjoy.

---

114. Instant Pot Chicken and Dumplings

(Servings: 4, Cooking time: 20 minutes)

Ingredients:

- 2 pounds chicken breasts, cut into cubes
- 2 cloves of garlic, minced
- 1 cup chopped onion
- 1 cup chopped celery
- 1 teaspoon dried thyme
- 1 tablespoon bouillon
- 2 cups frozen vegetables (peas and carrots)
- 3 cups chicken stock
- 2 cans cream of chicken
- Salt and pepper to taste
- 1 can Southern Homestyle biscuits
- ¼ cup parsley, chopped

Nutrition information:

Calories per serving:739; Carbohydrates: 51.2g; Protein: 63.8g; Fat: 29.6g; Sugar: 8.3g; Sodium: 1165mg

Directions for Cooking:

1. Press the Sauté button on the Instant Pot and stir in the chicken, garlic, onion, celery, and thyme. Stir constantly and allow the onions to sweat.
2. Stir in bouillon, vegetables, stock, and cream of chicken. Stir in the cream of chicken and season with salt and pepper to taste. Allow to simmer for a few minutes.
3. Add the biscuits on top.
4. Close Instant Pot, press the Manual button, choose high settings, and set time to 15 minutes.
5. Once done cooking, do a QPR.
6. Garnish with parsley.
7. Serve and enjoy.

---

115. Instant Pot Mississippi Chicken

(Servings: 6, Cooking time: 20 minutes)

Ingredients:

- 3 pounds chicken thighs
- ½ cup chicken broth,
- ½ jar pepperoncini, not drained
- 1 packet brown gravy mix
- 1 packet ranch dressing
- ½ stick butter
- Salt and pepper to taste
- 1 cup rice
- 2 cups water

Nutrition information:

Calories per serving: 714; Carbohydrates: 13.1g; Protein: 46.7g; Fat: 54.3g; Sugar: 0.6g; Sodium: 571mg

Directions for Cooking:

1. Place all ingredients in the Instant Pot except for the rice and water. Give a good stir.
2. Place a trivet on top of the chicken. In a heat-proof dish, place the rice and water. Place the bowl on the trivet.
3. Close Instant Pot, press the Manual button, choose high settings, and set time to 20 minutes.
4. Once done cooking, do a QPR.
5. Take the bowl of cooked rice and the trivet.
6. Ladle the chicken on to cooked rice.
7. Serve and enjoy.

---

116. Instant Pot Butter Chicken

(Servings: 2, Cooking time: 20 minutes)

Ingredients:

- 4 ounces butter, cut into cubes
- 1-pound boneless chicken breast, cut into cubes
- 6 cloves of garlic, minced
- 2 teaspoons grated ginger
- 1 teaspoon turmeric powder
- ½ teaspoon cayenne pepper
- 1 teaspoon paprika
- 1 teaspoon garam masala
- 1 teaspoon ground cumin
- 1 can diced tomatoes
- 4 ounces heavy cream
- Salt to taste
- ¼ cup chopped cilantro

Directions for Cooking:

1. Press the Sauté button on the Instant Pot and heat the butter.
2. Stir in chicken breast, garlic, ginger, turmeric powder, cayenne pepper, paprika, garam masala, and cumin. Stir for 3 minutes until well-combined,
3. Add the diced tomatoes and heavy cream. Season with salt and pepper to taste.
4. Close Instant Pot, press the Manual button, choose high settings, and set time to 15 minutes.
5. Once done cooking, do a QPR.
6. Garnish with chopped cilantro
7. Serve and enjoy.

Nutrition information:

Calories per serving:918; Carbohydrates: 10.6g; Protein: 54.6g; Fat: 73.7g; Sugar: 4.4g; Sodium: 703mg

---

117. Chinese Takeout Sweet and Sour Chicken

(Servings: 4, Cooking time: 15 minutes)

Ingredients:

- 2 pounds chicken breasts
- 1 cup potato starch
- ¼ teaspoon Chinese five-spice powder
- Salt and pepper to taste
- 3 tablespoons vegetable oil
- 2 cloves of garlic, minced
- 1 onion, chopped
- ½ cup water
- ¾ cup sugar
- ½ cup ketchup
- ¾ cup apple cider vinegar
- ¼ cup soy sauce

Nutrition information:

Calories per serving: 696; Carbohydrates: 46.8g; Protein: 50.7g; Fat: 34.5g; Sugar: 16.4g; Sodium: 663mg

Directions for Cooking:

1. In a mixing bowl, combine the chicken, potato starch, and Chinese five spice powder. Season with salt and pepper to taste.
2. Press the Sauté button on the Instant Pot and heat the oil. Fry the chicken on all sides until lightly brown.
3. Stir in the garlic and onion until fragrant.
4. Add the rest of the ingredients.
5. Close Instant Pot, press the Manual button, choose high settings, and set time to 10 minutes.
6. Once done cooking, do a QPR.
7. Serve and enjoy.

---

118. Instant Pot Honey Garlic Chicken

(Servings: 3, Cooking time: 20 minutes)

Ingredients:

- 1 tablespoon olive oil
- 3 chicken breasts, cut into chunks
- Salt and pepper to taste
- 6 cloves of garlic, minced
- 1/3 cup honey
- 1 tablespoon soy sauce
- ¾ cup water
- 1 teaspoon lemon juice
- 1 tablespoon cornstarch + 2 tablespoons cold water

Nutrition information:

Calories per serving:683; Carbohydrates: 35.8g; Protein: 61.5g; Fat: 32.5g; Sugar: 21g; Sodium: 265mg

Directions for Cooking:

1. Press the Sauté button on the Instant Pot.
2. Heat the oil and stir in the chicken. Season with salt and pepper to taste and continue stirring until lightly golden. Add garlic until fragrant.
3. Stir in the honey, soy sauce, water, and lemon juice.
4. Close Instant Pot, press the Manual button, choose high settings, and set time to 15 minutes.
5. Once done cooking, do a QPR.
6. Open the lid and press the Sauté button. Stir in the cornstarch slurry and allow to simmer until the sauce thickens.
7. Serve and enjoy.

---

119. Instant Pot Orange Chicken

(Servings: 4, Cooking time: 20 minutes)

Ingredients:

- 4 boneless chicken breasts, cubed
- ¼ cup water
- ½ cup orange juice
- ¼ cup brown sugar
- 1/3 cup soy sauce
- 2 tablespoons ketchup
- 1 tablespoon apple cider vinegar
- 2 cloves of garlic, minced
- ½ teaspoon ground ginger
- Salt and pepper to taste
- 2 tablespoons cornstarch + 3 tablespoons water

Directions for Cooking:

1. Place all ingredients in the Instant Pot except for the cornstarch mixture.
2. Close Instant Pot, press the Manual button, choose high settings, and set time to 20 minutes.
3. Once done cooking, do a QPR.
4. Open the lid and press the Sauté button. Stir in the cornstarch slurry and allow to simmer for the sauce to thicken.
5. Serve and enjoy.

Nutrition information:

Calories per serving: 431; Carbohydrates: 26.8g; Protein: 60.2g; Fat: 9.7g; Sugar: 12.6g; Sodium: 486mg

---

120. One Pot Chicken Curry

(Servings: 6, Cooking time: 15 minutes)

Ingredients:

- 6 chicken drumsticks
- 1 onion, chopped
- 2 cloves of garlic, minced
- 1 thumb-size ginger
- 1 tablespoon curry powder or garam masala
- ½ cup chicken broth
- 1cup heavy cream

Directions for Cooking:

1. Place all ingredients in the Instant Pot and give a good stir.
2. Close Instant Pot, press the Manual button, choose high settings, and set time to 15 minutes.
3. Once done cooking, do a QPR.
4. Serve and enjoy.

Nutrition information:

Calories per serving: 270; Carbohydrates: 3.4g; Protein: 30.3g; Fat: 15.2g; Sugar: 1.4g; Sodium: 214mg

---

121. Instant Pot Ranch Chicken

(Servings: 4, Cooking time: 17 minutes)

Ingredients:

- 1 tablespoon olive oil
- 2 pounds boneless chicken breasts
- 2 tablespoon taco seasoning
- 1 cup coconut cream
- ½ teaspoon garlic powder
- ½ teaspoon onion powder
- ½ teaspoon black pepper
- Salt and pepper to taste
- 1 tablespoon red wine vinegar
- ¾ cup chicken broth
- 1 cup parsley, chopped

Directions for Cooking:

1. Press the Sauté button on the Instant Pot and heat the oil.
2. Stir in the chicken and season with the taco seasoning. Keep stirring for 2 minutes.
3. Add the rest of the ingredients except for the parsley.
4. Close Instant Pot, press the Manual button, choose high settings, and set time to 15 minutes.
5. Once done cooking, do a QPR.
6. Garnish with chopped parsley.
7. Serve and enjoy.

Nutrition information:

Calories per serving:322; Carbohydrates: 3.5g; Protein: 28.6g; Fat: 20.9g; Sugar: 1.3g; Sodium: 229mg

---

122. Instant Pot Gingered Orange Chicken

(Servings: 2, Cooking time: 20 minutes)

Ingredients:

- ¼ cup chicken broth
- 1/3 cup soy sauce
- ½ cup rice vinegar
- ½ cup honey
- 1 tablespoon ginger
- 1 teaspoon red pepper, crushed
- 2 cloves of garlic, minced
- 1 peeled orange, segmented and seeds removed
- A dash of orange zest
- 2 large chicken breasts

Directions for Cooking:

1. Place all ingredients in the Instant Pot and give a good stir.
2. Close Instant Pot, press the Manual button, choose high settings, and set time to 20 minutes.
3. Once done cooking, do a QPR.
4. Serve and enjoy.

Nutrition information:

Calories per serving: 1127; Carbohydrates: 97.1g; Protein: 103.2g; Fat: 34.9g; Sugar: 46.3g; Sodium: 891mg

---

123. Instant Pot Cashew Chicken

(Servings: 2, Cooking time: 20 minutes)

Ingredients:

- 2 chicken breasts
- ½ cup chicken stock
- 2 tablespoons soy sauce
- 2 tablespoons rice vinegar
- 2 tablespoons hoisin sauce
- 1 tablespoon honey
- 2 teaspoons sesame oil
- 1 teaspoon fresh ginger, grated
- 1 clove of garlic, minced
- Salt and pepper to taste
- ½ red bell pepper, diced
- 1 ½ cups broccoli cut into florets
- 2 tablespoons cornstarch + 3 tablespoons water
- ½ cup whole cashews

Directions for Cooking:

1. Place the chicken breasts, chicken stock, soy sauce, rice vinegar, hoisin sauce, honey, sesame oil, ginger, and garlic in the Instant Pot. Give a good stir.
2. Close Instant Pot, press the Manual button, choose high settings, and set time to 15 minutes.
3. Once done cooking, do a QPR.
4. Open the lid and press the Sauté button. Stir in the red peppers and broccoli florets. Allow to simmer until the vegetables are cooked through. Stir in the cornstarch slurry and stir until the sauce thickens.
5. Garnish with cashew nuts on top.
6. Serve and enjoy.

Nutrition information:

Calories per serving:1090; Carbohydrates: 46g; Protein: 73.7g; Fat: 69.4g; Sugar: 24g; Sodium: 971mg

---

124. Taiwanese Chicken San Bei Ji

(Servings: 4, Cooking time: 20 minutes)

Ingredients:

- ¼ cup sesame oil
- 5 dried chilies
- ¼ cup garlic, smashed
- 2 tablespoons sliced ginger
- 2 pounds chicken breasts, cut into half
- ¼ cup soy sauce
- ¼ cup rice wine
- Salt to taste
- ¼ cup chopped Thai basil
- 1 tablespoon cornstarch + 2 tablespoons water

Nutrition information:

Calories per serving: 596; Carbohydrates: 11.1g; Protein: 50.1g; Fat: 39.1g; Sugar: 5.2g; Sodium: 459mg

Directions for Cooking:

1. Place in the Instant Pot the sesame oil, dried chilies, garlic, ginger, chicken, soy sauce, and rice wine.
2. Close Instant Pot, press the Manual button, choose high settings, and set time to 15 minutes.
3. Once done cooking, do a QPR.
4. Open the lid and press the Sauté button. Stir in the Thai basil and cornstarch slurry and allow to simmer until the sauce thickens.
5. Serve and enjoy.

---

125. Instant Pot Teriyaki Chicken

(Servings: 4 , Cooking time: 25 minutes)

Ingredients:

- 1 cup soy sauce
- 1 cup brown sugar
- ½ cup ketchup
- 1 teaspoon ground ginger
- 2 pounds chicken breasts
- 1 tablespoon cornstarch + 2 tablespoons water

Nutrition information:

Calories per serving:816; Carbohydrates: 78.3g; Protein: 52.5g; Fat: 32.5g; Sugar: 25.2g; Sodium: 1395mg

Directions for Cooking:

1. Place the soy sauce, brown sugar, ketchup, ginger, and chicken breasts in the Instant Pot and give a good stir.
2. Close Instant Pot, press the Manual button, choose high settings, and set time to 20 minutes.
3. Once done cooking, do a QPR.
4. Open the lid and press the Sauté button. Stir in the cornstarch slurry and allow to simmer until the sauce thickens.
5. Serve and enjoy.

---

126. Spicy Chicken Rice Meal

(Servings: 6, Cooking time: 25 minutes)

Ingredients:

- 1 tablespoon oil
- 1 tablespoon minced garlic
- 1 onion, chopped
- 2 chicken breasts, cut into cubes
- 1 tablespoon chili powder
- 1 teaspoon cayenne pepper
- 1 cup long grain rice
- 2 cups prepared salsa
- 1 ½ cups water
- Salt and pepper to taste
- 1 can beans
- 1 cup corn
- cilantro

Nutrition information:

Calories per serving: 444; Carbohydrates: 53.9g; Protein: 27.1g; Fat: 13.8g; Sugar: 5g; Sodium: 759mg

Directions for Cooking:

1. Press the Sauté button on the Instant Pot and heat the oil. Stir in the garlic and onions and cook until fragrant. Add n the chicken breasts and season with chili powder and cayenne powder.
2. Stir in the rice, salsa, and water. Season with salt and pepper to taste.
3. Close Instant Pot, press the Manual button, choose high settings, and cook for 20 minutes.
4. Once done cooking, do a QPR.
5. Open the lid and stir in the beans, corn, and cilantro.
6. Serve and enjoy.

---

127. Instant Pot Chicken and Corn Soup

(Servings: 2, Cooking time: 15 minutes)

Ingredients:

- 1 tablespoon oil
- 2 chicken breasts, cut in half
- 1 tablespoon garlic, minced
- 1 tablespoon chili powder
- Salt and pepper to taste
- 1 cup corn
- 4 cups chicken broth
- 1 cup cilantro, chopped

Nutrition information:

Calories per serving: 1649; Carbohydrates: 71.1g; Protein: 173.5g; Fat: 71.3g; Sugar: 2g; Sodium: 2309mg

Directions for Cooking:

1. Press the Sauté button on the Instant Pot and heat the oil.
2. Stir in the chicken, garlic, and chili powder. Stir to combine everything.
3. Season with salt and pepper to taste.
4. Add the corn and chicken broth.
5. Close Instant Pot, press the Manual button, choose high settings, and set time to 15 minutes.
6. Once done cooking, do a QPR.
7. Open the lid and stir in the cilantro.
8. Serve and enjoy.

---

128. Instant Pot Hawaiian Chicken

(Servings: 9, Cooking time: 15 minutes)

Ingredients:

- 2 tablespoons coconut oil
- 4 cloves of garlic, minced
- 1 onion, chopped
- 4 ½ pounds skinless chicken thighs
- 2 cups yellow corn, cut
- 2 cups red bell pepper, chopped
- 2 cups yellow bell pepper, chopped
- 1 can pineapple chunks
- 1 ¼ cups pineapple juice
- ¾ cup soy sauce
- 2 tablespoons apple cider vinegar
- 1 cup dark brown sugar
- 2 tablespoons cornstarch + 3 tablespoons water

Nutrition information:

Calories per serving: 855; Carbohydrates: 76.8g; Protein: 57.8g; Fat: 35.6g; Sugar: 28g; Sodium: 1306mg

Directions for Cooking:

1. Press the Sauté button and heat the oil. Stir the garlic and onion until fragrant.
2. Stir in the chicken for three minutes until lightly golden.
3. Stir in the corn, bell peppers, pineapple chunks, pineapple juice, soy sauce, apple cider vinegar, and sugar.
4. Close Instant Pot, press the Manual button, choose high settings, and set time to 10 minutes.
5. Once done cooking, do a QPR.
6. Open the lid and press the Sauté button. Stir in the cornstarch slurry and allow to simmer until the sauce thickens.
7. Serve and enjoy.

---

129. Greek Chicken Rice

(Servings: 4 , Cooking time: 20 minutes)

Ingredients:

- 1 ½ cups uncooked white rice
- 1 cup chicken stock
- A dash of lemon zest
- 4 chicken breasts, cubed
- ½ cup chicken stock
- 1 tablespoon oregano
- ½ teaspoon rosemary
- ½ teaspoon thyme
- 3 cloves of garlic, minced
- Juice from 1 lemon, freshly squeezed

Nutrition information:

Calories per serving: 432; Carbohydrates: 60g; Protein: 31g; Fat: 4g; Sugar: 1g; Sodium: 264mg

Directions for Cooking:

1. Prepare the rice by placing the rice, chicken stock, and lemon zest in a heat-proof dish that will fit inside the Instant Pot. Set aside.
2. Press the Sauté button on the Instant Pot and Add the rest of the ingredients.
3. Place a trivet on top of the chicken and place the dish with the prepared rice.
4. Close Instant Pot, press the Manual button, choose high settings, and set time to 20 minutes.
5. Once done cooking, do a QPR.
6. Serve rice with chicken and enjoy.

---

130. Instant Pot Butter Chicken

(Servings: 4, Cooking time: 15 minutes)

Ingredients:

- 2 tablespoons coconut oil
- 4 teaspoon garlic paste
- 5 teaspoon tomato paste
- 1 cup tomato pasta
- 4 tablespoons garam masala
- ½ teaspoon coriander
- ½ teaspoon cumin
- 1 tablespoon smoked paprika
- 1 teaspoon turmeric
- 2-pound chicken thighs
- 1 cup chicken stock
- 1 cup milk
- 2 tablespoons cornstarch + 3 tablespoons water

Nutrition information:

Calories per serving: 678; Carbohydrates: 17.8g; Protein: 43.1g; Fat: 47.8g; Sugar: 7.4g; Sodium: 464mg

Directions for Cooking:

1. Press the Sauté button on the Instant Pot and heat the oil.
2. Stir in the garlic paste, tomato paste, pasta, garam masala, coriander, cumin, smoked paprika, and turmeric. Toast for a minute until fragrant.
3. Place the chicken and stir for 2 minutes.
4. Add the chicken stock and milk.
5. Close Instant Pot, press the Manual button, choose high settings, and set time to 10 minutes.
6. Once done cooking, do a QPR.
7. Open the lid and stir in the cornstarch slurry. Allow to simmer until the sauce thickens.
8. Serve and enjoy.

---

131. Honey Mustard Curry Chicken

(Servings: 4 , Cooking time: 20 minutes)

Ingredients:

- 1 tablespoon olive oil
- 4 tablespoons butter
- 1 teaspoon onion, minced
- 4 boneless skinless chicken breasts
- Salt and pepper to taste
- ½ cup honey
- ¼ cup Dijon mustard
- 1 ½ teaspoon curry powder
- ½ cup water

Nutrition information:

Calories per serving:586; Carbohydrates: 43.6g; Protein: 54.9g; Fat: 21.9g; Sugar: 38g; Sodium: 891mg

Directions for Cooking:

1. Press the Sauté button on the Instant Pot and heat the oil and butter.
2. Sauté the onion until fragrant and add the chicken. Season with salt and pepper to taste.
3. Stir in the rest of the ingredients.
4. Close Instant Pot, press the Manual button, choose high settings, and set time to 15 minutes.
5. Once done cooking, do a QPR.
6. Serve and enjoy.

---

132. Instant Pot Simple Chicken Dinner

(Servings: 4, Cooking time: 15 minutes)

Ingredients:

- 1 can crushed pineapple
- 2 pounds boneless chicken breasts
- 3 cans fire-roasted tomatoes
- Salt and pepper to taste

Directions for Cooking:

1. Place all ingredients in the Instant Pot. Give a good stir.
2. Close Instant Pot, press the Manual button, choose high settings, and set time to 15 minutes.
3. Once done cooking, do a QPR.
4. Serve and enjoy.

Nutrition information:

Calories per serving: 396; Carbohydrates: 29.9g; Protein: 53.1g; Fat: 6.3g; Sugar: 13.2g; Sodium: 391mg

---

133. Instant Pot Chicken Pot Pie

(Servings: 4, Cooking time: 20 minutes)

Ingredients:

- 4 chicken breasts
- 1 can cream of chicken soup
- 1 cup milk
- 1 cup chicken broth
- ½ onion, chopped
- 4 potatoes, peeled and diced
- 1 bag frozen mixed vegetables
- ½ cup celery, chopped
- ¼ teaspoon poultry seasoning
- Salt and pepper to taste
- Canned biscuits

Directions for Cooking:

1. In the Instant Pot, place the chicken, chicken soup, milk, chicken broth, onion, potatoes, vegetables, celery, and poultry seasoning. Season with salt and pepper to taste.
2. Close Instant Pot, press the Manual button, choose high settings, and set time to 20 minutes.
3. Once done cooking, do a QPR.
4. Open the lid and serve with biscuits on top.
5. Serve and enjoy.

Nutrition information:

Calories per serving:1028; Carbohydrates: 80.9g; Protein: 85.7g; Fat: 38.8g; Sugar: 7g; Sodium: 1086mg

---

134. Creamy Salsa Chicken

(Servings: 5, Cooking time: 15 minutes)

Ingredients:

- 2 ½ pounds chicken breasts
- ½ cup chicken broth
- 4-ounce cream cheese
- ½ cup cottage cheese
- 1 cup salsa
- 2 teaspoon taco seasoning
- ¼ cup shredded cheese

Directions for Cooking:

1. Place all ingredients in the Instant Pot except for the cheese.
2. Close Instant Pot, press the Manual button, choose high settings, and set time to 15 minutes.
3. Once done cooking, do a QPR.
4. Open the lid and garnish with cheese on top.
5. Serve and enjoy.

Nutrition information:

Calories per serving: 559; Carbohydrates: 5.8g; Protein: 58.8g; Fat: 32.1g; Sugar: 3.5g; Sodium: 906mg

---

135. Balsamic Ginger Chicken

(Servings: 8, Cooking time: 15 minutes)

Ingredients:

- 8 chicken thighs
- 1/3 cup balsamic vinegar
- 3 tablespoons mustard
- 2 tablespoons ginger garlic paste
- 4 cloves of garlic, minced
- 2-inches fresh ginger root
- 4 tablespoons honey
- Salt and pepper to taste

Directions for Cooking:

1. Place all ingredients in the Instant Pot. Stir to combine everything.
2. Close Instant Pot, press the Manual button, choose high settings, and set time to 15 minutes.
3. Once done cooking, do a QPR.
4. Serve and enjoy.

Nutrition information:

Calories per serving: 477; Carbohydrates:12.5g; Protein: 32.4g; Fat: 32.9g; Sugar: 10.5g; Sodium: 244mg

---

136. Buffalo Chicken Wings

(Servings: 8, Cooking time: 20 minutes)

Ingredients:

- 4 pounds chicken wings
- 2 teaspoon salt
- ½ teaspoon garlic powder
- 1 teaspoon black pepper
- ½ teaspoon cayenne pepper
- 1 tablespoon smoked paprika
- 1 cup red hot sauce
- 1 stick butter

Nutrition information:

Calories per serving:439; Carbohydrates: 2.1g; Protein: 51.2g; Fat: 23.8g; Sugar: 0.8g; Sodium: 908mg

Directions for Cooking:

1. In a mixing bowl, combine the chicken wings, salt, garlic powder, black pepper, cayenne pepper, and paprika. Place in the fridge to marinate for at least 2 hours.
2. Press the Sauté button on the Instant Pot and stir in the chicken. Cook for at least 3 minutes until the chicken lightly turns golden.
3. Stir in the hot sauce and butter.
4. Close Instant Pot, press the Manual button, choose high settings, and set time to 15 minutes.
5. Once done cooking, do a QPR.
6. Serve and enjoy.

---

137. Instant Pot Korean Chicken

(Servings: 4, Cooking time: 25 minutes)

Ingredients:

- ½ cup gochujang paste
- ¼ cup hoisin sauce
- ¼ cup ketchup
- ¼ cup mirin
- ¼ cup soy sauce
- ¼ cup rice wine
- 1 tablespoon rice vinegar
- 2 pounds chicken thighs
- 2 tablespoons vegetable oil
- 1 tablespoon minced garlic
- 1 onion, chopped
- 1 cup chicken broth
- 2 teaspoons cornstarch + 3 teaspoons water

Nutrition information:

Calories per serving:817; Carbohydrates: 29.3g; Protein: 55.1g; Fat: 53.7g; Sugar: 51.3g; Sodium: 1140mg

Directions for Cooking:

1. In a mixing bowl, combine the gochujang paste, hoisin sauce, ketchup, mirin, soy sauce, rice wine, rice vinegar, and chicken thighs. Allow to marinate overnight.
2. Press the Sauté button and heat the oil. Sauté the garlic and onion. Stir in the chicken and cook for 3 minutes. Stir in the chicken broth.
3. Close Instant Pot, press the Manual button, choose high settings, and set time to 15 minutes.
4. Once done cooking, do a QPR.
5. Open the lid and Add the cornstarch slurry. Press the Sauté button and allow the sauce to thicken.
6. Serve and enjoy.

---

138. Chipotle Chicken Tacos

(Servings: 4, Cooking time: 20 minutes)

Ingredients:

- 2 pounds chicken breasts, chopped
- Salt and pepper to taste
- 1 tablespoon avocado oil
- 2 cloves of garlic, minced
- 1 onion, chopped
- 1 teaspoon oregano
- 1 tablespoon chipotle pepper
- ¼ cup chicken broth
- ¼ cup lime juice
- 4 cassava tortillas
- 1 avocado, peeled and sliced
- 2 roman tomatoes, chopped
- 1 can black olives

Nutrition information:

Calories per serving: 657; Carbohydrates: 29.6g; Protein: 55.9g; Fat: 35.1g; Sugar: 4g; Sodium: 456mg

Directions for Cooking:

1. Season the chicken breasts with salt and pepper to taste.
2. Press the Sauté button on the Instant Pot and heat the oil.
3. Sauté the garlic and onion until fragrant. Add the chicken breasts. Stir for 3 minutes and add the oregano and chipotle pepper. Stir in the chicken broth and lime juice.
4. Close Instant Pot, press the Manual button, choose high settings, and set time to 15 minutes.
5. Once done cooking, do a QPR. Open the lid and take the chicken out.
6. Assemble the taco by placing the chicken on the tortillas. Garnish with avocado slices, tomatoes, and black olives.
7. Serve and enjoy.

---

139. BBQ Pulled Chicken Sliders

(Servings: 6, Cooking time: 35 minutes)

Ingredients:

- 2 tablespoons butter
- 2 cloves of garlic
- 3 chicken breasts
- 1 cup chicken broth
- 1 cup BBQ sauce
- 24 slider buns, sliced

Directions for Cooking:

1. Press the Sauté button on the Instant Pot and melt the butter. Sauté the garlic until fragrant and stir in the chicken breasts until lightly golden. Stir in the chicken broth and BB sauce.
2. Close Instant Pot, press the Manual button, choose high settings, and set time to 30 minutes.
3. Once done cooking, do a QPR.
4. Open the lid and take the chicken out. Shred the chicken using forks.
5. Serve chicken on slider buns and add the sauce.
6. Serve and enjoy.

Nutrition information:

Calories per serving:573; Carbohydrates: 43.1g; Protein: 46.7g; Fat: 22.8g; Sugar: 6.2g; Sodium: 984mg

---

140. Instant Pot Salsa Verde Chicken

(Servings: 6, Cooking time: 20 minutes)

Ingredients:

- 3 pounds boneless chicken breasts
- 1 teaspoon salt
- 1 cup commercial salsa Verde

Nutrition information:

Calories per serving: 287; Carbohydrates: 2.5g; Protein: 51.4g; Fat: 6.3g; Sugar: 1.4g; Sodium: 839mg

Directions for Cooking:

1. Place all ingredients in the Instant Pot.
2. Close Instant Pot, press the Manual button, choose high settings, and set time to 20 minutes.
3. Once done cooking, do a QPR.
4. Serve and enjoy.

---

141. Instant Pot Ginger Garlic Drumsticks

(Servings: 8, Cooking time: 20 minutes)

Ingredients:

- 8 chicken drumsticks
- ¼ cup water
- ½ cup soy sauce
- 2 tablespoons honey
- 2 tablespoons brown sugar
- 2 tablespoons rice wine vinegar
- 2 cloves of garlic, minced
- 1 teaspoon minced ginger
- 1 onion, chopped

Directions for Cooking:

1. Place all ingredients in the Instant Pot.
2. Close Instant Pot, press the Manual button, choose high settings, and set time to 20 minutes.
3. Once done cooking, do a QPR.
4. Serve and enjoy.

Nutrition information:

Calories per serving: 288; Carbohydrates: 12.3g; Protein: 24.8g; Fat: 14.6g; Sugar: 4.3g; Sodium:381 mg

---

142. Instant Pot Whole Chicken

(Servings: 6, Cooking time: 40 minutes)

Ingredients:

- 3 pounds whole chicken
- ½ tbsp butter, melted
- Salt and pepper to taste
- ½ teaspoon smoked paprika
- ½ teaspoon onion powder
- ½ teaspoon garlic powder
- ¼ teaspoon dried oregano
- 1 cup water
- 1 lemon, sliced

Nutrition information:

Calories per serving: 470; Carbohydrates: 46.3g; Protein: 36.8g; Fat: 15.8g; Sugar: 8.7g; Sodium: 835mg

Directions for Cooking:

1. In a small bowl, mix together butter, paprika, onion powder, garlic powder, oregano, pepper and salt.
2. Rub butter and spice mixture all over the chicken.
3. Pour water into the instant pot and place trivet into the pot.
4. Place chicken on the trivet.
5. Close Instant Pot, press the Manual button, choose high settings, and set time to 40 minutes.
6. Once done cooking, do a QPR.
7. Garnish with lemon slices
8. Serve and enjoy.

---

143. Instant Pot Chicken Adobo

(Servings: 4, Cooking time: 35 minutes)

Ingredients:

- 2 pounds boneless chicken thighs
- 1/3 cup white vinegar
- ½ cup water
- 1/3 cup soy sauce
- 1 head garlic, peeled and smashed
- 3 bay leaves
- ½ teaspoon pepper
- 1 tablespoon oil

Nutrition information:

Calories per serving: 805; Carbohydrates: 3.2g; Protein: 43.9g; Fat: 58.3g; Sugar: 0.8g; Sodium: 892mg

Directions for Cooking:

1. Place all ingredients in the Instant Pot.
2. Close Instant Pot, press the Manual button, choose high settings, and set time to 30 minutes.
3. Once done cooking, do a QPR.
4. Open the lid and press the Sauté button. Allow the sauce to reduce so that the chicken is fried slightly in its oil.
5. Serve and enjoy.

---

144. Instant Pot Kung Pao Chicken

(Servings: 5, Cooking time: 20 minutes)

Ingredients:

- 1 tablespoon olive oil
- 3 cloves of garlic, minced
- 1 teaspoon grated ginger
- 1 teaspoon crushed red pepper
- 1 onion, chopped
- 2 pounds chicken breasts, cut into bite-sized pieces
- ½ cup soy sauce
- ¼ cup honey
- ¼ cup hoisin sauce
- 1 zucchini, diced
- 1 red bell pepper, chopped

Directions for Cooking:

1. Press the Sauté button on the Instant Pot and heat the oil. Sauté the garlic, ginger, red pepper, and onion until fragrant.
2. Add the chicken breasts and stir for 3 minutes until lightly golden.
3. Stir in the soy sauce, honey, and hoisin sauce.
4. Close Instant Pot, press Manual button, choose high settings, and set time to 10 minutes.
5. Once done cooking, do a QPR.
6. Open the lid and press the Sauté button. Stir in the zucchini and bell pepper. Allow to simmer until the vegetables are cooked.
7. Serve and enjoy.

Nutrition information:

Calories per serving:506; Carbohydrates: 29.4g; Protein: 40.7g; Fat: 24.5g; Sugar: 15.3g; Sodium: 918mg

---

145. Instant Pot Shredded Buffalo Chicken

(Servings: 4, Cooking time: 20 minutes)

Ingredients:

- 4 chicken breasts
- 4 tablespoons butter
- ½ bottle buffalo wing sauce
- 2 tablespoons honey
- 2 teaspoons cider vinegar
- 2 tablespoons Tabasco sauce

Directions for Cooking:

1. Place all ingredients in the Instant Pot.
2. Close Instant Pot, press the Manual button, choose high settings, and set time to 20 minutes.
3. Once done cooking, do a QPR.
4. Once cooked, take the chicken out and shred using forks.
5. Serve and enjoy.

Nutrition information:

Calories per serving: 695; Carbohydrates: 23.2g; Protein: 61g; Fat: 38.6g; Sugar: 20g; Sodium: 852mg

---

146. Instant Pot Chicken Saag

(Servings: 2, Cooking time: 18 minutes)

Ingredients:

- 1-pound chicken breasts, cut into 3 pieces
- Salt and pepper to taste
- 1 tablespoon oil
- ½ teaspoon cumin seeds
- 1-inch ginger, chopped
- 6 cloves of garlic, minced
- 2 onion, chopped
- ¼ cup water
- ¼ teaspoon turmeric
- ½ teaspoon red chili powder
- 2 teaspoon coriander powder

Nutrition information:

Calories per serving: 327; Carbohydrates: 10g; Protein: 21g; Fat: 22g; Sugar: 2g; Sodium: 732mg

Directions for Cooking:

1. Season the chicken with salt and pepper to taste.
2. Press the Sauté button and heat the oil. Toast the cumin, ginger, garlic, and onion until fragrant.
3. Stir in the chicken and sauté for at least 3 minutes until lightly golden.
4. Add the rest of the ingredients.
5. Close Instant Pot, press the Manual button, choose high settings, and set time to 15 minutes.
6. Once done cooking, do a QPR.
7. Garnish with chopped green onions.
8. Serve and enjoy.

---

147. Instant Pot Chicken Tacos

(Servings: 6 , Cooking time: 20 minutes)

Ingredients:

- 6 chicken breasts
- 1 tablespoon chili powder
- 1 cup salsa
- ½ cup Pico de gallo
- Salt and pepper to taste
- Corn tortillas
- Diced avocado
- Mexican cheese, shredded

Nutrition information:

Calories per serving:683; Carbohydrates: 16.9g; Protein: 67.4g; Fat: 37.8g; Sugar: 8.3g; Sodium: 700mg

Directions for Cooking:

1. In the Instant Pot, place the chicken, chili powder, salsa, and Pico de gallo. Season with salt and pepper to taste.
2. Close Instant Pot, press the Manual button, choose high settings, and set time to 20 minutes.
3. Once done cooking, do a QPR.
4. Serve with corn tortillas, avocado and Mexican cheese
5. Serve and enjoy.

---

148. Coconut Chicken Curry

(Servings: 3, Cooking time: 20 minutes)

Ingredients:

- 1 tablespoon olive oil
- 1 ½ pound chicken breasts
- 1 onion, diced
- 2 cloves of garlic, minced
- 5 tablespoons red curry paste
- ½ inch fresh ginger, minced
- 2 tablespoon fish sauce
- Salt and pepper to taste
- 1 cup coconut milk
- ¾ cup bone broth
- 2 red bell peppers, sliced
- 3 carrots, chopped
- 1 ½ cup green beans, chopped
- Juice from ½ lime

Directions for Cooking:

1. Press the Sauté button on the Instant Pot and heat the oil.
2. Stir in the chicken breasts, onion, garlic, red curry paste, ginger, and fish sauce.
3. Season with salt and pepper to taste.
4. Add the coconut milk and water. Stir in the rest of the ingredients.
5. Close Instant Pot, press the Manual button, choose high settings, and set time to 15 minutes.
6. Once done cooking, do a QPR.
7. Serve and enjoy.

Nutrition information:

Calories per serving: 732; Carbohydrates: 28.4g; Protein: 54.1g; Fat: 46.6g; Sugar: 10g; Sodium: 1156mg

---

149. One-Pot Thai Red Curry

(Servings: 3, Cooking time: 20 minutes)

Ingredients:

- 3 tablespoon Thai red curry paste
- 1 can coconut milk
- 1-pound chicken breasts, sliced into chunks
- ¼ cup chicken broth
- 2 tablespoon fish sauce
- 2 teaspoon brown sugar
- 1 tablespoon lime juice
- 1 cup red and green bell pepper
- 1 cup carrots, peeled and sliced
- ½ cup cubed onion
- ½ cup bamboo shoots, sliced
- 4 lime leaves
- 12 Thai Basil leaves

Directions for Cooking:

1. Place all ingredients in the Instant Pot and give a good stir.
2. Close Instant Pot, press the Manual button, choose high settings, and set time to 20 minutes.
3. Once done cooking, do a QPR.
4. Serve and enjoy.

Nutrition information:

Calories per serving:733; Carbohydrates: 26.1g; Protein: 42.5g; Fat: 54.3g; Sugar: 12.1g; Sodium:553mg

---

150. Jamaican Chicken Curry

(Servings: 2, Cooking time: 25 minutes)

Ingredients:

- 2 tablespoons oil
- 1 tablespoon minced garlic
- 1 cup chopped onion
- 1 ½ tablespoon Jamaican curry powder
- 1 scotch bonnet pepper, sliced
- ½ teaspoon ground allspice
- 3 sprigs of thyme
- 1-pound boneless chicken thighs, chunked
- Salt and pepper to taste
- 1 large potato, cut into chunks
- 1 cup water

Nutrition information:

Calories per serving: 1084; Carbohydrates: 78.5g; Protein: 48.6g; Fat: 65.6g; Sugar: 6.3g; Sodium: 1866mg

Directions for Cooking:

1. Press the Sauté button on the Instant Pot and sauté the garlic, onion, curry powder, scotch bonnet pepper, allspice, and thyme until fragrant.
2. Stir in the chicken thighs and cook until lightly golden. Season with salt and pepper to taste.
3. Add the potatoes and water.
4. Close Instant Pot, press the Manual button, choose high settings, and set time to 20 minutes.
5. Once done cooking, do a QPR.
6. Serve and enjoy.

---

151. Instant Pot Chicken Tetrazzini

(Servings: 6, Cooking time: 15 minutes)

Ingredients:

- 3 tablespoons butter
- 3 tablespoons flour
- ½ cup heavy cream
- 1 cup parmesan cheese
- ¼ cup cheddar cheese
- 4 chicken thighs, boneless and sliced
- 2 cups chicken broth
- Salt and pepper to taste
- ½ box spaghetti, cooked according to package instructions

Nutrition information:

Calories per serving:737; Carbohydrates: 32.7g; Protein: 50.5g; Fat: 43.6g; Sugar: 14.2g; Sodium: 929mg

Directions for Cooking:

1. Press the Sauté button on the Instant Pot and melt the butter. Whisk in the flour until it dissolves. Stir in the heavy cream, parmesan cheese, and cheddar cheese. Stir until melted. Set aside and clean the Instant Pot.
2. Still with the Sauté button on, stir in the chicken thighs and allow to sear until lightly golden. Season with salt and pepper to taste. Stir in chicken broth and spaghetti.
3. Pour over the cheese sauce.
4. Close Instant Pot, press the Manual button, choose high settings, and set time to 10 minutes.
5. Once done cooking, do a QPR.
6. Serve and enjoy.

---

152. Instant Pot Chicken Shawarma

(Servings: 4, Cooking time: 20 minutes)

Ingredients:

- ¼ teaspoon coriander
- ¼ teaspoon cumin
- ½ teaspoon paprika
- 1 teaspoon cardamom
- ½ teaspoon cinnamon powder
- ¼ teaspoon cloves
- ¼ teaspoon nutmeg
- ¼ cup lemon juice
- ¼ cup yogurt
- 2 tablespoons garlic, minced
- 2 pounds boneless chicken breasts, cut into strips
- 2 bay leaves
- Salt and pepper to taste
- 4 pita bread
- ¼ cup Greek yogurt
- For garnish: tomatoes, lettuce, and cucumber

Directions for Cooking:

1. Place in the Instant Pot the coriander, cumin, paprika, cardamom, cinnamon powder, cloves, nutmeg, lemon juice, yogurt, garlic, and chicken breasts. Add the bay leaves and season with salt and pepper to taste.
2. Close Instant Pot, press the button, choose high settings, and set time to 20 minutes.
3. Once done cooking, do a QPR.
4. Place the chicken in the pita bread and drizzle with Greek yogurt. Garnish with tomatoes, lettuce, and cucumber.
5. Serve and enjoy.

Nutrition information:

Calories per serving: 383; Carbohydrates: 21.8g; Protein: 55.1g; Fat: 7.1g; Sugar: 2.5g; Sodium: 262mg

---

153. One-Pot Mediterranean Chicken Paste

(Servings: 6, Cooking time: 15 minutes)

Ingredients:

- 3 skinless chicken breasts
- 1 cup chicken broth
- 2 cups marinara sauce
- 1 can diced tomatoes
- 1 tablespoon roasted peppers, chopped
- ½ cup sun-dried tomatoes
- ½ cup kalamata olives
- 9-ounce penne pasta

Directions for Cooking:

1. Place all ingredients in the Instant Pot. Mix to combine everything.
2. Close Instant Pot, press the Manual button, choose high settings, and set time to 15 minutes.
3. Once done cooking, do a QPR.
4. Garnish with chopped green onions.
5. Serve and enjoy.

Nutrition information:

Calories per serving: 483; Carbohydrates: 24.1g; Protein: 38.6g; Fat: 8.8g; Sugar: 7.5g; Sodium: 398mg

---

154. Creamy Garlic Tuscan Chicken Pasta

(Servings: 1C, Cooking time: 20 minutes)

Ingredients:

- 2 tablespoons olive oil
- 4 tablespoons butter
- 1 onion, divided
- 6 cloves of garlic, minced
- 3 chicken breasts, sliced into strips
- 1 tablespoon paprika
- Salt and pepper to taste
- ¼ cup white wine
- 1 jar sun-dried tomatoes
- 2 teaspoons Italian seasoning
- 4 cups chicken broth
- 1 cup milk
- 3 ½ cups dry elbow macaroni pasta
- 1 cup parmesan cheese, grated
- 1 cup mozzarella cheese, grated
- 1 ½ cup half and half
- Fresh basil leaves for garnish

Directions for Cooking:

1. Press the Sauté button on the Instant Pot and heat the oil and butter. Sauté the onion and garlic until fragrant. Add the chicken and stir until lightly golden. Season with salt and pepper to taste.
2. Stir in the rest of the ingredients. Give a stir to combine.
3. Close Instant Pot, press the Manual button, choose high settings, and set time to 15 minutes.
4. Once done cooking, do a QPR.
5. Serve and enjoy.

Nutrition information:

Calories per serving: 609; Carbohydrates: 37.1g; Protein: 52.3g; Fat: 26.7g; Sugar: 5.1g; Sodium: 782mg

---

155. Instant Pot Chicken Soup

(Servings: 12, Cooking time: 25 minutes)

Ingredients:

- 2 tablespoons olive oil
- 2 cups chopped onion
- 2 tablespoons minced garlic
- 1 cup chopped celery
- 1 tablespoon turmeric
- 1 tablespoon Italian seasoning
- 1 4-pound whole chicken, cut into pieces
- Salt and pepper to taste
- 2 cups carrots
- 3 cups baby red potatoes
- 4 cups chicken broth

Directions for Cooking:

1. Press the Sauté button on the Instant Pot and heat the oil. Sauté the onion, garlic, and celery until fragrant. Add the turmeric, Italian seasoning.
2. Stir in the chicken and season with salt and pepper to taste.
3. Add the carrots, potatoes, and chicken broth.
4. Close Instant Pot, press the button, choose high settings, and set time to 20 minutes.
5. Once done cooking, do a QPR.
6. Serve and enjoy.

Nutrition information:

Calories per serving: 506; Carbohydrates:41.8g; Protein: 43.6g; Fat: 18.5g; Sugar: 7.4g; Sodium: 981mg

---

156. Instant Pot Chicken Chowder

(Servings: 4, Cooking time: 20 minutes)

Ingredients:

- 1-pound chicken thighs, cut into bite-sized pieces
- 6 strips of bacon, chopped
- ½ cup diced onions
- ½ cup chopped celery
- 2 teaspoons minced garlic
- ½ teaspoon dried thyme
- ½ teaspoon dried oregano
- 4 cups chicken stock
- 1 cup heavy cream
- Salt and pepper to taste
- 2 cups spinach

Directions for Cooking:

1. Press the Sauté button on the Instant Pot and stir in the chicken and bacon. Add the onions, celery, garlic, thyme, and oregano until fragrant.
2. Add the stock and heavy cream. Season with salt and pepper to taste.
3. Close Instant Pot, press the Manual button, choose high settings, and set time to 15 minutes.
4. Once done cooking, do a QPR.
5. Open the lid and stir in the spinach last.
6. Serve and enjoy.

Nutrition information:

Calories per serving: 482; Carbohydrates: 13.9g; Protein: 27.2g; Fat: 35.6g; Sugar: 6.1g; Sodium:709mg

---

157. Instant Pot Chicken and Rice Soup

(Servings: 6, Cooking time: 20 minutes)

Ingredients:

- 1-pound chicken breast
- 1 cup carrots, peeled and diced
- 1 cup chopped celery
- 1 box wild rice
- 1 cup chopped onion
- 3 cups chicken broth
- 1 cup water
- 2 bay leaves
- 2 teaspoons butter
- 2 teaspoons minced garlic
- 3 cups light cream
- Salt and pepper to taste

Directions for Cooking:

1. Place all ingredients in the Instant Pot and give a good stir.
2. Close Instant Pot, press the Manual button, choose high settings, and set time to 20 minutes.
3. Once done cooking, do a QPR.
4. Serve and enjoy.

Nutrition information:

Calories per serving: 874; Carbohydrates: 70.3g; Protein: 57.4g; Fat: 40.7g; Sugar: 8.6g; Sodium: 845mg

---

158. Instant Pot Chicken Fajita Soup

(Servings: 3, Cooking time: 20 minutes)

Ingredients:

- 1 tablespoon butter
- 1 cup onion, minced
- 1 tablespoon minced garlic
- 1-pound chicken breasts, chopped
- 1 jalapeno, diced
- 1 cup red bell pepper
- 1 cup green bell pepper
- 4 tomato, diced
- 2 cups chicken broth
- 1 tablespoon lemon juice
- 2 tablespoons sour cream

Nutrition information:

Calories per serving:620; Carbohydrates: 15.8g; Protein: 69.1g; Fat: 30.2g; Sugar: 5.3g; Sodium: 803mg

Directions for Cooking:

1. Press the Sauté button on the Instant Pot.
2. Heat the butter and sauté the onion and garlic until fragrant.
3. Stir in the chicken breasts until lightly golden.
4. Add the rest of the ingredients.
5. Close Instant Pot, press the Manual button, choose high settings, and set time to 20 minutes.
6. Once done cooking, do a QPR.
7. Garnish with chopped green onions.
8. Serve and enjoy.

---

159. Instant Pot Chicken Stock

(Servings: 4, Cooking time: 30 minutes)

Ingredients:

- 1 chicken carcass
- 1 onion, quartered
- 2 bay leaves
- 15 whole peppercorns
- 2 tablespoons apple cider vinegar
- Salt and pepper to taste
- Veggie scraps
- 4 cups water

Nutrition information:

Calories per serving: 284; Carbohydrates: 4.5g; Protein: 49.2g; Fat: 6.5g; Sugar: 0.6g; Sodium: 623mg

Directions for Cooking:

1. Place all ingredients in the Instant Pot and give a good stir.
2. Close Instant Pot, press the Manual button, choose high settings, and set time to 30 minutes.
3. Once done cooking, do a QPR.
4. Serve and enjoy.

---

160. White Bean Chicken Chili

(Servings: 9, Cooking time: 40 minutes)

Ingredients:

- 3 tablespoons coconut oil
- 2 cups chopped onions
- 4 cloves of garlic, minced
- 6 boneless chicken breasts, cubed
- 2 teaspoons chili powder
- 1 teaspoon ground cumin
- ½ teaspoon ground coriander
- ½ teaspoon dried oregano
- 1-pound dried great northern beans, soaked overnight then drained
- Salt and pepper to taste
- 1 can diced tomatoes
- 7 ounces diced green chilies
- 4 cups chicken broth

Directions for Cooking:

1. Press the Sauté button on the Instant Pot and heat the oil. Sauté the onions and garlic until fragrant.
2. Stir in the chicken for 3 minutes until lightly golden.
3. Add the chili powder, cumin, coriander, and oregano.
4. Stir in the rest of the ingredients.
5. Close Instant Pot, press the Manual button, choose high settings, and set time to 35 minutes.
6. Once done cooking, do a QPR.
7. Garnish with chopped green onions.
8. Serve and enjoy.

Nutrition information:
Calories per serving: 402; Carbohydrates: 37.3g; Protein: 34.9g; Fat: 12.7g; Sugar: 2.4g; Sodium: 442mg

---

161. Low Carb Poblano Chicken Soup

(Servings: 5, Cooking time: 40 minutes)

Ingredients:

- ½ cup navy beans, soaked in hot water
- 1 cup onion, diced
- 3 poblano peppers, chopped
- 5 cloves of garlic, minced
- 1 cup cauliflower, diced
- 1 ½ pounds chicken breasts, cut into chunks
- 1 teaspoon ground coriander
- 1 teaspoon ground cumin
- 1 ½ cups water
- Salt and pepper to taste
- 1 cup cream cheese

Directions for Cooking:

1. Place all ingredients in the Instant Pot except for the cream cheese.
2. Close Instant Pot, press the Manual button, choose high settings, and set time to 40 minutes.
3. Once done cooking, do a QPR.
4. Open the lid and stir in the cream cheese. Press the Sauté button and allow to simmer until the cheese is dissolved.
5. Serve and enjoy.

Nutrition information:
Calories per serving: 208; Carbohydrates: 13g; Protein: 22g; Fat: 5g; Sugar: 2g; Sodium: 423mg

---

162. Instant Pot Chicken Curry Soup

(Servings: 6, Cooking time: 20 minutes)

Ingredients:

- 2 tablespoons butter
- 1 cup onion, chopped
- 2 tablespoons garlic, minced
- 2 tablespoons ginger, chopped
- 1 jalapeno, sliced
- 2 tablespoons curry powder
- 2 pounds boneless chicken thighs
- Salt and pepper to taste
- 4 cups chicken broth
- 1 cup diced tomatoes
- 1 cup coconut milk
- 3 cups fresh spinach, chopped
- ¼ cup cilantro, chopped

Nutrition information:

Calories per serving: 920; Carbohydrates: 32.4g; Protein: 65.4g; Fat: 58.9g; Sugar: 4g; Sodium: 1914mg

Directions for Cooking:

1. Press the Sauté button on the Instant Pot and heat the butter. Sauté the onion, garlic, and ginger until fragrant. Add the jalapeno and curry powder. Stir in the chicken and season with salt and pepper to taste.
2. Stir in the chicken broth, tomatoes, and coconut milk.
3. Close Instant Pot, press the Manual button, choose high settings, and set time to 15 minutes.
4. Once done cooking, do a QPR.
5. Open the lid and press the Sauté button. Add the spinach and cilantro.
6. Serve and enjoy.

---

163. Instant Pot Chicken Taco Soup

(Servings: 5, Cooking time: 40 minutes)

Ingredients:

- 2 boneless chicken breasts
- 1 onion, chopped
- 2 can diced tomatoes, undrained
- 1 can corn, drained
- 1 can black beans, drained and rinsed
- 1 can great northern beans, drained and rinsed
- 1 can tomato paste
- 1 tablespoon taco seasoning
- 2 tablespoons dry Ranch seasoning
- 2 teaspoons cumin

Directions for Cooking:

1. Place all ingredients in the Instant Pot and mix everything.
2. Close Instant Pot, press the Manual button, choose high settings, and set time to 40 minutes.
3. Once done cooking, do a QPR.
4. Serve and enjoy.

Nutrition information:

Calories per serving: 473; Carbohydrates: 47.6g; Protein: 47.5g; Fat: 11.4g; Sugar: 10.5g; Sodium: 1094mg

---

164. Healthy Chicken Stew

(Servings: 6, Cooking time: 20 minutes)

Ingredients:

- 2 pounds boneless chicken thighs
- ¾ cup water
- 1 cup carrot, peeled and chopped
- 1 cup chopped onion
- 1 cup bell pepper, sliced
- ¼ cup soy sauce

Directions for Cooking:

1. Place all ingredients in the Instant Pot.
2. Close Instant Pot, press the Manual button, choose high settings, and set time to 20 minutes.
3. Once done cooking, do a QPR.
4. Serve and enjoy.

Nutrition information:

Calories per serving: 392; Carbohydrates: 13g; Protein: 27g; Fat: 25g; Sugar: 6g; Sodium: 696mg

---

165. Paleo Buffalo Chicken Chili

(Servings: 5， Cooking time: 20 minutes)

Ingredients:

- 1 ½ pounds boneless chicken breasts
- 1 onion, chopped
- 5 cloves of garlic, minced
- 2 stalks of celery, chopped
- 2 carrots, chopped
- 1 tablespoon tomato paste
- 1 teaspoon chili powder
- 1 teaspoon cumin
- 1 teaspoon coriander
- 1 teaspoon onion powder
- Salt and pepper to taste
- 3 cups bone broth
- 1 can diced tomatoes
- ¼ cup hot sauce

Directions for Cooking:

1. Place all ingredients in the Instant Pot. Mix until well-combined.
2. Close Instant Pot, press the Manual button, choose high settings, and set time to 20 minutes.
3. Once done cooking, do a QPR.
4. Serve and enjoy.

Nutrition information:

Calories per serving:229; Carbohydrates: 9.9g; Protein: 35.1g; Fat: 4.9g; Sugar: 2.1g; Sodium: 918mg

---

166. Buffalo Chicken Meatballs

(Servings: 5, Cooking time: 15 minutes)

Ingredients:

- 1 ½ pounds ground chicken
- ¾ cup almond meal
- 1 teaspoon salt
- 2 cloves of garlic, minced
- 2 green onions, sliced thinly
- 2 tablespoons ghee
- 4 tablespoons coconut oil, melted
- ½ cup water
- 6 tablespoons hot sauce
- Salt and pepper to taste
- 1 tablespoon cornstarch + 2 tablespoons water

Nutrition information:

Calories per serving: 357; Carbohydrates: 3g; Protein: 23g; Fat: 28g; Sugar: 0.8g; Sodium: 867mg

Directions for Cooking:

1. Place all ingredients in the mixing bowl except for the hot sauce and coconut oil.
2. Mix until well combined and form small balls using your hands. Allow to set in the fridge for at least 3 hours.
3. Press the Sauté button on the Instant Pot and heat the oil. Slowly add the meatballs and allow to sear on all sides. Add water, hot sauce, salt and pepper.
4. Close Instant Pot, press the Manual button, choose high settings, and set time to 10 minutes.
5. Once done cooking, do a QPR.
6. Open the lid and press the Sauté button. Stir in the cornstarch slurry and allow to simmer until the sauce thickens.
7. Serve and enjoy.

---

167. Instant Pot Frozen Chicken

(Servings: 10, Cooking time: 50 minutes)

Ingredients:

- 5 pounds whole chicken, frozen
- 1 cup chicken broth
- 2 cloves of garlic, minced
- 1 onion, chopped
- Salt and pepper to taste

Nutrition information:

Calories per serving: 508; Carbohydrates: 46.3g; Protein: 42.1g; Fat: 17.5g; Sugar: 8.8g; Sodium: 923mg

Directions for Cooking:

1. Place all ingredients in the Instant Pot.
2. Close Instant Pot, press the Manual button, choose high settings, and set time to 50 minutes.
3. Once done cooking, do a QPR.
4. Garnish with chopped green onions.
5. Serve and enjoy.

Instant Pot Seafood Recipes

168. Miso & Bokchoy on Sesame-Ginger Salmon

(Servings: 1, Cooking Time:6 minutes)

Ingredients:

- 1 tablespoon toasted sesame oil
- 1 tablespoons rice vinegar
- 2 tablespoons brown sugar
- 1/2 cup Shoyu (soy sauce)
- 1 garlic clove, pressed
- 1 tablespoon freshly grated ginger
- 1 tablespoon toasted sesame seed
- 2 green onions, sliced reserve some for garnish
- 1 7-oz Salmon filet
- 2 baby Bok Choy washed well
- 1 teaspoon Miso paste mixed with a 1/2 cup of water

Directions for Cooking:

1. On a loaf pan that fits inside your Instant Pot, place salmon with skin side down.
2. In a small bowl whisk well sesame oil, rice vinegar, brown sugar, shoyu, garlic, ginger, and sesame seed. Pour over salmon.
3. Place half of sliced green onions over salmon. Securely cover pan with foil.
4. On a separate loaf pan, place Bok Choy. In a small bowl, whisk well water and miso paste. Pour over Bok choy and seal pan securely with foil.
5. Add water to Instant Pot and place trivet. Place pan of salmon side by side the Bok choy pan on trivet.
6. Close Instant Pot, press manual button, choose high settings, and set time to 6 minutes.
7. Once done cooking, do a QPR.
8. Serve and enjoy.

Nutrition information:
Calories per serving:610; Carbohydrates: 30.4g; Protein: 56.0g; Fat: 29.2g; Sugar: 19.3g; Fiber: 2.9g; Sodium: 4872mg

---

169. Alaskan Crab Legs in Instant Pot

(Servings: 3, Cooking Time: 5 minutes)

Ingredients:

- 2 pounds frozen crab legs
- 1 cup water
- 1/2 tablespoon salt
- 1 stick butter, melted for serving
- 1 medium lemon, for serving

Directions for Cooking:

1. Add a cup of water and salt in Instant Pot.
2. Place steamer basket in pot and add crab legs.
3. Close Instant Pot, press manual button, choose high settings, and set time to 4 minutes.
4. Meanwhile in a Pyrex measuring cup, melt butter in microwave. Juice the lemon and stir in melted butter. Keep warm.
5. Once done cooking, do a QPR.
6. Serve and enjoy with lemon butter sauce.

Nutrition information:
Calories per serving:578; Carbohydrates: 66.4g; Protein: 10.4g; Fat: 31.5g; Sugar: 60.6g; Fiber: 0g; Sodium: 1523mg

---

170. Easy Shrimp Pasta

(Servings: 6, Cooking Time: 7 minutes)

Ingredients:

- 1-pound dried spaghetti
- 3 cloves garlic, minced
- 1 teaspoon coconut oil
- 4 1/4 cup water
- 1-pound raw deveined jumbo shrimp
- 3/4 cup light mayonnaise
- 3/4 cup Thai sweet chili sauce
- 1/4 cup lime juice
- 1+ tablespoon sriracha sauce
- 1/2 cup chopped scallions
- Salt and pepper

Directions for Cooking:

1. Break the spaghetti noodles in half and place in the Instant Pot. Add the garlic, coconut oil, 1 teaspoon salt, and water.
2. Close Instant Pot, press pressure cook button, choose high settings, and set time to 4 minutes.
3. Meanwhile, mix well sriracha, lime juice, Thai sweet chili sauce, and mayonnaise in a medium bowl and set aside.
4. Once done cooking, do a QPR.
5. Press sauté button.
6. Mix in the sriracha sauce, scallions, and shrimps. Mix thoroughly. And cook for 3 minutes.
7. Serve and enjoy.

Nutrition information:
Calories per serving:485; Carbohydrates: 63.6g; Protein: 24.5g; Fat: 13.7g; Sugar: 14.1g; Sodium: 562mg

---

171. Salmon Quickie

(Servings: 4, Cooking Time: 10 minutes)

Ingredients:

- 3 medium lemon
- 3/4 cup water
- 4 4-oz salmon fillet
- 1 bunch dill weed, fresh
- 1 tablespoon butter, unsalted
- 1/4 teaspoon salt
- 1/4 teaspoon black pepper, ground

Directions for Cooking:

1. Place 1/4 cup fresh lemon juice, plus 3/4 cup water in the bottom of the Instant Pot. Add the metal steamer insert.
2. Place the (Sockeye) salmon fillets, frozen, on top of the steamer insert.
3. Sprinkle fresh dill on top of the salmon, then place one slice of fresh lemon on top of each one.
4. Close Instant Pot, press manual button, choose high settings, and set time to 5 minutes.
5. Meanwhile, in a Pyrex measuring cup, melt butter in microwave. Mix in pepper, salt, excess lemon, and excess dill.
6. Once done cooking, do a QPR.
7. Serve and enjoy with a drizzle of the butter lemon sauce.

Nutrition information:
Calories per serving:530; Carbohydrates: 49.0g; Protein: 45.0g; Fat: 16.0g; Sugar: 3.0g; Sodium: 1119mg

---

172. Creamy Parmesan-Herb Sauce Over Salmon

(Servings: 4, Cooking Time: 10 minutes)

Ingredients:

- 4 frozen salmon filets
- 1/2 cup water
- 1 1/2 tsp minced garlic
- 1/2 cup heavy cream
- 1 cup parmesan cheese grated
- 1 tbsp chopped fresh chives
- 1 tbsp chopped fresh parsley
- 1 tbsp fresh dill
- 1 tsp fresh lemon juice
- Salt and pepper to taste

Directions for Cooking:

1. Add water and trivet in pot. Place fillets on top of trivet.
2. Close Instant Pot, press manual button, choose high settings, and set time to 4 minutes.
3. Once done cooking, do a QPR.
4. Transfer salmon to a serving plate. And remove trivet.
5. Press cancel and then press sauté button on Instant Pot. Stir in heavy cream once water begins to boil. Boil for 3 minutes. Press cancel and then stir in lemon juice, parmesan cheese, dill, parsley, and chives. Season with pepper and salt to taste. Pour over salmon.
6. Serve and enjoy.

Nutrition information:

Calories per serving:429; Carbohydrates: 6.4g; Protein: 43.1g; Fat: 25.0g; Sugar: 1.1g;Sodium: 1196 mg

---

173. Easy Steamed Mussels

(Servings: 4, Cooking Time: 10 minutes)

Ingredients:

- 2 Tablespoons butter
- 2 shallots chopped
- 4 garlic cloves minced
- 1/2 cup broth
- 1/2 cup white wine
- 2-lbs mussels cleaned
- Lemon optional for serving
- Parsley optional for serving

Directions for Cooking:

1. Press sauté button and melt butter.
2. Sauté garlic and shallots for 5 minutes.
3. Stir in broth and wine. Deglaze pot.
4. Add mussels.
5. Close Instant Pot, press pressure cook button, choose high settings, and set time to 5 minutes.
6. Once done cooking, do a QPR.
7. Discard unopened mussels.
8. Serve and enjoy.

Nutrition information:

Calories per serving: 189; Carbohydrates: 8.0g; Protein: 14.0g; Fat: 8.0g; Sugar: 1.0g; Sodium: 501mg

---

174. Easy Fish Tacos

(Servings: 2, Cooking Time:8 minutes)

Ingredients:

- 2 4-oz tilapia fillets
- 1 teaspoon canola oil
- 1 pinch of salt
- 2 tablespoons smoked paprika
- juice of one lime
- 1-2 sprigs of fresh cilantro
- 2 8-inch corn tortilla

Directions for Cooking:

1. Place tilapia in the middle of a large piece of parchment paper. Drizzle with canola oil, sprinkle with salt and paprika, squeeze lime juice on the tilapia and sprinkle with some cilantro. Fold your parchment paper into a packet, as not to let any air in.
2. Add 1 cup of water in pot and place trivet. Place packets on trivet.
3. Close Instant Pot, press pressure cook button, choose high settings, and set time to 8 minutes.
4. Once done cooking, do a QPR.
5. Warm tortilla in microwave for 10 seconds each. Place 1 packet of fish in each tortilla, add cilantro and dressing of choice.
6. Serve and enjoy.

Nutrition information:

Calories per serving: 206; Carbohydrates: 16.3g; Protein: 25.2g; Fat: 5.8g; Sugar: 1.3g; Sodium: 153mg

---

175. Mascarpone-Salmon Risotto

(Servings: 4, Cooking Time: 5 minutes)

Ingredients:

- 2 tbsp olive oil
- 1 onion finely chopped
- 1 garlic clove finely chopped
- 1 1/2 cups Arborio rice
- 3 1/2 cups gluten free chicken broth
- 1/2 tsp lemon zest
- 3 tbsp Italian parsley chopped
- 1/2 cup mascarpone cheese
- 4-oz smoked salmon chopped
- salt to taste
- pepper to taste
- lemon juice to taste

Directions for Cooking:

1. Press sauté button and heat oil.
2. Stir in garlic and onions. Sauté for 5 minutes. Press cancel.
3. Stir in rice and broth. Mix well.
4. Close Instant Pot, press pressure cook button, choose high settings, and set time to 5 minutes.
5. Once done cooking, do a QPR.
6. Stir in smoked salmon, mascarpone cheese, parsley, and lemon zest. Mix well.
7. Season with pepper and salt to taste.
8. Serve and enjoy.

Nutrition information:

Calories per serving: 503; Carbohydrates: 63.0g; Protein: 11.0g; Fat: 21.0g; Sugar: 1.0g; Sodium: 928mg

---

176. Shrimp Scampi in Instant Pot

(Servings: 6, Cooking Time: 15 minutes)

Ingredients:

- 2-pounds shrimp
- 2 tablespoons extra virgin olive oil
- 2 tablespoons pastured butter
- 1 tablespoon minced organic garlic
- 1/2 cup white wine
- 1/2 cup homemade chicken stock
- 1-pound gluten free pasta, cooked
- 1 tablespoon fresh squeezed lemon juice
- Sea salt and pepper, to taste
- Parsley, optional garnish

Directions for Cooking:

1. Press sauté button and heat oil.
2. Add garlic and sauté for a minute. Stir in butter and let it melt for a minute.
3. Stir in wine and stock. Mix well.
4. Stir in shrimps and cook for 5 minutes.
5. Add pasta and continue tossing well to coat and cooking for another 5 minutes or until heated through.
6. Adjust seasoning to taste.
7. Turn pot off.
8. Serve and enjoy.

Nutrition information:

Calories per serving: 308; Carbohydrates: 20.1g; Protein: 35.2g; Fat: 8.7g; Sugar: 0.3g; Sodium: 1458mg

---

177. Salmon with Pepper-Lemon

(Servings: 4, Cooking Time: 10 minutes)

Ingredients:

- ¾ cup water
- A few sprigs of parsley dill, tarragon, basil or a combo
- 1-pound salmon filet skin on
- 3 teaspoons ghee or other healthy fat divided
- ¼ teaspoon salt or to taste
- ½ teaspoon pepper or to taste
- 1/2 lemon thinly sliced
- 1 zucchini julienned
- 1 red bell pepper julienned
- 1 carrot julienned

Directions for Cooking:

1. Add water and herb sprigs in Instant pot. Place trivet and add salmon with skin side down.
2. Season salmon with peppers, salt, and oil. Add lemon slices on top.
3. Close Instant Pot, press steam button, and set time to 3 minutes.
4. Once done cooking, do a QPR.
5. Remove salmon and trivet.
6. Add zucchini, pepper, and carrots in pot. Cover and let it sit for 5 minutes. Fish out the vegetables and place on serving tray. Add salmon on top.
7. Serve and enjoy.

Nutrition information:

Calories per serving: 202; Carbohydrates: 2.7g; Protein: 24.7g; Fat: 9.8g; Sugar: 1.3g; Sodium: 281mg

---

178. Feta & Tomatoes on Shrimp

(Servings: 6, Cooking Time: 12 minutes)

Ingredients:

- 2 tablespoons Butter
- 1 tablespoon garlic
- 1/2 teaspoon red pepper flakes adjust to taste
- 1.5 cups chopped onion
- 1 14.5-oz can tomatoes
- 1 teaspoon oregano
- 1 teaspoons salt
- 1-pound frozen shrimp 21-25 count, shelled
- 1 cup crumbled feta cheese
- 1/2 cup sliced black olives
- 1/4 cup parsley

Directions for Cooking:

1. Press sauté button and melt butter. Add red pepper flakes and garlic. Sauté for a minute.
2. Stir in salt, oregano, tomatoes, and onions. Cook for 5 minutes.
3. Add shrimp. Mix well and press cancel.
4. Close Instant Pot, press pressure cook button, choose low settings, and set time to 1 minute.
5. Once done cooking, do a QPR.
6. Transfer to plates. Sprinkle feta cheese, olives and parsley.
7. Serve and enjoy.

Nutrition information:

Calories per serving: 211; Carbohydrates: 6.0g; Protein: 19.0g; Fat: 11.0g; Sugar: 2.0g; Sodium: 1468mg

---

179. Salmon on Rice Pilaf

(Servings: 2, Cooking Time:5 minutes)

Ingredients:

- ½ cup Jasmine Rice
- ¼ cup dried vegetable soup mix
- 1 cup chicken bone-broth or water
- 1 tablespoon butter
- ¼ teaspoon sea salt
- 1 pinch saffron
- 2 4-6-ounce wild caught salmon filet FROZEN

Directions for Cooking:

1. Except for salmon, add all ingredients in Instant Pot and mix well.
2. Place steamer rack on top of ingredients.
3. Season salmon with pepper and salt. Place salmon on steamer rack.
4. Close Instant Pot, press pressure cook button, choose high settings, and set time to 5 minutes.
5. Once done cooking, do a QPR.
6. Serve and enjoy.

Nutrition information:

Calories per serving: 440; Carbohydrates: 40.6g; Protein: 32.2g; Fat: 15.3g; Sugar: 0.7g; Sodium: 860mg

---

180. Lemon-Tahini Sauce over Salmon

(Servings: 2, Cooking Time: 3 minutes)

Ingredients:

- 1 tablespoon red wine vinegar
- 1 tablespoon freshly squeezed lemon juice (from ½ medium lemon)
- 1 clove garlic, minced
- ¼ teaspoon dried oregano
- ¼ teaspoon kosher salt
- ⅛ teaspoon freshly ground black pepper
- ¼ cup olive oil
- 1 tbsp feta cheese, crumbled
- 1lb salmon filets, fresh or frozen
- 2 sprigs fresh rosemary
- 2 slices of lemon

Directions for Cooking:

1. In a lidded jar, add vinegar, lemon juice, garlic, oregano, salt, pepper, feta cheese, and olive oil. Close jar and shake well until emulsified to make the lemon-tahini sauce. Set aside.
2. Add a cup of water in Instant Pot. Place trivet and add salmon on top. Season salmon with pepper and salt. Drizzle ¼ of the lemon-tahini sauce over salmon. Place lemon slices and rosemary sprigs on top of salmon.
3. Close Instant Pot, press manual button, choose low settings, and set time to 3 minutes.
4. Once done cooking, do a QPR.
5. Serve and enjoy with the remaining sauce drizzled over the salmon.

Nutrition information:

Calories per serving: 557; Carbohydrates: 4.9g; Protein: 47.5g; Fat: 38.2g; Sugar: 1.6g; Sodium: 506mg

---

181. Salmon Over Potatoes & Broccoli

(Servings: 1, Cooking Time: 10 minutes)

Ingredients:

- 3-oz Salmon Fillet
- 1 cup Broccoli florets
- 1 medium New Potatoes, cubed into ½-inch slices
- 1 tsp Rosemary, 1 tsp dill
- 1 tsp lemon juice
- 1 garlic clove, smashed
- 1 tbsp butter
- Pepper and salt to taste

Directions for Cooking:

1. In a heatproof dish that fits inside your Instant Pot, place potatoes on the sides and then the broccoli florets in the middle. Top with salmon fillet with skin side down.
2. Season salmon generously with salt and pepper. Season salmon with lemon juice, rosemary, dill, smashed garlic, and place butter on top of salmon. Securely cover top with foil.
3. Add a cup of water in Instant Pot, place trivet, and place dish of salmon on trivet.
4. Close Instant Pot, press pressure cook button, choose high settings, and set time to 5 minutes.
5. Once done cooking, do a 5-minute natural release and then do a QPR.
6. Serve and enjoy.

Nutrition information:

Calories per serving: 418; Carbohydrates: 41.1g; Protein: 23.8g; Fat: 18.4g; Sugar: 2.0g; Sodium: 487mg

---

182. Crab Quiche without Crust

(Servings: 4, Cooking Time: 50 minutes)

Ingredients:

- 4 eggs
- 1 cup half and half
- 1/2 -1 tsp salt
- 1 teaspoon pepper
- 1 teaspoon sweet smoked paprika
- 1 teaspoon Simply Organic Herbs de Provence
- 1 cup shredded parmesan or swiss cheese
- 1 cup chopped green onions green and white parts
- 8 oz imitation crab meat about 2 cups OR
- 8 oz real crab meat, or a mix of crab and chopped raw shrimp

Directions for Cooking:

1. In a large bowl, beat together eggs and half-and-half with a whisk.
2. Add salt, pepper, sweet smoked paprika, Herb de Provence, and shredded cheese. Stir with a fork to mix.
3. Stir in chopped green onions.
4. Mix in crab meat with fork.
5. Lay out a sheet of aluminum foil that is cut bigger than the pan you intend to use. Place the springform pan on this sheet and crimp the sheet around the bottom.
6. Pour in the egg mixture into your spring form pan. Cover loosely with foil or a silicone lid.
7. Add 2 cups of water in Instant Pot and place a steamer rack inside.
8. Place the covered spring form pan on the trivet.
9. Close Instant Pot, press pressure cook button, choose high settings, and set time to 40 minutes.
10. Once done cooking, do a 10-minute natural release and then do a QPR.
11. Serve and enjoy.

Nutrition information:
Calories per serving: 395; Carbohydrates: 19.0g; Protein: 22.0g; Fat: 14.0g; Sugar: 3.0g; Sodium: 526mg

---

183. Ginger-Orange Sauce over Salmon

(Servings: 4, Cooking Time: 15 minutes)

Ingredients:

- 1-pound salmon
- 1 tablespoon dark soy sauce
- 2 teaspoons minced ginger
- 1 teaspoon minced garlic
- 1 teaspoon salt
- 1 1/2 tsp ground pepper
- 2 tablespoons low sugar marmalade

Directions for Cooking:

1. In a heatproof pan that fits inside your Instant Pot, add salmon.
2. Mix all the sauce ingredients and pour over the salmon. Allow it to marinate for 15-30 minutes. Cover pan with foil securely.
3. Put 2 cups of water in Instant Pot and add trivet.
4. Place the pan of salmon on trivet.
5. Close Instant Pot, press pressure cook button, choose low settings, and set time to 3 minutes.
6. Once done cooking, do a QPR.
7. Serve and enjoy.

Nutrition information:
Calories per serving: 179; Carbohydrates: 8.8g; Protein: 24.0g; Fat: 5.0g; Sugar: 6.9g; Sodium: 801mg

---

184. Salmon with Shoyu-Pineapple Sauce

(Servings: 1, Cooking Time: 6 minutes)

Ingredients:

- 1 6-oz Salmon filet
- 1/4 cup soy sauce
- 1/8 cup water
- 1/8 cup pineapple juice
- 3 slices of ginger julienned
- 1 clove of garlic chopped
- 5-6 pineapple chunks
- 1 cup broccoli florets
- ¼ cup carrots sliced thinly
- 1 small red onion peeled and quartered

Directions for Cooking:

1. Place salmon in a loaf pan that fits inside your Instant Pot.
2. Mix the soy sauce, pineapple juice and water in a small bowl then pour over the salmon. Sprinkle on the garlic and ginger and set aside.
3. Place all the veggies into a second pan that fits inside Instant Pot. Pour the water and soy sauce over the veggies then add the sesame oil. Season with salt and pepper to taste. Cover veggie pan tightly with foil.
4. Add 1 cup of water and the trivet to your pot.
5. Place your salmon pan on the trivet then stack the veggies pan on top.
6. Close Instant Pot, press pressure cook button, choose high settings, and set time to 6 minutes.
7. Once done cooking, do a QPR.
8. Serve and enjoy.

Nutrition information:

Calories per serving: 405; Carbohydrates: 32.8g; Protein: 47.0g; Fat: 10.1g; Sugar: 18.8g; Sodium: 4254mg

---

185. Clams in Pale Ale

(Servings: 4, Cooking Time: 4minutes)

Ingredients:

- 1/4 cup olive oil
- 2 cloves garlic, peeled and minced
- 1/4 cup finely chopped fresh basil
- 2 cups pale ale
- 1 cup water
- 1/2 cup chicken broth
- 1/4 cup dry white wine
- 3 pounds fresh clams, scrubbed
- 2 tablespoons freshly squeezed lemon juice

Directions for Cooking:

1. Press sauté button and heat oil. Once oil is hot, sauté garlic until lightly browned around a minute.
2. Stir in basil and sauté for half a minute. Add pale ale, water, chicken broth, and white win. Mix well.
3. Add clams.
4. Close Instant Pot, press pressure cook button, choose high settings, and set time to 4 minutes.
5. Once done cooking, do a QPR.
6. Discard any unopened clams. Mix well.
7. Serve and enjoy with freshly squeezed lemon juice.

Nutrition information:

Calories per serving: 479; Carbohydrates: 24.1g; Protein: 51.6g; Fat: 18.3g; Sugar: 11.0g; Sodium: 2286mg

---

186. Shrimps with Spiced Pineapples

(Servings: 4, Cooking Time: 12 minutes)

Ingredients:

- 1 large Red Bell Pepper cleaned and sliced
- 12-oz Calrose Rice or Quinoa
- 3/4 cup Unsweetened Pineapple Juice
- 1/4 cup Dry White Wine
- 2 Tablespoons Soy Sauce
- 2 Tablespoons Thai Sweet Chili Sauce
- 1 Tablespoon Sambal Oelek Ground Chili Paste
- 1-pound Large Shrimp, tails on frozen
- 4 Scallions chopped, White and Greens separated
- 1 1/2 cups Unsweetened Pineapple Chunks drained

Directions for Cooking:

1. Drain Juice from Pineapple and set Pineapple Chunks aside. Measure out 3/4 cup of Pineapple Juice.
2. Add Red Bell Peppers, Pineapple Juice, Wine, Chili Sauce, Soy Sauce, Sambal Oelek, Rice and chopped Scallions (the white part) to Pressure Cooker cooking pot. Place frozen Shrimp on top.
3. Close Instant Pot, press pressure cook button, choose high settings, and set time to 2 minutes.
4. Once done cooking, do a 10-minute natural release and then do a QPR.
5. Stir in green scallions and pineapple chunks.
6. Serve and enjoy.

Nutrition information:

Calories per serving: 282; Carbohydrates: 35.6g; Protein: 26.4g; Fat: 4.8g; Sugar: 27.9g; Sodium: 572mg

---

187. Citrusy Salmon en Papilote

(Servings: 4, Cooking Time: 15 minutes)

Ingredients:

- 4 – 4 oz. salmon fillets
- Salt and pepper
- 1 tsp dill
- 1 orange, sliced thinly
- 1 lemon, sliced thinly
- 1 lime, sliced thinly
- 4 pieces foil
- 8 Asparagus spears, quartered
- 12 Cremini mushrooms, halved

Directions for Cooking:

1. Add a cup of water in Instant Pot and add trivet.
2. In each foil, place ¼ of Asparagus spears and mushrooms in each foil.
3. Top veggies with one salmon fillet and season generously with pepper and salt.
4. Add slices of orange, lemon, and lime on top of each salmon. Season with dill.
5. Securely seal foil packets and place on top of trivet.
6. Close Instant Pot, press pressure cook button, choose high settings, and set time to 5 minutes.
7. Once done cooking, do a 10-minute natural release and then do a QPR.
8. Serve and enjoy.

Nutrition information:

Calories per serving: 216; Carbohydrates: 18.3g; Protein: 26.0g; Fat: 5.4g; Sugar: 5.7g;Sodium: 131mg

---

188. Easy Sweet-Soy Salmon

(Servings: 2, Cooking Time: 8 minutes)

Ingredients:

- 2 8-oz salmon fillets
- ½ cup soy sauce
- ¼ cup water
- ¼ cup mirin (can substitute sake or sherry)
- 1 tablespoon sesame oil
- 2 teaspoons sesame seeds
- 1 clove garlic, minced
- 1 tablespoon freshly grated ginger
- 2 tablespoons brown sugar
- 2-3 green onions, minced, (reserve some for garnish)

Directions for Cooking:

1. In a heatproof casserole dish that fits inside the Instant Pot, mix well soy sauce, water, mirin, sesame oil, sesame seeds, garlic, ginger, brown sugar, and green onions.
2. Add salmon fillets and coat well in marinade. Keep in the fridge for at least an hour.
3. Cover dish with foil securely.
4. In Instant Pot, add a cup of water, place trivet, and put dish of salmon top of trivet.
5. Close Instant Pot, press pressure cook button, choose high settings, and set time to 8 minutes.
6. Once done cooking, do a QPR.
7. Serve and enjoy with a sprinkle of remaining green onions.

Nutrition information:

Calories per serving: 483; Carbohydrates: 16.0g; Protein: 53.3g; Fat: 18.7g; Sugar: 9.7g; Sodium: 2472mg

---

189. Asparagus & Salmon with Buttered Garlic Sauce

(Servings: 3, Cooking Time: 4 minutes)

Ingredients:

- 1-lb Salmon Filet, divided equally into 3
- 1-lb Asparagus (small - medium stalks)
- 1/4 cup Lemon Juice
- 3 tbsp Butter
- 1 1/2 tbsp garlic (minced)
- Salt to taste
- Red Pepper Flakes

Directions for Cooking:

1. In a heatproof baking dish that fits in your Instant Pot, place asparagus. Season with salt.
2. Place salmon fillets on top of asparagus.
3. Season and drizzle with lemon juice, garlic, red pepper flakes. Season well with salt.
4. Cover dish securely with foil.
5. Add a cup of water in Instant Pot, place trivet, and add dish of salmon on trivet.
6. Close Instant Pot, press pressure cook button, choose high settings, and set time to 4 minutes.
7. Once done cooking, do a QPR.
8. Serve and enjoy.

Nutrition information:

Calories per serving: 360; Carbohydrates: 10.0g; Protein: 36.6g; Fat: 19.6g; Sugar: 4.2g; Sodium: 915mg

---

190. Olive & Tuna Rigatoni

(Servings: 4, Cooking Time: 10 minutes)

Ingredients:

- 1 tablespoon olive oil
- 2 cloves garlic, minced
- 16 oz package rigatoni pasta
- 4 cups water
- 2 teaspoons salt
- 3 pouches Star-Kist Selects E.V.O.O. Yellow fin Tuna
- 1 cup cherry tomatoes, halved
- ¼ cup Kalamata olives, roughly chopped
- ¼ teaspoon black pepper
- ½ cup freshly grated Parmesan cheese

Directions for Cooking:

1. Press sauté button and heat oil.
2. Sauté garlic for a minute.
3. Stir in Salt, water, and rigatoni.
4. Close Instant Pot, press pressure cook button, choose high settings, and set time to 4 minutes.
5. Once done cooking, do a QPR.
6. Stir in Parmesan, black pepper, olives, tomatoes, and tuna. Mix well and let it rest for 5 minutes while covered.
7. Serve and enjoy.

Nutrition information:

Calories per serving: 267; Carbohydrates: 37.1g; Protein: 17.0g; Fat: 5.8g; Sugar: 0.4g; Sodium: 1363mg

---

191. Orange-Ginger Sauce over Fish

(Servings: 4, Cooking Time: 7 minutes)

Ingredients:

- 4 white fish fillets
- Juice and zest from 1 orange
- Thumb size piece of ginger, chopped
- 3 to 4 spring onions
- Olive oil
- Salt and pepper
- 1 cup of fish stock or white wine

Directions for Cooking:

1. Pat dry fish with paper towel and rub olive oil all over. Lightly season with pepper and salt. Place in steamer basket.
2. Add remaining ingredients in Instant Pot and add steamer basket.
3. Add a cup of water in Instant Pot, place trivet, and add dish of salmon on trivet.
4. Close Instant Pot, press pressure cook button, choose high settings, and set time to 7 minutes.
5. Once done cooking, do a QPR.
6. Serve and enjoy.

Nutrition information:

Calories per serving: 243; Carbohydrates: 7.1g; Protein: 21.7g; Fat: 14.1g; Sugar: 4.7g; Sodium: 123mg

---

192. Salmon Croquette

(Servings: 2, Cooking Time: 10 minutes)

Ingredients:

- 2 6-oz salmon filets
- 1/4 cup Chopped onion
- 2 stalks green onion, chopped
- 1 egg
- 1/2 cup Panko, place in bowl
- Salt and pepper
- 2 tablespoons of cooking oil

Directions for Cooking:

1. Add a cup of water in Instant Pot, place trivet, and salmon on trivet.
2. Close Instant Pot, press pressure cook button, choose high settings, and set time to 3 minutes.
3. Once done cooking, do a QPR.
4. Remove salmon and let it cool.
5. Meanwhile, in a large mixing bowl, whisk well egg. Stir in green onion and yellow onion.
6. With two forks shred salmon and add to bowl of eggs.
7. Place a medium skillet on medium high fire and heat oil.
8. Divide salmon mixture into two patties. Roll in bowl of Panko until thoroughly covered. Pan fry for 3 minutes per side or until golden brown.
9. Serve and enjoy.

Nutrition information:

Calories per serving: 433; Carbohydrates: 23.9g; Protein: 41.8g; Fat: 17.9g; Sugar: 4.4g; Sodium: 446mg

---

193. Dill & Lemon Salmon

(Servings: 2, Cooking Time: 5 minutes)

Ingredients:

- 2 3-oz salmon filets
- 1 tsp fresh dill chopped
- 1/2 tsp salt
- 1/4 tsp pepper
- 1 cup Water
- 2 tbsp lemon juice
- 1/2 lemon sliced

Directions for Cooking:

1. Place salmon fillets on a steamer rack. Season with dill, salt, and pepper.
2. Add a cup of water in Instant Pot. Place steamer rack on Instant Pot. Squeeze lemon juice over salmon fillets and add lemon slices on top.
3. Close Instant Pot, press pressure cook button, choose high settings, and set time to 5 minutes.
4. Once done cooking, do a QPR.
5. Serve and enjoy.

Nutrition information:

Calories per serving: 305; Carbohydrates: 3.0g; Protein: 51.9g; Fat: 10.0g; Sugar: 1.0g;Sodium: 628mg

---

194. Asian Style Salmon Soy-Free

(Servings: 2, Cooking Time: 7 minutes)

Ingredients:

- 2 6-oz salmon fillets
- 1 tbsp coconut oil
- 1 tbsp brown sugar
- 3 tbsp coconut aminos (soy-free alternative)
- 2 tbsp maple syrup
- 1 tsp paprika
- ¼ tsp ginger
- 1 tsp sesame seeds (optional)
- Fresh scallions

Directions for Cooking:

1. Press sauté and heat coconut oil. Add brown sugar and melt for 4 minutes.
2. Stir in maple, coconut aminos, ginger, and paprika. Cook for a minute.
3. Add frozen salmon fillets with skin side down. Season with pepper and salt.
4. Close Instant Pot, press pressure cook button, choose low settings, and set time to 2 minutes.
5. Once done cooking, do a 5-minute natural release and then do a QPR.
6. Serve and enjoy with a garnish of sesame seeds and fresh scallion.

Nutrition information:
Calories per serving: 396; Carbohydrates: 20.4g; Protein: 38.8g; Fat: 17.4g; Sugar: 16.9g; Sodium: 963mg

---

195. Easy Tuna Pasta Casserole

(Servings: 4, Cooking Time: 10 minutes)

Ingredients:

- 1 can cream-of-mushroom soup
- 3 cups water
- 2 1/2 cups macaroni pasta
- 2 cans tuna
- 1 cup frozen peas
- 1/2 t each salt and pepper
- 1 cup shredded cheddar cheese

Directions for Cooking:

1. Mix soup and water in pressure cooker.
2. Add remaining ingredients except for cheese. Stir.
3. Close Instant Pot, press pressure cook button, choose high settings, and set time to 4 minutes.
4. Once done cooking, do a QPR.
5. Stir in cheese and let it sit for 5 minutes.
6. Serve and enjoy.

Nutrition information:
Calories per serving: 382; Carbohydrates: 34.0g; Protein: 28.0g; Fat: 14.1g; Sugar: 2.2g; Sodium: 407mg

---

196. Mahi-Mahi in Sweet Spicy sauce

(Servings: 2, Cooking Time: 5 minutes)

Ingredients:

- 2 6-oz mahi-mahi fillets
- Salt, to taste
- black pepper, to taste
- 1-2 cloves garlic, minced or crushed
- 1" piece ginger, finely grated
- ½ lime, juiced
- 2 tablespoons honey
- 1 tablespoon Nanami Togarashi
- 2 tablespoons sriracha
- 1 tablespoon orange juice

Nutrition information:

Calories per serving: 201; Carbohydrates: 20.1g; Protein: 28.1g; Fat: 0.8g; Sugar: 18.1g;Sodium: 442mg

Directions for Cooking:

1. In a heatproof dish that fits inside the Instant Pot, mix well orange juice, sriracha, nanami togarashi, honey lime juice, ginger, and garlic.
2. Season Mahi-mahi with pepper and salt. Place in bowl of sauce and cover well in sauce. Seal dish securely with foil.
3. Add a cup of water in Instant Pot, place trivet, and add dish of mahi-mahi on trivet.
4. Close Instant Pot, press pressure cook button, choose high settings, and set time to 5 minutes.
5. Once done cooking, do a QPR.
6. Serve and enjoy.

---

197. Caramel Salmon Vietnamese Style

(Servings: 4, Cooking Time: 10 minutes)

Ingredients:

- 1 tablespoon extra-virgin olive oil
- 1/3 cup packed light brown sugar
- 3 tablespoons Asian fish sauce
- 1 1/2 tablespoons soy sauce or low-sodium soy sauce
- 1 teaspoon grated peeled fresh ginger
- Finely grated zest of 1 lime (about 2 teaspoons)
- Juice of 1/2 lime (about 1 tablespoon)
- 1/2 teaspoon freshly ground black pepper
- 4 8-oz salmon fillets
- Sliced scallions (white and green parts), for garnish
- Fresh cilantro leaves, for garnish

Directions for Cooking:

1. Press sauté and heat oil. Whisk in black pepper, lime juice, lime zest, ginger, soy sauce, fish sauce, brown sugar, and oil. Cook until it simmers, around 2 minutes. Press cancel.
2. Add fish with skin side down. Cover in sauce.
3. Close Instant Pot, press pressure cook button, choose low settings, and set time to 1 minute.
4. Once done cooking, do a 5-minute natural release and then do a QPR.
5. Remove fish and transfer to a plate.
6. Press cancel, press sauté, and the cook sauce until thick, around 3 minutes. Pour over fish.
7. Serve and enjoy.

Nutrition information:

Calories per serving: 426; Carbohydrates: 22.2g; Protein: 49.8g; Fat: 14.3g; Sugar: 19.9g; Sodium: 722mg

---

198. Tilapia with Basil-Tomato Dressing

(Servings: 4, Cooking Time: 4 minutes)

Ingredients:

- 4 (4 oz) tilapia fillets
- Salt and pepper
- 3 roma tomatoes, diced
- 2 minced garlic cloves
- 1/4 cup chopped basil (fresh)
- 2 Tbsp olive oil
- 1/4 tsp salt
- 1/8 tsp pepper
- Balsamic vinegar (optional)

Directions for Cooking:

1. Add a cup of water in Instant Pot, place steamer basket, and add tilapia in basket. Season with pepper and salt.
2. Close Instant Pot, press pressure cook button, choose high settings, and set time to 2 minutes.
3. Meanwhile, in a medium bowl toss well to mix pepper, salt, olive oil, basil, garlic, and tomatoes. If desired, you can add a tablespoon of balsamic vinegar. Mix well.
4. Once done cooking, do a QPR.
5. Serve and enjoy with the basil-tomato dressing.

Nutrition information:

Calories per serving: 170; Carbohydrates: 2.0g; Protein: 20.0g; Fat: 12.0g; Sugar: 0g; Sodium: 223mg

---

199. Cod the Mediterranean Way

(Servings: 6, Cooking Time: 15 minutes)

Ingredients:

- 6 pieces of frozen or fresh cod (about 1.5 pounds)
- 3 tablespoons butter
- 1 lemon, juiced
- 1 onion, sliced
- 1 teaspoon salt
- 1/2 teaspoon black pepper
- 1 teaspoon oregano
- 1- 28 oz. can diced tomatoes

Nutrition information:

Calories per serving: 145; Carbohydrates: 3.3g; Protein: 18.4g; Fat: 6.4g; Sugar: 2.0g; Sodium: 864mg

Directions for Cooking:

1. Press sauté and melt butter. Stir in lemon juice, onion, salt, black pepper, oregano and diced tomatoes. Cook for 8 minutes.
2. Add fish and spoon sauce over it. Press cancel.
3. Close Instant Pot, press pressure cook button, choose high settings, and set time to 5 minutes.
4. Once done cooking, do a QPR.
5. Serve and enjoy.

Instant Pot Vegetarian Recipes

200. Instant Pot Black Bean Chili

(Servings: 4, Cooking time: 13 minutes)

Ingredients:

- 2 teaspoons olive oil
- 1 onion, diced
- 1 bell pepper, diced
- 1 teaspoon dried oregano
- 2 cloves of garlic, minced
- 2 tablespoons chili powder
- 2 teaspoons ground cumin
- 2 cans cooked black beans, drained
- 1 can tomatoes
- 1 jalapeno pepper, minced
- Salt and pepper to taste
- 1 cup water

Directions for Cooking:

1. Press the Sauté button on the Instant Pot and heat the olive oil.
2. Once hot, stir in the onion, bell pepper, oregano, and garlic until fragrant.
3. Stir in the rest of the ingredients.
4. Close Instant Pot, press the Manual button, choose high settings, and set time to 10 minutes.
5. Once done cooking, do a QPR.
6. Serve and enjoy.

Nutrition information:

Calories per serving: 294; Carbohydrates: 50.4g; Protein: 17.2g; Fat: 4.3g; Sugar: 4.1g; Sodium: 177mg

---

201. Vegetarian Mushroom Bourguignon

(Servings: 2, Cooking time: 10 minutes)

Ingredients:

- 1 teaspoon oil
- 1 onion, chopped
- 3 cloves of garlic, minced
- 2 carrots, cut into thick strips
- 5 cups mushrooms, halved
- 1 cup red wine
- 4 tablespoons tomato paste
- 1 teaspoon dried marjoram
- 1 cup vegetable broth
- 3 teaspoons Italian herbs
- Salt and pepper to taste
- 1 tablespoon cornstarch + 2 tablespoons water

Directions for Cooking:

1. Press the Sauté button on the Instant Pot and heat the oil. Stir in the onion and garlic until fragrant.
2. Add the carrots and mushrooms and allow to soften. Stir in the rest of the ingredients except for the cornstarch slurry.
3. Close Instant Pot, press the Manual button, choose high settings, and set time to 5 minutes.
4. Once done cooking, do a QPR.
5. Open the lid and press the Sauté button. Stir in the cornstarch slurry and allow to simmer until the sauce thickens.
6. Serve and enjoy.

Nutrition information:

Calories per serving: 168; Carbohydrates: 25.1g; Protein: 10.2g; Fat: 3.3g; Sugar: 13g; Sodium: 323mg

---

202. Vegetarian Fajita Pasta

(Servings: 6. Cooking time: 9 minutes)

Ingredients:

- 1 teaspoon oil
- 6 cloves of garlic, minced
- 1 cup chopped bell peppers
- 1 cup black beans, cooked
- 1 teaspoon taco seasoning mix
- 4 cups pasta, cooked according to package instruction
- 2 cups commercial enchilada sauce
- Salt and pepper to taste

Directions for Cooking:

1. vPress the Sauté button on the Instant Pot and heat the oil. Stir in the garlic and bell peppers and allow to wilt for 3 minutes.
2. Add the rest of the ingredients.
3. Close Instant Pot, press the Manual button, choose high settings, and set time to 6 minutes.
4. Once done cooking, do a QPR.
5. Serve and enjoy.

Nutrition information:

Calories per serving: 275; Carbohydrates: 52.1g; Protein: 10.4g; Fat: 3.5g; Sugar: 3.4g; Sodium: 257mg

---

203. Instant Pot Tomato Soup

(Servings: 3, Cooking time: 9 minutes)

Ingredients:

- 2 tablespoons olive oil
- 1 onion, chopped
- 3 medium carrots, peeled and chopped
- 1 cans fire roasted tomatoes
- ¾ cup vegetable broth
- 2 teaspoons dried basil
- 1 teaspoon salt
- 2 teaspoons sugar
- 1 cup cashew nuts, soaked

Directions for Cooking:

1. Press the Sauté button on the Instant Pot and heat the oil.
2. Stir in the onions and carrots for 3 minutes
3. Add the rest of the ingredients.
4. Close Instant Pot, press the Manual button, choose high settings, and set time to 6 minutes.
5. Once done cooking, do a QPR.
6. Open the lid and transfer the contents into a blender. Pulse until smooth.
7. Serve and enjoy.

Nutrition information:

Calories per serving: 390; Carbohydrates: 27.7g; Protein: 8.8g; Fat: 29.9g; Sugar: 10g; Sodium: 1162mg

---

204. One-Pot Refried Black Beans

(Servings: 2, Cooking time: 40 minutes)

Ingredients:

- 1 ¼ cups dried black beans, soaked overnight
- 3 cups water
- 1 onion, chopped
- 2 cloves of garlic, minced
- ½ teaspoons ground cumin
- 2 tablespoons chilies, chopped
- Salt to taste

Directions for Cooking:

1. Place all ingredients in the Instant Pot.
2. Close Instant Pot, press the Manual button, choose high settings, and set time to 40 minutes.
3. Once done cooking, do a QPR.
4. Using potato masher mash beans until get desired consistency.
5. Serve and enjoy.

Nutrition information:

Calories per serving:465; Carbohydrates: 85.1g; Protein: 28.1g; Fat: 3.1g; Sugar: 5.5g; Sodium: 329mg

---

205. Pasta Mediterranean

(Servings: 3, Cooking time: 25 minutes)

Ingredients:

- 1 tablespoon olive oil
- 1 red onion, chopped
- 2 cloves of garlic, chopped
- 1 eggplant, chopped
- 1 can chopped tomatoes
- 1-pound pasta
- Enough vegetable broth to cover the pasta
- ¼ cup black olives, pitted and sliced
- Salt and pepper to taste

Nutrition information:

Calories per serving: 399; Carbohydrates: 73g; Protein: 12g; Fat: 6g; Sugar: 8g; Sodium: 362mg

Directions for Cooking:

1. Press the Sauté button on the Instant Pot and heat the oil. Sauté the onions and garlic until fragrant before adding the eggplants Allow the eggplants to wilt before adding the rest of the ingredients.
2. Close Instant Pot, press the Manual button, choose high settings, and set time to 20 minutes.
3. Once done cooking, do a QPR.
4. Serve and enjoy.

---

206. Cilantro Lime Quinoa Salad

(Servings: 2, Cooking time: 15 minutes)

Ingredients:

- 1 cup quinoa, rinsed and drained
- 1 ¼ cups vegetable broth
- 2 tablespoons lime juice
- Zest from one lime, grated
- ½ cup chopped cilantro
- Salt to taste

Nutrition information:

Calories per serving: 108; Carbohydrates: 19g; Protein: 4g; Fat: 1g; Sugar: 3.2g; Sodium: 197mg

Directions for Cooking:

1. In the Instant Pot, place the quinoa and vegetable broth.
2. Close Instant Pot, press the Manual button, choose high settings, and set time to 15 minutes.
3. Once done cooking, do a QPR.
4. Open the lid and fluff the quinoa using fork. Transfer to a bowl and let it cool.
5. Assemble the salad by adding into the quinoa the remaining ingredients.
6. Serve and enjoy.

---

207. Mashed Cauliflower Casserole

(Servings: 3, Cooking time: 10 minutes)

Ingredients:

- 1 head of cauliflower, cut into florets
- 2 tablespoons salted butter, melted
- 4 ounces cream cheese
- ½ cup sour cream
- ½ cup heavy cream
- Salt to taste
- 2 cups cheddar cheese, grated

Directions for Cooking:

1. Place a trivet in the Instant Pot and pour a cup of water.
2. Place the cauliflower on the trivet.
3. Close Instant Pot, press the Steam button, choose high settings, and set time to 10 minutes.
4. Once done cooking, do a QPR.
5. Open the lid and transfer the cauliflower into a food processor.
6. Add in the rest of the ingredients. Pulse until a bit coarse.
7. Serve and enjoy.

Nutrition information:

Calories per serving:606 ; Carbohydrates: 10g; Protein: 24.3g; Fat: 53.1g; Sugar: 1.3g; Sodium: 757mg

---

208. Instant Pot Creamy Garlic and Veggies Pasta

(Servings: 6, Cooking time: 20 minutes)

Ingredients:

- 16-ounce ziti pasta
- 2 cups chopped zucchini
- 1 cup frozen peas
- 3 cloves of garlic, minced
- 1 cup white wine
- 2 cups chicken broth
- Salt and pepper to taste
- 1 cup mozzarella cheese, grated
- 1 cup milk

Directions for Cooking:

1. Place the pasta, zucchini, peas, garlic, white wine, and chicken broth in the Instant Pot. Season with salt and pepper to taste.
2. Close Instant Pot, press the Manual button, choose high settings, and set time to 15 minutes.
3. Once done cooking, do a QPR.
4. Open the lid then press the Sauté button. Stir in the cheese and milk. Allow to simmer for 5 minutes.
5. Serve and enjoy.

Nutrition information:

Calories per serving: 291; Carbohydrates: 27.7g; Protein: 26.9g; Fat: 7.5g; Sugar: 3.1g; Sodium: 491mg

---

209. Instant Pot Black Bean Soup

(Servings: 5, Cooking time: 45 minutes)

Ingredients:

- 1 tablespoon olive oil
- 1 onion, chopped
- 3 cloves of garlic, minced
- 1 red pepper, diced
- 1 tablespoon cumin
- 2 tablespoons chili powder
- ½ teaspoon cayenne pepper
- 14 ounces dry black beans, soaked overnight
- 3 cups vegetable broth
- Juice and zest from 1 lemon
- Salt to taste

Directions for Cooking:

1. Press the Sauté button on the Instant Pot and heat the oil.
2. Sauté the onion and garlic until fragrant.
3. Stir in the rest of the ingredients.
4. Close Instant Pot, press the Manual button, choose high settings, and set time to 40 minutes.
5. Once done cooking, do a QPR.
6. Serve and enjoy.

Nutrition information:

Calories per serving: 165; Carbohydrates:27.4 g; Protein: 7.6g; Fat: 3.8g; Sugar: 4.5g; Sodium: 201mg

---

210. Cauliflower and Pasta Alfredo

(Servings: 6, Cooking time: 6 minutes)

Ingredients:

- 1 head cauliflower, cut into florets and boiled
- 2 tablespoons butter
- 4 cloves of garlic, minced
- 1 cup chicken broth
- ¼ cup half and half
- 1 teaspoon onion powder
- 2 teaspoons garlic powder
- Salt and pepper to taste
- 1 box fettuccini noodles, cooked according to package instructions

Directions for Cooking:

1. Place the cauliflower in the food processor and pulse until smooth. Set aside.
2. Press the Sauté button on the Instant Pot and heat the butter. Sauté the garlic until fragrant and add in the cauliflower puree.
3. Stir in the half and half, onion, and garlic. Season with salt and pepper to taste.
4. Close Instant Pot, press the Manual button, choose high settings, and set time to 6 minutes.
5. Once done cooking, do a QPR.
6. Open the lid and press the Sauté button and stir in the fettuccini noodles. Allow to simmer until the pasta is soaked with the sauce.
7. Serve and enjoy.

Nutrition information:

Calories per serving: 248; Carbohydrates: 29.4g; Protein: 16.1g; Fat: 7.7g; Sugar: 6.4g; Sodium: 523mg

---

211. Instant Pot Mushroom Risotto

(Servings: 3, Cooking time: 25 minutes)

Ingredients:

- 1 ½ tablespoons olive oil
- 2 tablespoons vegan butter, divided
- 1 onion, diced
- 3 cloves of garlic, minced
- 8 ounces cremini mushrooms, diced
- ¾ teaspoon dried thyme
- 1 ½ cups Arborio rice
- ½ cup dry white wine
- 4 cups vegetable broth
- Salt and pepper to taste
- 1 cup frozen peas, thawed

Directions for Cooking:

1. Press the Sauté button on the Instant Pot and heat the oil and half of the butter. Stir in the onions, garlic, mushrooms, and thyme until fragrant.
2. Add the rice and stir to coat well. Pour in the wine and allow to simmer for 2 minutes.
3. Pour in the rest of the ingredients.
4. Close Instant Pot, press the Manual button, choose high settings, and set time to 20 minutes.
5. Once done cooking, do a QPR.
6. Open the lid and stir in the remaining butter before serving.
7. Serve and enjoy.

Nutrition information:

Calories per serving:3 79; Carbohydrates: 59g; Protein:10 g; Fat: 9g; Sugar: 3g; Sodium: 646mg

212. Instant Pot Pulled BBQ Jackfruit

(Servings: 6, Cooking time: 10 minutes)

Ingredients:

- 2 20-ounces cans young green jackfruit in water
- 1 can barbecue sauce
- 6 hamburger buns
- 1 head of cabbage, shredded

Directions for Cooking:

1. Mash or shred the jackfruit using fork.
2. Place the jackfruit and barbecue sauce in the Instant Pot.
3. Close Instant Pot, press the Manual button, choose high settings, and set time to 10 minutes.
4. Once done cooking, do a QPR.
5. Remove from the Instant Pot and allow to cool.
6. Serve on hamburger buns with shredded cabbage.
7. Serve and enjoy.

Nutrition information:

Calories per serving: 508; Carbohydrates: 72.4g; Protein: 20.7g; Fat: 16.9g; Sugar: 23.4g; Sodium: 1113mg

---

213. Easy Autumn Soup

(Servings: 6, Cooking time: 15 minutes)

Ingredients:

- 2 cups vegetable stock
- 2 cloves of garlic, minced
- 1 carrot, diced
- 1 Granny Smith apple, cored and diced
- 1 medium squash, seeded and diced
- 1 onion, diced
- Salt and pepper to taste
- A pinch of ground cinnamon
- ½ cup canned coconut milk
- A pinch of paprika powder

Directions for Cooking:

1. In the Instant Pot, put in the vegetable stock, garlic, carrots, apples, and squash. Season with salt and pepper to taste and sprinkle with cinnamon.
2. Close Instant Pot, press the Manual button, choose high settings, and set time to 15 minutes.
3. Once done cooking, do a QPR.
4. Open the lid and press the Sauté button. Stir in the coconut milk.
5. Using an immersion blender, pulse until the mixture becomes smooth.
6. Sprinkle with paprika on top.
7. Serve and enjoy.

Nutrition information:

Calories per serving: 83; Carbohydrates: 9.7g; Protein: 1.4g; Fat: 4.9g; Sugar: 0.8g; Sodium: 12mg

---

214. Veggie Spanish rice

(Servings: 12, Cooking time: 25 minutes)

Ingredients:

- 2 tablespoons olive oil
- 1 large onion, chopped
- 4 cloves of garlic, minced
- 4 cups rice, uncooked
- 1 can diced tomatoes with chilies
- Salt and pepper to taste
- 4 ½ cups rice

Directions for Cooking:

1. Press the Sauté button on the Instant Pot and heat the oil.
2. Sauté the onion and garlic for 5 minutes until the onions start to caramelize.
3. Place the rest of the ingredients and give a good stir.
4. Close Instant Pot, press the Manual button, choose high settings, and set time to 20 minutes.
5. Once done cooking, do a QPR.
6. Serve and enjoy.

Nutrition information:

Calories per serving:298; Carbohydrates: 44.8g; Protein: 11.7g; Fat: 19.7g; Sugar: 1.4g; Sodium: 166mg

---

215. Instant Pot Steamed Cauliflower

(Servings: 2, Cooking time: 8 minutes)

Ingredients:

- 1 head of cauliflower, cut into florets
- Salt and pepper to taste

Directions for Cooking:

1. Place a trivet in the Instant Pot and pour a cup of water.
2. Place the cauliflower florets on the trivet.
3. Close Instant Pot, press the button, choose high settings, and set time to 8 minutes.
4. Once done cooking, do a QPR.
5. Place the cauliflower florets in a bowl and season with salt and pepper to taste.
6. Serve and enjoy.

Nutrition information:

Calories per serving: 42; Carbohydrates: 8.7g; Protein: 2.9g; Fat: 0.4g; Sugar: 0g; Sodium: 12mg

---

216. Lemon Butter Broccoli

(Servings: 3, Cooking time: 8 minutes)

Ingredients:

- 1 large head of broccoli, cut into florets
- 1 stick melted butter
- 1 teaspoon garlic powder
- 2 tablespoons lemon juice
- Salt and pepper to taste

Directions for Cooking:

1. Place a trivet in the Instant Pot and pour a cup of water.
2. Place the cauliflower florets on the trivet.
3. Close Instant Pot, press the button, choose high settings, and set time to 8 minutes.
4. Once done cooking, do a QPR.
5. Place the cauliflower florets in a bowl and stir in the rest of the seasonings.

Nutrition information:

Calories per serving: 32; Carbohydrates: 4.1g; Protein: 1.8g; Fat: 1.5g; Sugar: 1.2g; Sodium: 25mg

---

217. Sweet Potato Hash

(Servings: 8, Cooking time: 20 minutes)

Ingredients:

- 1 large sweet potato, sliced
- 3 cups butternut squash, cubed
- 1 cup water
- 2 tablespoons butter
- 4 cloves of garlic, minced
- 1 onion, sliced
- Salt and pepper to taste
- 1 teaspoon parsley, chopped

Directions for Cooking:

1. Place the potatoes and squash in the Instant Pot and pour in water.
2. Close Instant Pot, press the button, choose high settings, and set time to 15 minutes.
3. Once done cooking, do a QPR.
4. Open the lid and set the sweet potatoes and squash aside.
5. Remove the water from the Instant Pot.
6. Heat the Sauté button and melt the butter.
7. Sauté the garlic and onion until fragrant.
8. Add in the cooked vegetables and season with salt and pepper.
9. Garnish with parsley.
10. Serve and enjoy.

Nutrition information:

Calories per serving: 74; Carbohydrates: 11.9g; Protein: 1.2g; Fat: 2.9g; Sugar: 2.9g; Sodium: 39mg

---

218. Indian Green Bean Curried Potatoes

(Servings: 5, Cooking time: 15 minutes)

Ingredients

- 2 teaspoons cooking oil
- ½ teaspoon mustard seed
- ¼ teaspoon asofetida
- 3 cloves of garlic, minced
- ½ teaspoon ground turmeric
- ¼ teaspoon cayenne powder
- 2 ½ teaspoons ground coriander
- 2 cups long green beans
- 2 medium-sized potatoes, peeled and quartered
- ¼ cup water
- Juice from ½ lemon, freshly squeezed
- Salt and pepper to taste

Directions for Cooking:

1. Press the Sauté button on the Instant Pot and heat the oil.
2. Toast the mustard and asafetida until fragrant. Add in the garlic, turmeric, cayenne powder, and coriander. Toast for another minute.
3. Stir in the rest of the ingredients.
4. Close Instant Pot, press the Manual button, choose high settings, and set time to 10 minutes.
5. Once done cooking, do a QPR.
6. Serve and enjoy.

Nutrition information:

Calories per serving: 99; Carbohydrates: 14g; Protein: 6g; Fat: 2g; Sugar: 2.1g; Sodium: 1mg

---

219. Easy Rustic Lentil Soup

(Servings: 6, Cooking time: 35 minutes)

Ingredients:

- 1 teaspoon olive oil
- 1 onion, diced
- 3 cloves of garlic, minced
- 3 stalks of celery, chopped
- 3 carrots, peeled and chopped
- 1 large potato, peeled and diced
- 2 teaspoons herbs de Provence
- 1 can diced tomatoes
- 6 cups vegetable broth
- 2 cups green lentils, soaked overnight
- Salt and pepper to taste
- 3 cups kale, torn

Directions for Cooking:

1. Press the Sauté button on the Instant Pot and heat the oil.
2. Sauté the onion, garlic, and celery until fragrant.
3. Stir in the carrots, potatoes, herbs, tomatoes, vegetable broth and lentils. Season with salt and pepper to taste.
4. Close Instant Pot, press the Manual button, choose high settings, and set time to 30 minutes.
5. Once done cooking, do a QPR.
6. Open the lid and stir in the kale while still hot.
7. Serve and enjoy.

Nutrition information:

Calories per serving: 326; Carbohydrates: 53g; Protein: 23g; Fat: 3g; Sugar: 3.1g; Sodium: 131mg

---

220. Organic Spinach Pasta

(Servings: 6, Cooking time: 9 minutes)

Ingredients:

- 1 tablespoon olive oil
- 4 cloves of garlic, minced
- 1-pound organic pasta
- 5 cups water
- Salt and pepper to taste
- 5 cups organic spinach
- 3 tablespoons butter

Directions for Cooking:

1. Press the Sauté button on the Instant Pot and heat the oil. Sauté the garlic until fragrant.
2. Add in the pasta and water. Season with salt and pepper to taste.
3. Close Instant Pot, press the Manual button, choose high settings, and set time to 6 minutes.
4. Once done cooking, do a QPR.
5. Open the lid and stir in the spinach and butter. Allow to simmer for additional 2 minutes.
6. Serve and enjoy.

Nutrition information:

Calories per serving: 137; Carbohydrates: 10.4g; Protein: 2.3g; Fat: 9.9g; Sugar: 3.1g; Sodium: 355mg

---

221. Vegan Pasta Puttanesca

(Servings: 4, Cooking time: 15 minutes)

Ingredients

- 1 tablespoon olive oil
- 3 cloves of garlic, minced
- 4 cups pasta sauce
- 3 cups water
- 4 cups penne pasta
- ¼ teaspoon crushed red pepper flakes
- 1 tablespoon capers
- ½ cup kalamata olives, sliced
- Salt and pepper to taste

Directions for Cooking:

1. Press the Sauté button on the Instant Pot and heat the oil.
2. Sauté the garlic until fragrant and add in the rest of the ingredients. Give a good stir.
3. Close Instant Pot, press the Manual button, choose high settings, and set time to 10 minutes.
4. Once done cooking, do a QPR.
5. Serve and enjoy.

Nutrition information:

Calories per serving: 504; Carbohydrates: 98g; Protein: 18g; Fat: 4g; Sugar: 13g; Sodium: 1620mg

---

222. Broccoli Macaroni and Cheese

(Servings: 5, Cooking time: 10 minutes)

Ingredients:

- 1-pound whole wheat macaroni pasta
- ¾ pounds broccoli, cut into florets
- 4 cups water
- 2 tablespoons unsalted butter
- 1 ½ cups whole milk
- 6 ounces cheddar cheese, grated
- 8 ounces provolone cheese, grated
- Salt and pepper to taste

Directions for Cooking:

1. Place all ingredients in the Instant Pot. Give a good stir.
2. Close Instant Pot, press the button, choose high settings, and set time to 10 minutes.
3. Once done cooking, do a QPR.
4. Open the lid and stir to combine everything.
5. Serve and enjoy.

Nutrition information:

Calories per serving:444; Carbohydrates: 40.9g; Protein: 25.7g; Fat: 21.3g; Sugar: 12g; Sodium: 447mg

---

223. Instant Pot Garlic Hummus

(Servings: 12, Cooking time: 50 minutes)

Ingredients:

- 1 ½ cups dried chickpeas, soaked overnight
- 6 cups water
- ½ cup tahini
- 2 cloves of garlic, minced
- 3 tablespoons lemon juice
- 1 ½ teaspoon salt to taste
- Crushed red pepper
- Chopped parsley
- Ground paprika

Directions for Cooking:

1. Place the chickpeas and water in the Instant Pot.
2. Close Instant Pot, press the Manual button, choose high settings, and set time to 50 minutes.
3. Once done cooking, do a QPR.
4. Open the lid and strain the chickpeas. Set aside.
5. In a food processor, place the chickpeas, tahini, garlic, and lemon juice. Season with salt and pepper to taste. Pulse until smooth. If the hummus is too thick, add water if necessary.
6. Garnish with crushed red pepper, parsley, and paprika.
7. Serve and enjoy.

Nutrition information:

Calories per serving: 159; Carbohydrates: 18.9g; Protein: 7.1g; Fat: 6.9g; Sugar: 3.1g; Sodium: 314mg

---

224. Cauliflower and Potato Soup

(Servings: 4, Cooking time: 7 minutes)

Ingredients:

- 1 head cauliflower, cut into florets
- 2 small red potatoes, peeled and sliced
- 4 cups vegetable stock
- 6 cloves of garlic, minced
- 1 onion, diced
- 1 cup heavy cream
- 2 bay leaves
- Salt and pepper to taste
- 2 stalks of green onions

Nutrition information:

Calories per serving: ; Carbohydrates: g; Protein: g; Fat: g; Sugar: g; Sodium: mg

Directions for Cooking:

1. Place the cauliflower, potatoes, vegetable stock, garlic, onion, heavy cream, and bay leaves in the Instant Pot. Season with salt and pepper to taste.
2. Close Instant Pot, press the Manual button, choose high settings, and set time to 6 minutes.
3. Once done cooking, do a QPR.
4. Open the lid and stir in the green onions.
5. Serve and enjoy.

---

225. One-Pot Vegetarian Lentil Tortilla Soup

(Servings: 6, Cooking time: 40 minutes)

Ingredients:

- 1 cup diced onion
- 1 bell pepper, diced
- 1 jalapeno pepper, diced
- 2 ½ cups vegetable broth
- 1 can tomato sauce
- ½ cup salsa Verde
- 1 tablespoon tomato paste
- 1 can black beans, drained and rinsed
- 1 can pinto beans, drained and rinsed
- 1 cup fresh corn kernels
- ½ teaspoon chili powder
- ½ teaspoon garlic powder
- Salt and pepper to taste
- ¼ cup heavy cream

Directions for Cooking:

1. Place all ingredients in the Instant Pot except for the heavy cream and give a good stir.
2. Close Instant Pot, press the Manual button, choose high settings, and set time to 35 minutes.
3. Once done cooking, do a QPR.
4. Open the lid and press the Sauté button. Stir in the heavy cream and allow to simmer for 5 minutes.
5. Serve and enjoy.

Nutrition information:

Calories per serving:321 ; Carbohydrates: 48.7g; Protein: 8.6g; Fat: 12.4g; Sugar: 13.8g; Sodium: 496mg

---

226. Vegan BBQ Meatballs

(Servings: 4, Cooking time: 10 minutes)

Ingredients:

- ¼ cup water
- 2 pounds frozen vegan meatballs
- 1 ½ cup barbecue sauce
- 1 can cranberry sauce
- Salt and pepper to taste

Directions for Cooking:

1. Place all ingredients in the Instant Pot and give a good stir.
2. Close Instant Pot, press the Manual button, choose high settings, and set time to 10 minutes.
3. Once done cooking, do a QPR.
4. Serve and enjoy.

Nutrition information:

Calories per serving: 347; Carbohydrates: 68.1g; Protein: 17.1g; Fat: 1.8g; Sugar: 23.1g; Sodium: 675mg

---

227. Simple Garden Pasta

(Servings: 4, Cooking time: 10 minutes)

Ingredients:

- 1 onion, diced
- 2 cloves of garlic, minced
- 1 carrot, peeled and chopped
- 2 teaspoons dried basil
- ¾ teaspoon dried thyme
- 1 can diced tomatoes
- 2 tablespoons tomato paste
- 4 cups vegetable broth
- 1 medium zucchini, chopped
- ¼ cup shell pasta
- Salt and pepper to taste
- 1 cup baby spinach
- 1 teaspoon balsamic vinegar

Directions for Cooking:

1. Place all ingredients in the Instant Pot except for the spinach and balsamic vinegar.
2. Close Instant Pot, press the Manual button, choose high settings, and set time to 10 minutes.
3. Once done cooking, do a QPR.
4. Open the lid and press the Sauté button. Stir in the baby spinach and simmer until wilted.
5. Drizzle with balsamic vinegar.
6. Serve and enjoy.

Nutrition information:

Calories per serving:86 ; Carbohydrates: 18g; Protein: 4g; Fat: 1g; Sugar: 6g; Sodium: 678mg

---

228. Vegan Lasagna Soup

(Servings: 3, Cooking time: 12 minutes)

Ingredients:

- 1 teaspoon oil
- ½ onion, chopped
- 4 cloves of garlic, minced
- 1 cup packaged vegetables
- ¼ cup red lentils, cooked
- 1 cup tomato puree
- 2 teaspoons Italian seasoning mix
- 2 cups veggie broth
- 5 ounces lasagna sheets, broken into small pieces
- Salt and pepper to taste
- 1 tablespoon nutritional yeast

Directions for Cooking:

1. Press the Sauté button on the Instant Pot and heat the oil. Sauté the onion and garlic until fragrant.
2. Stir in the rest of the ingredients.
3. Close Instant Pot, press the button, choose high settings, and set time to 10 minutes.
4. Once done cooking, do a QPR.
5. Serve and enjoy.

Nutrition information:

Calories per serving: 223; Carbohydrates: 35.3g; Protein: 11.4g; Fat: 4.8g; Sugar: 9.3g; Sodium: 472mg

---

229. Vegan "Buttered" Chicken

(Servings: 3, Cooking time: 10 minutes)

Ingredients:

- 3 large ripe tomatoes, diced
- 4 cloves of garlic
- ½ inch ginger, minced
- 1 green chili, chopped
- ¾ cup water
- ½ teaspoon garam masala
- Salt and pepper to taste
- 1 cup cooked chickpeas
- 1 cup soy curls, rehydrated
- ½ teaspoon sugar
- Salt and pepper to taste

Directions for Cooking:

1. Place all ingredients in the Instant Pot and give a good stir.
2. Close Instant Pot, press the Manual button, choose high settings, and set time to 10 minutes.
3. Once done cooking, do a QPR.
4. Serve and enjoy.

Nutrition information:

Calories per serving: 191; Carbohydrates: 31.4g; Protein: 14.9g; Fat: 2.1g; Sugar: 14.2g; Sodium: 689mg

---

230. One-Pot Cauliflower Cheddar Pasta

(Servings: 4, Cooking time: 10 minutes)

Ingredients:

- 1-pound pasta, dry
- 4 cups water
- 16 ounces cheddar cheese
- 1 cup frozen cauliflower
- 1 cup half and half
- Salt and pepper to taste
- A dash of paprika

Directions for Cooking:

1. Place all ingredients in the Instant Pot and give a good stir.
2. Close Instant Pot, press the button, choose high settings, and set time to 10 minutes.
3. Once done cooking, do a QPR.
4. Serve and enjoy.

Nutrition information:

Calories per serving:964 ; Carbohydrates: 90g; Protein: 45g; Fat: 46g; Sugar: 4g; Sodium: 755mg

---

231. Instant Pot Tempeh Tajine

(Servings: 6, Cooking time: 15 minutes)

Ingredients:

- 1 teaspoon each of ground cumin, cinnamon, turmeric and ground ginger
- 2 packs tempeh, cubed
- 2 teaspoons soy sauce
- 4 cloves of garlic, minced
- 1 tablespoon oil
- 1 onion, chopped
- 2 carrots, peeled and chopped
- 1 sweet potato, peeled and chopped
- ½ cup prunes, pitted and chopped
- 1 can diced tomatoes
- 1 cup vegetable stock
- Salt and pepper to taste

Directions for Cooking:

1. In a mixing bowl, combine the herbs with the tempeh, soy sauce, and garlic. Allow to marinate in the fridge for at least 3 hours.
2. Press the Sauté button and heat the oil. Stir in the marinated tempeh and onions. Stir until lightly brown.
3. Stir in the rest of the ingredients.
4. Close Instant Pot, press the Manual button, choose high settings, and set time to 10 minutes.
5. Once done cooking, do a QPR.
6. Serve and enjoy.

Nutrition information:

Calories per serving: 242; Carbohydrates: 24.4g; Protein: 15.4g; Fat: 11.5g; Sugar: 3.4g; Sodium: 99mg

---

232. Veggie Shepherd's Pie

(Servings: 6, Cooking time: 4 hours and 5 minutes)

Ingredients:

- 4 red potatoes, boiled and peeled
- ¾ cup almond milk
- 4 tablespoons olive oil, divided
- ¼ cup nutritional yeast
- ½ teaspoon garlic powder
- Salt and pepper to taste
- 1 white onion, chopped
- 1 cup carrot, chopped
- 1 block extra firm tofu, chopped
- 1 bunch dinosaur kale, chopped
- ½ cup corn kernels
- ½ cup frozen peas
- ½ cup water

Directions for Cooking:

1. In a bowl, mash the potatoes, milk, half of the olive oil, nutritional yeast, and garlic powder. Season with salt and pepper to taste. Set aside.
2. Press the Sauté button on the Instant Pot and heat the remaining oil. Sauté the onion until fragrant and add in the carrots, tofu, kale, corn, and peas. Season with salt and pepper to taste.
3. Pour in water. Pack the vegetable mixture firmly and spread the potato mash on top.
4. Close Instant Pot but do not seal the vent.
5. Press the Slow Cook button and set time to 4 hours.
6. Serve and enjoy.

Nutrition information:

Calories per serving: 389; Carbohydrates: 51.4g; Protein: 16.2g; Fat: 14.5g; Sugar: 17.3g; Sodium: 446mg

---

233. Vegan Baked Beans

(Servings: 10, Cooking time: 50 minutes)

Ingredients:

- 1-pound dry navy beans
- 6 cups water
- ¾ cup molasses
- ½ cup brown sugar
- ¾ cup ketchup salt and pepper to taste
- 1 ½ tablespoon Worcestershire sauce
- 2 tablespoons apple cider vinegar
- 1 onion, chopped
- 3 cloves of garlic, minced
- 1 bay leaf

Directions for Cooking:

1. Place the beans and water in the Instant Pot.
2. Close Instant Pot, press the Manual button, choose high settings, and set time to 40 minutes.
3. Once done cooking, do a QPR.
4. Open the lid and strain the beans. Discard the water.
5. In the Instant Pot, place all ingredients including the beans.
6. Close the lid and seal the vent. Press the Manual button and set time to 10 minutes.
7. Serve and enjoy.

Nutrition information:

Calories per serving: 135; Carbohydrates: 34.1g; Protein: 0.7g; Fat: 0.2g; Sugar: 12.9g; Sodium: 42mg

---

234. One-Pot Vegetable Barley Soup

(Servings: 3, Cooking time: 30 minutes)

Ingredients:

- 2 garlic cloves, minced
- 1 leek, sliced
- 3 carrots, peeled and sliced
- 3 stalks of celery, minced
- 8 ounces mushrooms, sliced
- 7 cups water
- 2 cubes of vegetable bouillon
- ½ cup dried pearled barley
- Salt and pepper to taste

Directions for Cooking:

1. Place all ingredients in the Instant Pot and give a good stir.
2. Close Instant Pot, press the button, choose high settings, and set time to 30 minutes.
3. Once done cooking, do a QPR.
4. Serve and enjoy.

Nutrition information:

Calories per serving:372; Carbohydrates:73.2g; Protein: 11.5g; Fat: 1g; Sugar: 2.1g; Sodium: 47mg

---

235. Creamy Tomato Soup

(Servings: 4, Cooking time: 12 minutes)

Ingredients:

- 4 tablespoons olive oil
- 1 onion, diced
- 2 cans crushed tomatoes
- 6 cups vegetable stock
- Salt and pepper to taste
- ½ cup fresh basil
- 1 ½ cups whole raw cashews

Directions for Cooking:

1. Press the Sauté button on the Instant Pot and heat the oil. Sauté the onion until slightly caramelized.
2. Stir in the rest of the ingredients.
3. Close Instant Pot, press the Manual button, choose high settings, and set time to 10 minutes.
4. Once done cooking, do a QPR.
5. Open the lid and use an immersion blender to smoothen the texture.
6. Serve and enjoy.

Nutrition information:

Calories per serving: 735; Carbohydrates: 36.1g; Protein: 13.1g; Fat: 64.7g; Sugar: 12.9g; Sodium: 395mg

---

236. One-Pot Veggie Curry Dish

(Servings: 4, Cooking time: 7 minutes)

Ingredients:

- 3 potatoes, peeled and chopped
- 1 cup broccoli florets
- 1 cup cauliflower florets
- 1 red bell pepper, sliced
- ½ cup frozen corn
- ½ cup frozen peas

Directions for Cooking:

1. Place all ingredients in the Instant Pot.
2. Close Instant Pot, press the Manual button, choose high settings, and set time to 7 minutes.
3. Once done cooking, do a QPR.

- 2 tablespoons green curry paste
- 1 teaspoon onion powder
- 1 teaspoon garlic powder
- 1 cup coconut milk
- 2 cups vegetable stock
- Salt to taste

4. Serve and enjoy.

Nutrition information:

Calories per serving:410 ; Carbohydrates: 63g; Protein: 9.8g; Fat: 15.4g; Sugar: 6g; Sodium: 42mg

---

237. Vegan Carrot Ginger Soup

(Servings: 5, Cooking time: 8 minutes)

Ingredients:

- 1 ½ tablespoons olive oil
- 1 onion, diced
- 4 cloves of garlic, minced
- 1 ½ tablespoons fresh ginger, grated
- 1 teaspoon dried thyme
- ½ teaspoon ground coriander
- ½ teaspoon crushed red pepper
- 2 bay leaves
- 2 pounds carrots, chopped
- 4 cups vegetable broth
- Salt and pepper to taste
- 1 cup coconut milk
- 2 tablespoons lime juice

Directions for Cooking:

1. Press the Sauté button on the Instant Pot and heat the oil.
2. Sauté the onion and garlic until fragrant. Stir in the rest of the ingredients.
3. Close Instant Pot, press the Manual button, choose high settings, and set time to 6 minutes.
4. Once done cooking, do a QPR.
5. Serve and enjoy.

Nutrition information:

Calories per serving: 268; Carbohydrates: 26g; Protein: 7g; Fat: 16g; Sugar: 11g; Sodium: 584mg

---

238. Split Pea Soup

(Servings: 4, Cooking time: 40 minutes)

Ingredients:

- 1 tablespoon olive oil
- 1 onion, diced
- 2 stalks of celery, chopped
- 3 cloves of garlic, minced
- 3 carrots, sliced
- 2 teaspoons curry power
- 1 teaspoon ground cumin
- ½ teaspoon ground coriander
- 2 cups yellow split peas
- 4 cups vegetable broth
- 2 cups water
- Salt and pepper to taste

Directions for Cooking:

1. Press the Sauté button on the Instant Pot and sauté the onion, celery, and garlic until fragrant.
2. Stir in the carrots, curry powder, cumin, coriander, and peas.
3. Add in the rest of the ingredients.
4. Close Instant Pot, press the Manual button, choose high settings, and set time to 35 minutes.
5. Once done cooking, do a QPR.
6. Serve and enjoy.

Nutrition information:

Calories per serving: 383; Carbohydrates: 29g; Protein: 25g; Fat: 5g; Sugar: 13g; Sodium: 582mg

---

239. Three Cheese Mushroom and Tortellini

(Servings: 8, Cooking time: 15 minutes)

Ingredients:

- 2 teaspoons butter
- 2 stalks of celery, chopped
- 3 cloves of garlic, minced
- 1 carrot, peeled and chopped
- 8 cups vegetable broth
- 5 ounces shiitake mushrooms, sliced
- 8 ounces baby Bella mushrooms, sliced
- 1 cup parmigiana Reggiano, grated
- 1 cup three cheese tortellini
- 1 cup mozzarella cheese, grated
- Salt to taste

Directions for Cooking:

1. Press the Sauté button on the Instant Pot and sauté the celery and garlic until fragrant.
2. Add in the rest of the ingredients. Stir to combine everything.
3. Close Instant Pot, press the Manual button, choose high settings, and set time to 15 minutes.
4. Once done cooking, do a QPR.
5. Serve and enjoy.

Nutrition information:

Calories per serving: 182; Carbohydrates: 19.5g; Protein: 10g; Fat: 12g; Sugar: 2.5g; Sodium: 605mg

---

240. Curried Black Eyed Peas

(Servings: 5, Cooking time: 52 minutes)

Ingredients:

- 1 tablespoon olive oil
- 4 cloves of garlic, minced
- ½ onion, minced
- 1 cup dried black-eyed peas
- 2 cups water
- 3 dried curry leaves
- 1/8 teaspoon mustard seeds
- 2 ½ tablespoons tomato paste
- 1 teaspoon ground cumin
- 1 teaspoon ground coriander
- ¼ teaspoon ground turmeric
- 3 teaspoons brown sugar
- 2 teaspoons fresh lemon juice

Directions for Cooking:

1. Press the Sauté button on the Instant Pot and heat the oil.
2. Sauté the garlic and onion until fragrant. Stir in the rest of the ingredients.
3. Close Instant Pot, press the Manual button, choose high settings, and set time to 50 minutes.
4. Once done cooking, do a QPR.
5. Serve and enjoy.

Nutrition information:

Calories per serving:131; Carbohydrates: 24g; Protein: 8g; Fat: 3.2g; Sugar: 4g; Sodium: 753mg

---

241. Quinoa Burrito Bowls

(Servings: 5, Cooking time: 33 minutes)

Ingredients:

- 1 teaspoon olive oil
- ½ red onion, diced
- 1 bell pepper, diced
- 1 teaspoon ground cumin
- 1 cup quinoa, rinsed
- 1 cup commercial salsa
- 1 cup water
- 1 ½ cups cooked black beans
- Salt and pepper to taste
- Avocado slices
- Fresh cilantro, chopped
- Lime wedges

Directions for Cooking:

Press the Sauté button and heat the oil. Sauté the onion until fragrant.

1.
2. Stir in the bell pepper, cumin, quinoa, commercial salsa, water, and black beans. Season with salt and pepper to taste.
3. Close Instant Pot, press the Manual button, choose high settings, and set time to 30 minutes.
4. Once done cooking, do a QPR.
5. Open the lid and ladle the mixture into bowls. Add in avocado slices, cilantro, and lime wedges.
6. Serve and enjoy.

Nutrition information:

Calories per serving: 296; Carbohydrates: 44.5g; Protein: 11.5g; Fat: 9.4g; Sugar: 3.8g; Sodium: 375mg

---

242. Instant Pot Veggie Clear Soup

(Servings: 4, Cooking time: 10 minutes)

Ingredients:

- 1 onion, diced
- 2 cloves of garlic, minced
- 1 carrot, chopped
- 1 stalk of celery, chopped
- 2 teaspoons dried basil
- 1 teaspoon dried oregano
- ¾ teaspoon dried thyme
- 1 yellow zucchini, chopped
- 2 tablespoons nutritional yeast
- Salt and pepper to taste

Directions for Cooking:

1. Place all ingredients in the Instant Pot. Mix to combine.
2. Close Instant Pot, press the Manual button, choose high settings, and set time to 10 minutes.
3. Once done cooking, do a QPR.
4. Serve and enjoy.

Nutrition information:

Calories per serving: 62; Carbohydrates: 11.4g; Protein: 4.4g; Fat: 0.6g; Sugar: 2.4g; Sodium: 292mg

---

243. Cheesy Lentils and Brown Rice

(Servings: 5, Cooking time: 25 minutes)

Ingredients:

- 1 onion, diced
- 4 cloves of garlic, minced
- 1 red bell pepper, chopped
- ¾ cup brown rice
- ¾ cup brown lentils
- 2 ½ cups vegetable broth
- 1 can diced tomatoes
- 1 can diced green chilies
- 1 tablespoon taco seasoning
- Salt and pepper to taste
- 2 cups mozzarella cheese, shredded
- ¼ cup chopped cilantro

Directions for Cooking:

1. Place all ingredients except for the mozzarella cheese and cilantro.
2. Close Instant Pot, press the Manual button, choose high settings, and set time to 25 minutes.
3. Once done cooking, do a QPR.
4. Open the lid and stir in the mozzarella cheese and cilantro.
5. Serve and enjoy.

Nutrition information:

Calories per serving:530; Carbohydrates: 61g; Protein: 29g; Fat: 19g; Sugar: 6g; Sodium: 1125mg

---

244. Spicy Chili and Beer Macaroni

(Servings: 4, Cooking time: 15 minutes)

Ingredients:

- 3 ½ cups commercial chili
- 1 12-ounce beer
- ½ cup water
- 2 cups elbow pasta
- 1 cup coconut milk
- Salt and pepper to taste

Directions for Cooking:

1. Place all ingredients in the Instant Pot and give a good stir.
2. Close Instant Pot, press the Manual button, choose high settings, and set time to 15 minutes.
3. Once done cooking, do a QPR.
4. Serve and enjoy.

Nutrition information:

Calories per serving: 487; Carbohydrates: 47.8g; Protein: 14.2g; Fat: 28.5g; Sugar: 9g; Sodium: 1188mg

---

245. Vegetarian Quinoa Chili

(Servings: 9, Cooking time: 25 minutes)

Ingredients:

- 4 cups vegetable broth
- 2 cups canned crushed tomatoes
- 2 cups diced onions
- 1 green bell pepper, diced
- 1 red bell pepper, diced
- 1 cup corn
- 1 can spicy chili beans
- 1 cup cooked black beans
- 3 tablespoons chili powder
- 2 tablespoon cumin
- ½ cup quinoa
- ½ cup red lentils
- Salt and pepper to taste
- Avocado, sliced
- Cilantro for garnish
- Sour cream

Directions for Cooking:

1. Place the broth, tomatoes, onions, bell peppers, corn, chili beans, chili powder, cumin, quinoa, and red lentils. Season with salt and pepper to taste.
2. Close Instant Pot, press the Manual button, choose high settings, and set time to 25 minutes.
3. Once done cooking, do a QPR.
4. Open the lid and spoon into bowls. Top with avocado, cilantro, and sour cream.
5. Serve and enjoy.

Nutrition information:

Calories per serving: 241; Carbohydrates: 41.3g; Protein: 9.2g; Fat: 5.8g; Sugar: 4.1g; Sodium: 336mg

---

246. Instant Pot Acorn Squash

(Servings: 6, Cooking time: 25 minutes)

Ingredients:

- 1 tablespoon olive oil
- 1 shallot, chopped
- 3 large cloves of garlic, minced
- ½ cup wild rice, uncooked
- 8 ounces baby Bella mushrooms, chopped
- ½ teaspoon black pepper
- 1 can chickpeas, rinsed and drained
- 1/3 cup cranberries, chopped
- 1 tablespoon fresh thyme leaves, chopped
- Salt and pepper to taste
- 3 acorn squashes, halved and seeded
- ¼ cup pepitas, chopped

Nutrition information:

Calories per serving: 256; Carbohydrates: 47g; Protein: 7g; Fat: 4g; Sugar:3 g; Sodium: 253mg

Directions for Cooking:

1. Press the Sauté button on the Instant Pot and heat the oil. Sauté the shallot and garlic until fragrant. Stir in the rice, mushrooms, black pepper, chickpeas, cranberries, and thyme. Season with salt and pepper to taste.
2. Close Instant Pot, press the Manual button, choose high settings, and set time to 10 minutes.
3. Once done cooking, do a QPR.
4. Open the lid and spoon the quinoa into the hollows of the acorn squash. Sprinkle with pepitas on top.
5. Bake in a 350^{0}F preheated oven for 15 minutes.
6. Serve and enjoy.

247. Instant Pot Chickpea Gumbo

(Servings: 5, Cooking time: 12 minutes)

Ingredients:

- 1 tablespoon olive oil
- 1 teaspoon minced garlic
- 1 ½ cups chopped onion
- 2 celery ribs, chopped
- ½ tablespoon oregano
- ½ teaspoon cayenne pepper
- 1 cup cooked chickpeas
- 3 cups vegetable broth
- 2 cups frozen okra
- 1 red bell pepper, chopped
- 1 can diced tomatoes, drained
- 2 tablespoons apple cider vinegar
- ½ cups tomato sauce
- 1 cup cauliflower, cut into florets
- Salt and pepper to taste

Directions for Cooking:

1. Press the Sauté button on the Instant Pot and heat the oil. Sauté the garlic, onions, and celery until fragrant.
2. Stir in the rest of the ingredients.
3. Close Instant Pot, press the Manual button, choose high settings, and set time to 10 minutes.
4. Once done cooking, do a QPR.
5. Serve and enjoy.

Nutrition information:

Calories per serving: 221; Carbohydrates: 29.2g; Protein: 13.2g; Fat: 6.3g; Sugar: 3.5g; Sodium: 768mg

---

248. Instant Pot Pinto Beans

(Servings: 4, Cooking time: 42 minutes)

Ingredients:

- 1 tablespoon oil
- 1 onion, chopped
- 3 cloves of garlic, minced
- 1 cup dry pinto beans
- 4 cups water
- 1 teaspoon thyme
- Salt and pepper to taste

Directions for Cooking:

1. Press the Sauté button on the Instant Pot and heat the oil.
2. Sauté the onion and garlic until fragrant. Stir in the rest of the ingredients.
3. Close Instant Pot, press the Manual button, choose high settings, and set time to 40 minutes.
4. Once done cooking, do a QPR.
5. Serve and enjoy.

Nutrition information:

Calories per serving:111 ; Carbohydrates: 15.6g; Protein: 4.5g; Fat: 3.8g; Sugar: 1.9g; Sodium: 91mg

---

249. Instant Pot Hearty Vegetable and Brown Rice Soup

(Servings: 8, Cooking time: 25 minutes)

Ingredients:

- 1 tablespoon olive oil
- 1 onion, chopped
- 3 cloves of garlic, minced
- 2 fresh ginger, minced
- 4 celery sticks, chopped
- 1 cup dry brown rice
- 1-pound red potatoes, peeled and chopped
- 3 carrots, peeled and chopped
- 2 ½ cups French green beans, cut into 2-inch pieces
- 2 tablespoons tomato paste
- 1 tablespoon dried basil
- 4 cups vegetable broth
- Salt and pepper to taste

Directions for Cooking:

1. Press the Sauté button on the Instant Pot and heat the oil.
2. Stir in the onions, garlic, ginger, and celery until fragrant.
3. Stir in the rice and sauté for 1 minute. Add in the rest of the ingredients.
4. Close Instant Pot, press the Manual button, choose high settings, and set time to 20 minutes.
5. Once done cooking, do a QPR.
6. Serve and enjoy.

Nutrition information:

Calories per serving: 193; Carbohydrates: 37.1g; Protein: 8.9g; Fat: 2.3g; Sugar: 16.3g; Sodium: 637

---

250. Portobello Pot Roast

(Servings: 6, Cooking time: 20 minutes)

Ingredients:

- 1 ½ pounds gold potatoes, cut into bite-sized pieces
- 1-pound baby Bella mushrooms
- 2 large carrots, peeled and chopped
- 2 cups frozen pearl onions
- 4 cloves of garlic, minced
- 3 sprigs fresh thyme
- 3 cups vegetable stock
- ½ cup white wine
- 3 tablespoons tomato paste
- Salt and pepper to taste

Directions for Cooking:

1. Place all ingredients in the Instant Pot and give a good stir.
2. Close Instant Pot, press the Manual button, choose high settings, and set time to 20 minutes.
3. Once done cooking, do a QPR.
4. Serve and enjoy.

Nutrition information:

Calories per serving: 376; Carbohydrates:91.1 g; Protein:12 g; Fat: 0.9g; Sugar: 7.9g; Sodium: 367mg

---

251. Creamy Parsnips and Chive Soup

(Servings: 10, Cooking time: 10 minutes)

Ingredients:

- 3 pounds parsnips, trimmed and peeled
- 3 cloves of garlic, minced
- ½ cup raw cashews
- 6 cups vegetable broth
- Juice from 1 lemon, freshly squeezed
- ¼ cup fresh chives
- Salt and pepper to taste

Nutrition information:

Calories per serving: 186; Carbohydrates: 29.9g; Protein: 3.5g; Fat: 7.2g; Sugar: 9.3g; Sodium: 382mg

Directions for Cooking:

1. Place all ingredients in the Instant Pot
2. Close Instant Pot, press the Manual button, choose high settings, and set time to 10 minutes.
3. Once done cooking, do a QPR.
4. Open the lid and use the immersion blender to pulse everything until smooth.
5. Serve and enjoy.

---

252. Vegan Potato Corn Chowder

(Servings: 6, Cooking time: 10 minutes)

Ingredients:

- 1 cup diced onions
- 2 cloves of garlic, minced
- 1 cup diced carrots
- 1 cup diced celery
- 6 cups gold potatoes, peeled and quartered
- 1 bay leaf
- 1 teaspoon dried thyme
- 4 cups vegetable broth
- 2 cups frozen corns
- ½ cup coconut cream
- ½ cup water
- Salt and pepper to taste

Directions for Cooking:

1. Place all ingredients in the Instant Pot and mix until well combined.
2. Close Instant Pot, press the Manual button, choose high settings, and set time to 10 minutes.
3. Once done cooking, do a QPR.
4. Serve and enjoy.

Nutrition information:

Calories per serving: 243; Carbohydrates: 44g; Protein: 8g; Fat: 5g; Sugar: 4g; Sodium: 678mg

---

253. Smoky Pecan Brussels sprouts

(Servings: 3, Cooking time: 6 minutes)

Ingredients:

- 2 cups small baby Brussels sprouts
- ¼ cup water
- ½ teaspoon liquid smoke
- ¼ cup chopped pecans
- 2 tablespoons maple syrup
- Salt and pepper to taste

Nutrition information:

Calories per serving:124 ; Carbohydrates: 16.7g; Protein: 3.1g; Fat: 6.2g; Sugar: 10.5g; Sodium: 18mg

Directions for Cooking:

1. Place the Brussels sprouts, water and liquid smoke into the Instant Pot.
2. Close Instant Pot, press the Manual button, choose high settings, and set time to 6 minutes.
3. Once done cooking, do a QPR.
4. Open the lid and press the Sauté button. Stir in the pecans, and maple syrup. Season with salt and pepper to taste.
5. Serve and enjoy.

---

254. Maple Bourbon Sweet Potato Chili

(Servings: 4, Cooking time: 20 minutes)

Ingredients:

- 1 tablespoon cooking oil
- 1 onion, sliced thinly
- 3 cloves of garlic, minced
- 4 cups sweet potatoes, peeled and cubed
- 2 cups vegetable broth
- 1 ½ tablespoons chili powder
- 2 teaspoons cumin
- ½ teaspoon paprika
- 2 cans kidney beans, drained
- 1 can diced tomatoes
- ¼ cup bourbon
- 2 tablespoons maple syrup
- Salt and pepper to taste
- Green onions for garnish
- Tortillas, toasted and sliced

Directions for Cooking:

1. Press the Sauté button on the Instant Pot and heat the oil. Sauté the onion and garlic until fragrant.
2. Stir in the sweet potatoes, broth, chili powder, cumin, paprika, beans, tomatoes, bourbon, and maple syrup. Season with salt and pepper to taste.
3. Close Instant Pot, press the Manual button, choose high settings, and set time to 20 minutes.
4. Once done cooking, do a QPR.
5. Serve with green onions and tortillas.
6. Serve and enjoy.

Nutrition information:

Calories per serving: 239; Carbohydrates: 40g; Protein: 3g; Fat: 4g; Sugar: 13g; Sodium: 597mg

---

255. Cauliflower Tikka Masala

(Servings: 4, Cooking time: 10 minutes)

Ingredients:

- 1 tablespoon olive oil
- 1 onion, diced
- 3 cloves of garlic, minced
- 1 tablespoon grated ginger
- 2 teaspoons dried fenugreek leaves
- 2 teaspoons garam masala
- 1 teaspoon turmeric
- ½ teaspoon ground chili
- ¼ teaspoon ground cumin
- 1 28-ounce crushed tomatoes
- 1 tablespoon maple syrup
- 1 cauliflower head, cut into florets
- Salt and pepper to taste
- ½ cup non-dairy yogurt
- ½ cup roasted cashews

Directions for Cooking:

1. Press the Sauté button on the Instant Pot and sauté the onion and garlic until fragrant.
2. Add in the ginger, fenugreek leaves, garam masala, turmeric, ground chili, cumin, tomatoes, and maple syrup.
3. Stir in the cauliflower florets and season with salt and pepper to taste.
4. Add water if necessary.
5. Close Instant Pot, press the Manual button, choose high settings, and set time to 10 minutes.
6. Once done cooking, do a QPR.
7. Garnish with yogurt and roasted cashews.
8. Serve and enjoy.

Nutrition information:

Calories per serving:331; Carbohydrates:32 g; Protein: 9.4g; Fat: 21.2g; Sugar: 12g; Sodium: 222mg

---

256. Vegan Udon Noodles Bowl

(Servings: 3, Cooking time: 7 minutes)

Ingredients:

- 1-inch ginger, peeled
- 1 large carrot, peeled and sliced
- ½ cup water
- 1 teaspoon maple syrup
- 2 tablespoons miso paste
- 2 cups edamame, blanched
- ¾ cup green onions
- 2 ½ cups udon noodles, cooked

Directions for Cooking:

1. Place the ginger, carrots, water, maple syrup, and miso paste in the Instant Pot.
2. Close Instant Pot, press the Manual button, choose high settings, and set time to 7 minutes.
3. Once done cooking, do a QPR.
4. Open the lid and stir in the rest of the ingredients.
5. Serve and enjoy.

Nutrition information:

Calories per serving: 318; Carbohydrates: 51.1g; Protein: 15.3g; Fat: 6.4g; Sugar: 5.1g; Sodium: 582mg

---

257. Basmati Rice Pilaf

(Servings: 4 , Cooking time: 20 minutes)

Ingredients:

- 1 tablespoon oil
- 1 onion, sliced
- 1 teaspoon turmeric
- 1 pinch cinnamon
- 1 pinch ground cumin
- 2 cups basmati rice
- 1 can chickpeas
- ½ cup raisins
- ½ cup dates, chopped
- 4 cups water
- Salt and pepper to taste

Directions for Cooking:

1. Press the Sauté button on the Instant and heat the oil. Sauté the onion until fragrant. Add the turmeric, cinnamon, and cumin until toasted.
2. Stir in the basmati rice for a minute and stir in the rest of the ingredients.
3. Close Instant Pot, press the Manual button, choose high settings, and set time to 15 minutes.
4. Once done cooking, do a QPR.
5. Serve and enjoy.

Nutrition information:

Calories per serving:487; Carbohydrates: 104g; Protein: 7g; Fat: 4g; Sugar: 12g; Sodium: 11mg

Instant Pot Soup Recipes

258. Singaporean Prawn and Pork Ribs Noodle Soup

(Servings: 4, Cooking time: 40 minutes)

Ingredients:

- 3 pounds pork ribs
- 4 cloves of garlic, minced
- 3 cloves
- 1 star anise
- 1 tablespoon soy sauce
- 1 tablespoon sugar
- Salt and pepper to taste
- 6 cups water
- 1-pound Chinese yellow noodles, cooked
- 20 jumbo prawns, boiled and shelled
- 1 bunch water spinach, blanched
- 2 cups fresh bean sprouts
- 5 red chilies, chopped

Directions for Cooking:

1. In the Instant Pot, place the pork, garlic, cloves, star anise, soy sauce, sugar, salt, pepper, and water.
2. Close Instant Pot, press the Manual button, choose high settings, and set time to 40 minutes.
3. Once done cooking, do a QPR.
4. Assemble the noodles by place the noodles in a bowl and pouring in the beef and broth. Top with boiled prawns, spinach, and bean sprouts. Garnish with chilies on top.
5. Serve and enjoy.

Nutrition information:

Calories per serving: 600; Carbohydrates: 16.9g; Protein: 79.7g; Fat: 23.4g; Sugar: 3.2g; Sodium: 684mg

---

259. Chicken Wonton Soup

(Servings: 4, Cooking time: 20 minutes)

Ingredients

- 4 cups chicken stock
- 1 32-ounce pack frozen chicken wontons
- ½-inch ginger, peeled and sliced thinly
- 2 cloves of garlic, peeled and chopped
- 1 tablespoon rice vinegar
- 2 tablespoons soy sauce
- 1 tablespoon sambal oelek
- 1 teaspoon honey
- 1 tablespoon fish sauce
- 3 medium carrots, sliced
- 3 heads of Bok Choy
- ½ teaspoon sesame oil

Directions for Cooking:

1. In the Instant Pot, place the chicken stock, wonton, ginger, garlic, rice vinegar, soy sauce, sambal oelek, honey, fish sauce, and carrots.
2. Close Instant Pot, press the Manual button, choose high settings, and set time to 20 minutes.
3. Once done cooking, do a QPR.
4. Open the lid and press the Sauté button. Stir in the bok choy and allow to simmer until cooked.
5. Drizzle with sesame oil.
6. Serve and enjoy.

Nutrition information:

Calories per serving: 450; Carbohydrates: 12.9g; Protein: 46.5g; Fat: 23.2g; Sugar: 7.1g; Sodium: 955mg

---

260. Instant Pot Mexican Chicken Tomato Soup

(Servings: 5, Cooking time: 20 minutes)

Ingredients:

- 1 ½ cups tomatoes, crushed
- 1 cup chicken broth
- 1-ounce taco seasoning
- 1 red bell pepper, sliced
- 1 onion, sliced
- 1 ½ pounds chicken thighs
- Salt and pepper to taste

Directions for Cooking:

1. Place all ingredients in the Instant Pot.
2. Close Instant Pot, press the Manual button, choose high settings, and set time to 20 minutes.
3. Once done cooking, do a QPR.
4. Serve and enjoy.

Nutrition information:

Calories per serving: 411; Carbohydrates: 7.6g; Protein: 33.5g; Fat: 26.1g; Sugar: 2.7g; Sodium: 734mg

---

261. Instant Pot Chicken Rice Porridge

(Servings: 6, Cooking time: 40 minutes)

Ingredients:

- 1 tablespoon olive oil
- 1 onion, diced
- 3 cloves of garlic, minced
- 3 carrots, chopped
- 2 stalks of celery, chopped
- 2 chicken breasts, chopped
- 1 cup long grain rice
- 1 package button mushrooms
- 5 cups water
- Salt and pepper to taste

Nutrition information:

Calories per serving:328; Carbohydrates: 30.3g; Protein: 23.4g; Fat: 12.2g; Sugar: 3g; Sodium: 94mg

Directions for Cooking:

1. Press the Sauté button on the Instant Pot and heat the oil.
2. Sauté the onion and garlic until fragrant. Stir in the carrots, celery, and chicken breasts. Keep stirring for 2 minutes.
3. Add in the rest of the ingredients.
4. Close Instant Pot, press the Manual button, choose high settings, and set time to 35 minutes.
5. Once done cooking, do a QPR.
6. Serve and enjoy.

---

262. New England clam chowder

(Servings: 5, Cooking time: 15 minutes)

Ingredients:

- 3 pieces of bacon
- 1 onion, peeled and diced
- 1 stalk of celery, diced
- 2 cups clam juice
- 4 potatoes, peeled and cubed
- 2 cups water
- 1 bay leaf
- 1 teaspoon thyme
- Salt and pepper to taste
- 1-pound clam meat
- 1 cup cream

Directions for Cooking:

1. Press the Sauté button on the Instant Pot and stir in the bacon. Cook the bacon until crispy. Set aside.
2. Use the bacon grease and sauté the onion and celery until fragrant. Add in the potatoes, water, bay leaf, and thyme. Season with salt and pepper to taste.
3. Close Instant Pot, press the Manual button, choose high settings, and set time to 10 minutes.
4. Once done cooking, do a QPR.
5. Open the lid and press the Sauté button. Stir in the clam meat and cream. Allow to simmer until the clam is cooked.
6. Garnish with sliced bacon on top.
7. Serve and enjoy.

Nutrition information:

Calories per serving:433 ; Carbohydrates: 77.1g; Protein: 9.6g; Fat: 10.8g; Sugar: 11.7g; Sodium: 692mg

---

263. Vegan Ginger Noodle Soup

(Servings: 4, Cooking time: 23 minutes)

Ingredients:

- 2 tablespoons olive oil
- ¼ cup chopped onions
- 1 cup chopped celery
- 4 cloves of garlic, minced
- 1 cup kohlrabi, peeled and diced
- 1 cup sliced carrots
- 1 teaspoon of your favorite dried herbs
- 2 tablespoons fresh ginger, grated
- 3 bay leaves
- 8 cups vegetable broth
- 8 ounces fusilli noodles
- ¼ cup white wine
- Salt and pepper to taste

Directions for Cooking:

1. Press the Sauté button on the Instant Pot and heat the oil.
2. Stir in the onions, celery, and garlic until fragrant.
3. Add in the rest of the ingredients and give a good stir.
4. Close Instant Pot, press the Manual button, choose high settings, and set time to 20 minutes.
5. Once done cooking, do a QPR.
6. Serve and enjoy.

Nutrition information:

Calories per serving: 331; Carbohydrates: 53.1g; Protein: 9.4g; Fat: 8.5g; Sugar: 7.6g; Sodium: 1143mg

---

264. Instant Pot Salmon Tortellini Soup

(Servings: 4, Cooking time: 15 minutes)

Ingredients:

- 2 strips of bacon, diced
- 2/3 cup diced onions
- 2 cloves of garlic, minced
- 16 ounces boneless salmon, sliced
- 1 10-ounce packaged vegetables
- 10 ounces frozen tortellini
- 4 cups chicken broth
- 1 teaspoon Old Bay seasoning
- Salt and pepper to taste
- 3 handfuls of baby spinach

Directions for Cooking:

1. Press the Sauté button on the Instant Pot and stir in the bacon until the fat has rendered.
2. Sauté the onions and garlic until fragrant.
3. Add in the salmon, vegetables, tortellini, and chicken broth. Season with old bay seasoning, salt and pepper.
4. Close Instant Pot, press the Manual button, choose high settings, and set time to 15 minutes.
5. Once done cooking, do a QPR.
6. Open the lid and press the Sauté button. Stir in the baby spinach and allow to cook.
7. Serve and enjoy.

Nutrition information:

Calories per serving: 711; Carbohydrates: 30.6g; Protein: 80.2g; Fat: 28.2g; Sugar: 4.2g; Sodium: 1587mg

---

265. Instant Pot Chicken Ramen

(Servings: 3, Cooking time: 25 minutes)

Ingredients:

- 3 boneless, chicken breasts
- ½ onion, chopped
- 1 cup celery, chopped
- 1 cup carrots, chopped
- Salt and pepper to taste
- ¼ teaspoon thyme
- ½ teaspoon salt
- 1 teaspoon garlic
- 4 cups chicken broth
- 1 cup water
- 3 cups ramen noodles

Directions for Cooking:

1. Place all ingredients in the Instant Pot except for the ramen noodles.
2. Close Instant Pot, press the Manual button, choose high settings, and set time to 20 minutes.
3. Once done cooking, do a QPR.
4. Open the lid and press the Sauté button. Stir in the noodles and allow to simmer for additional 5 more minutes.
5. Serve and enjoy.

Nutrition information:

Calories per serving: 598; Carbohydrates: 11.3g; Protein: 76.6g; Fat: 24.1g; Sugar: 4.2g; Sodium: 884mg

---

266. Instant Pot Summer Soup

(Servings: 5, Cooking time: 25 minutes)

Ingredients:

- 1 tablespoon olive oil
- 1-pound chicken breasts
- 2 stalks of celery, chopped
- 3 cloves of garlic, minced
- 1 28-ounce can crushed tomatoes
- 4 carrots, peeled and chopped
- ½ cup farro
- 1 teaspoon basil
- ½ teaspoon onion powder
- 1 zucchini, chopped
- 6 cups chicken broth
- Salt and pepper to taste

Directions for Cooking:

1. Press the Sauté button on the Instant Pot and heat the oil. Stir in the chicken breasts, celery, and garlic. Keep stirring for 3 minutes.
2. Add in the tomatoes, carrots, farro, basil, onion powder, zucchini and chicken stock. Season with salt and pepper to taste.
3. Close Instant Pot, press the Manual button, choose high settings, and set time to 20 minutes.
4. Once done cooking, do a QPR.
5. Top with yogurt or parmesan cheese if desired.
6. Serve and enjoy.

Nutrition information:

Calories per serving:433 ; Carbohydrates: 9.4g; Protein: 52.2g; Fat: 19.7g; Sugar: 3.8g; Sodium: 845mg

---

267. Lebanese Chicken Soup

(Servings: 2, Cooking time: 6 minutes)

Ingredients:

- 2 large carrots, diced
- 1 onion, chopped
- 3 stalks of celery, diced
- 1 15-ounce can of chickpeas, drained
- 2 chicken breasts, sliced
- 1 teaspoon cinnamon
- 1 teaspoon garlic powder
- Salt and pepper to taste
- ¼ cup lemon juice
- 8 cups chicken broth
- 8 cups baby spinach

Directions for Cooking:

1. Place all ingredients in the Instant Pot except for the spinach.
2. Close Instant Pot, press the Manual button, choose high settings, and set time to 20 minutes.
3. Once done cooking, do a QPR.
4. Open the lid and press the Sauté button. Add in the spinach and allow to simmer.
5. Serve and enjoy.

Nutrition information:

Calories per serving: 236; Carbohydrates: 28g; Protein: 27.8g; Fat: 3.7g; Sugar: 7.1g; Sodium: 992mg

268. Fish and Potato Chowder

(Servings: 5, Cooking time: 23 minutes)

Ingredients:

- 2/3 pounds tilapia fillet, sliced
- 1 cup Yukon gold potatoes, peeled and quartered
- ½ cups diced celery
- ¾ cup diced onions
- Salt and pepper to taste
- 1 cup chicken broth
- 2 cups water
- 2 tablespoons diced bacon
- 2 tablespoons butter
- 1 1/3 cups cream

Nutrition information:

Calories per serving: 346; Carbohydrates: 10.9g; Protein: 25.7g; Fat: 22.4g; Sugar: 3.9g; Sodium:357mg

Directions for Cooking:

In the Instant Pot, place the tilapia fillets, potatoes, celery, and onions.

Season with salt and pepper to taste before pouring in the chicken broth and water.

1. Close Instant Pot, press the Manual button, choose high settings, and set time to 20 minutes.
2. Once done cooking, do a QPR.
3. Open the lid and press the Sauté button. Stir in the bacon, butter, and cream and allow to simmer for another 3 minutes.
4. Serve and enjoy.

---

269. Zuppa Toscana

(Servings: 5, Cooking time: 13 minutes)

Ingredients:

- 2 tablespoons olive oil
- 1 onion, chopped
- 3 cloves of garlic, minced
- 1-pound Italian sausages, sliced
- 3 large potatoes, peeled and cut into chunks
- 5 cups chicken broth
- 2 teaspoons dried basil
- 1 teaspoon dried fennel
- 2 cups fresh kale
- ½ cup heavy cream
- 1 tablespoon crushed red pepper
- Salt and pepper to taste

Directions for Cooking:

1. Press the Sauté button on the Instant Pot and heat the oil.
2. Sauté the onion and garlic until fragrant.
3. Stir in the Italian sausages, potatoes, and chicken broth.
4. Add in the rest of the ingredients.
5. Close Instant Pot, press the Manual button, choose high settings, and set time to 10 minutes.
6. Once done cooking, do a QPR.
7. Serve and enjoy.

Nutrition information:

Calories per serving: 974; Carbohydrates: 45.9g; Protein: 70.4g; Fat: 55.2g; Sugar: 3.7g; Sodium: 1674mg

---

270. Seattle Seafood Chowder

(Servings: 6, Cooking time: 15 minutes)

Ingredients:

- 2 tablespoons butter
- 2 cloves of garlic, minced
- 1 onion, chopped
- 2 stalks of celery, minced
- 1 teaspoon sage
- 4 cups vegetable broth
- 1 large potato, peeled and cubed
- 1 cup canned corn
- ½ pound frozen salmon
- Salt and pepper to taste
- 1 cup squid, cleaned and sliced
- 10 prawns, shelled and deveined
- 2 cups half-and half

Directions for Cooking:

1. Press the Sauté button on the Instant Pot and heat the butter.
2. Sauté the garlic, onion, celery, and sage until fragrant. Add in the broth, potatoes, and salmon. Season with salt and pepper to taste.
3. Close Instant Pot, press the Manual button, choose high settings, and set time to 10 minutes.
4. Once done cooking, do a QPR.
5. Open the lid and press the Sauté button. Stir in the rest of the ingredients and allow to simmer until cooked through.
6. Serve and enjoy.

Nutrition information:

Calories per serving: 444; Carbohydrates: 58.1g; Protein: 21.3g; Fat: 14.3g; Sugar: 6.5g; Sodium: 744mg

---

271. Chicken and Corn Chowder

(Servings: 4, Cooking time: 25 minutes)

Ingredients:

- 1-pound boneless chicken breasts, cut into cubes
- 1 cup frozen whole kernel corn
- ½ cup carrots, diced
- 3 stalks of celery, chopped
- 4 cups vegetable broth
- 1 can cream of chicken soup
- 1 tablespoon garlic powder
- 1 tablespoon onion powder
- 1 teaspoon dried parsley flakes
- Salt and pepper to taste

Directions for Cooking:

1. Place all ingredients in the Instant Pot and give a good stir.
2. Close Instant Pot, press the Manual button, choose high settings, and set time to 25 minutes.
3. Once done cooking, do a QPR.
4. Serve and enjoy.

Nutrition information:

Calories per serving: 285; Carbohydrates: 23.5g; Protein: 30.3g; Fat: 7.8g; Sugar: 2.1g; Sodium: 1284mg

---

272. Butternut Squash Apple Soup

(Servings: 4, Cooking time: 15 minutes)

Ingredients:

- 1 teaspoon olive oil
- 1 onion, diced
- 2 cloves of garlic, minced
- 1 butternut squash, peeled and cubed
- 1 large apple, peeled and cubed
- Salt and pepper to taste
- 2 cups chicken broth
- ¼ cup heavy cream
- 1 tablespoon maple syrup

Directions for Cooking:

1. Press the Sauté button on the Instant Pot and heat the oil. Sauté the onion and garlic until fragrant. Add in the rest of the ingredients.
2. Close Instant Pot, press the button, choose high settings, and set time to 10 minutes.
3. Once done cooking, do a QPR.
4. Open the lid and transfer the contents in a blender or food processor. Pulse until smooth.
5. Serve and enjoy.

Nutrition information:

Calories per serving: 301; Carbohydrates: 20.4g; Protein: 27.2g; Fat: 12.3g; Sugar: 11.5g; Sodium: 508mg

---

273. Spicy Tomato Chicken Soup

(Servings: 3, Cooking time: 20 minutes)

Ingredients:

- 3 boneless chicken breasts
- 2 teaspoons chili powder
- Salt and pepper to taste
- 1 28-ounce can diced tomatoes
- 3 cups chicken broth
- 1 tablespoon lime juice
- Salt and pepper to taste
- ¾ cup green onions, sliced

Directions for Cooking:

1. Place all ingredients in the Instant Pot except for the green onions.
2. Close Instant Pot, press the Manual button, choose high settings, and set time to 20 minutes.
3. Once done cooking, do a QPR.
4. Garnish with green onions.
5. Serve and enjoy.

Nutrition information:

Calories per serving:349 ; Carbohydrates: 14.3g; Protein: 56.3g; Fat: 7.2g; Sugar: 9.1g; Sodium:467mg

---

274. Buffalo Chicken Soup

(Servings: 4, Cooking time: 25 minutes)

Ingredients:

- 1 tablespoon olive oil
- 1 onion, diced
- ½ cup celery, chopped
- 4 cloves of garlic, minced
- 1-pound chicken, shredded
- 4 cups chicken broth
- 3 tablespoons buffalo sauce
- Salt and pepper to taste
- 6 ounces cream cheese
- ½ cup heavy cream

Directions for Cooking:

1. Press the Sauté button on the Instant Pot and heat the oil. Sauté the onion, celery, and garlic until fragrant before adding the chicken. Keep stirring for another minute.
2. Pour in the chicken broth and buffalo sauce. Season with salt and pepper to taste.
3. Close Instant Pot, press the Manual button, choose high settings, and set time to 20 minutes.
4. Once done cooking, do a QPR.
5. Open the lid and press the Sauté button. Stir in the cream cheese and heavy cream and allow to simmer for another 5 minutes.
6. Serve and enjoy.

Nutrition information:

Calories per serving: 756; Carbohydrates: 13.9g; Protein:79.1g; Fat: 40.3g; Sugar: 8.1g; Sodium: 1402mg

---

275. Broccoli Cheese Soup

(Servings: 5, Cooking time: 18 minutes)

Ingredients:

- 2 tablespoons butter
- 1 onion, chopped
- 2 cloves of garlic, minced
- 1 ½ teaspoon dry mustard
- 4 cups broccoli florets
- 4 cups chicken broth
- 2 cups spinach
- Salt and pepper to taste
- 1 cup cheddar cheese, shredded
- ½ cup parmesan cheese, shredded

Directions for Cooking:

1. Press the Sauté button on the Instant Pot and melt the butter. Sauté the onions and garlic until fragrant.
2. Add in the dry mustard, broccoli, chicken broth, and spinach. Season with salt and pepper to taste.
3. Close Instant Pot, press the Manual button, choose high settings, and set time to 15 minutes.
4. Once done cooking, do a QPR.
5. Open the lid and transfer contents into a blender. Blend until smooth.
6. Garnish with cheddar and parmesan cheese on top.
7. Serve and enjoy.

Nutrition information:

Calories per serving: 518; Carbohydrates: 7.9g; Protein: 52.6g; Fat: 29.9g; Sugar: 1.6g; Sodium: 1216mg

---

276. Instant Pot Vegetable Beef Soup

(Servings: 6, Cooking time: 45 minutes)

Ingredients:

- 2 tablespoons olive oil
- 2 pounds beef stew meat, cut into chunks
- 1 tablespoon onion powder
- 1 tablespoon garlic powder
- Salt and pepper to taste
- 1 can tomato paste
- 1 can green beans
- 2 cans sliced carrots
- 1 can sweet corn
- 2 cups diced potatoes
- 5 cups beef broth

Directions for Cooking:

1. Press the Sauté button on the Instant Pot and heat the oil.
2. Stir in the beef and season with onion powder, garlic powder, salt, and pepper. Stir until the beef turns lightly golden.
3. Add in the rest of the ingredients.
4. Close Instant Pot, press the Manual button, choose high settings, and set time to 40 minutes.
5. Once done cooking, do a QPR.
6. Serve and enjoy.

Nutrition information:

Calories per serving: 371; Carbohydrates: 51.1g; Protein: 5.8g; Fat: 17.9g; Sugar: 8.3g; Sodium: 897mg

---

277. Peasant Chicken and Veggie Soup

(Servings: 6, Cooking time: 25 minutes)

Ingredients:

- 1 tablespoon olive oil
- 1 onion, chopped
- 2 cloves of garlic, minced
- 1-pound chicken breasts, sliced
- 1 sweet potato, peeled and cubed
- 1 carrot, peeled and cubed
- 1 head cauliflower, cut into florets
- 1 can diced tomatoes
- 6 cups chicken stock
- Salt and pepper to taste

Directions for Cooking:

1. Press the Sauté button on the Instant Pot. Heat the oil and sauté the onion, garlic, and chicken until the chicken turns lightly golden.
2. Pour in the rest of the ingredients.
3. Close Instant Pot, press the Manual button, choose high settings, and set time to 20 minutes.
4. Once done cooking, do a QPR.
5. Serve and enjoy.

Nutrition information:

Calories per serving: 271; Carbohydrates: 16.1g; Protein: 23.5g; Fat: 12.4g; Sugar: 7.1g; Sodium: 449mg

---

278. Cabbage Soup with Ground Beef

(Servings: 6, Cooking time: 35 minutes)

Ingredients:

- 1 tablespoon avocado oil
- 1 onion, chopped
- 1-pound ground beef
- ½ teaspoon garlic powder
- Salt and pepper to taste
- 1 can diced tomatoes
- 6 cups bone broth
- 2 bay leaves
- 1-pound shredded cabbage

Directions for Cooking:

1. Press the Sauté button on the Instant Pot and heat oil.
2. Sauté the onion and beef. Season with garlic powder, salt and pepper. Stir for 2 minutes.
3. Add in the diced tomatoes, bone broth, bay leaves and cabbages.
4. Close Instant Pot, press the Manual button, choose high settings, and set time to 30 minutes.
5. Once done cooking, do a QPR.
6. Serve and enjoy.

Nutrition information:

Calories per serving: 428; Carbohydrates: 9.2g; Protein: 26.3g; Fat: 24.8g; Sugar: 3.2g; Sodium: 879mg

---

279. Instant Pot French Onion Soup

（Servings: 2, Cooking time: 23 minutes)

Ingredients:

- 4 tablespoons unsalted butter
- 2 large yellow onions, sliced thinly
- 3 cloves of garlic, minced
- Salt and pepper to taste
- 1 ½ cup chicken broth
- 1 ½ cup beef broth
- 2 tablespoons worcestershire sauce
- 3 slices of French bread, toasted and cubed
- 1 cup mozzarella cheese

Directions for Cooking:

1. Press the Sauté button on the Instant Pot and melt the butter. Sauté the onion and garlic. Keep stirring for 6 minutes until the onions have caramelized. Season with salt and pepper to taste.
2. Add in the chicken broth, beef broth, and Worcestershire sauce.
3. Close Instant Pot, press the button, choose high settings, and set time to 20 minutes.
4. Once done cooking, do a QPR.
5. Serve with slices of French bread on top and mozzarella cheese.
6. Serve and enjoy.

Nutrition information:

Calories per serving: 740; Carbohydrates: 54.8g; Protein: 63.8g; Fat: 29.8g; Sugar: 11g; Sodium: 1733mg

---

280. Vegan Red Lentil Soup

(Servings: 3, Cooking time: 60 minutes)

Ingredients:

- 1 tablespoon peanut oil
- 1 onion, chopped
- 1 tablespoon fresh ginger root, grated
- 1 clove of garlic, minced
- 1 pinch fenugreek seeds
- 1 cup dry red lentils, soaked overnight
- 2 cups water,2 tablespoons tomato paste
- 1 teaspoon curry powder
- Salt and pepper to taste
- 2 cups coconut milk

Directions for Cooking:

1. Press the Sauté button on the Instant Pot and heat oil. Stir in the onions, ginger, garlic, and fenugreek seeds until fragrant.
2. Stir in the lentils and pour in water and tomato paste. Season with curry powder, salt and pepper.
3. Close Instant Pot, press the Manual button, choose high settings, and set time to 40 minutes.
4. Once done cooking, do a QPR.
5. Open the lid and stir in the coconut milk.
6. Close the lid again and press the Manual button and set the time to 10 minutes.
7. Do QPR.
8. Serve and enjoy.

Nutrition information:

Calories per serving: 672; Carbohydrates: 57.1g; Protein: 20.2g; Fat: 44.5g; Sugar: 9.3g; Sodium: 481mg

---

281. Cream of Celery Soup

(Servings: 4, Cooking time: 20 minutes)

Ingredients:

- 6 cups chopped celery
- 1 onion, chopped
- 1 cup coconut milk
- 2 cups water
- ½ teaspoon dill
- Salt to taste

Directions for Cooking:

1. Place all ingredients in the Instant Pot.
2. Once done cooking, do a QPR.
3. Open the lid and transfer into a blender. Pulse until smooth.
4. Serve and enjoy.

Nutrition information:

Calories per serving:174 ; Carbohydrates: 10.5g; Protein: 2.8g; Fat: 14.6g; Sugar:5.2 g; Sodium: 672mg

---

282. Instant Pot Pork Shank Carrots Soup

(Servings: 4, Cooking time: 40 minutes)

Ingredients:

- 2 large carrots, chopped
- 1 green radish, peeled and chopped
- 2 pounds pork shank, cut into chunks
- 4 quarts water
- 1 thin slice of ginger
- 2 dried dates, pitted
- 1 small piece of chenpi (dried Mandarin peel)
- Salt to taste

Directions for Cooking:

1. Place all ingredients in the Instant Pot.
2. Close Instant Pot, press the Manual button, choose high settings, and set time to 40 minutes.
3. Once done cooking, do a QPR.
4. Serve and enjoy.

Nutrition information:

Calories per serving: 320; Carbohydrates: 12.1g; Protein: 50.2g; Fat: 6.9g; Sugar: 2.1g; Sodium: 128mg

---

283. Instant Pot Beef and Vegetable Soup

(Servings: 5, Cooking time: 30 minutes)

Ingredients:

- 2 pounds lean ground beef
- 1 onion, diced
- 2 teaspoons garlic, minced
- 1 can tomatoes
- 4 cups beef broth
- 4 carrots, peeled and chopped
- 3 stalks of celery, diced
- 4 large potatoes, peeled and cut into chunks
- 2 tablespoons tomato paste
- Salt and pepper to taste
- ½ teaspoon ground oregano

Directions for Cooking:

1. Press the Sauté button on the Instant Pot and stir in the beef, onion, and garlic. Stir until the beef slightly turns golden.
2. Add in the rest of the ingredients.
3. Close Instant Pot, press the Manual button, choose high settings, and set time to 25 minutes.
4. Once done cooking, do a QPR.
5. Serve and enjoy.

Nutrition information:

Calories per serving:735; Carbohydrates: 79.2g; Protein: 56.2g; Fat: 20.9g; Sugar: 7.3g; Sodium: 918mg

---

284. Unstuffed Cabbage Roll Soup

(Servings: 3, Cooking time: 25 minutes)

Ingredients:

- 1 ½ pounds ground beef
- ½ onion, diced
- 2 cloves of garlic, minced
- 1 14-ounce can diced tomatoes
- 1 cup tomato sauce
- ¼ cup liquid aminos
- 3 cups beef broth
- 1 cabbage, chopped
- 3 teaspoons Worcestershire sauce
- Salt and pepper to taste

Directions for Cooking:

1. Press the Sauté button on the Instant Pot and stir in the beef, onions, and garlic until fragrant.
2. Stir in the rest of the ingredients
3. Close Instant Pot, press the button, choose high settings, and set time to 20 minutes.
4. Once done cooking, do a QPR.
5. Serve and enjoy.

Nutrition information:

Calories per serving: 217; Carbohydrates: 6.4g; Protein: 15.6g; Fat: 14.8g; Sugar: 3.1g; Sodium: 731mg

---

285. Instant Pot Beef Borscht

(Servings: 9, Cooking time: 25 minutes)

Ingredients:

- 1 tablespoon oil
- 1-pound beef steak, cut into strips
- 2 cloves of garlic, minced
- 1 onion, diced
- 3 large beets, peeled and diced
- 3 stalks of celery, diced
- 2 carrots, diced
- 3 cups cabbage, shredded
- 6 cups beef stock
- 1 bay leaf
- Salt and pepper to taste
- ¼ cup fresh dill, chopped
- ½ cup sour cream

Directions for Cooking:

1. Press the Sauté button on the Instant Pot and heat the oil.
2. Stir in the beef steak, garlic, and onion until lightly golden.
3. Stir in the rest of the ingredients.
4. Close Instant Pot, press the Manual button, choose high settings, and set time to 20 minutes.
5. Once done cooking, do a QPR.
6. Serve and enjoy.

Nutrition information:

Calories per serving: 157; Carbohydrates: 10.9g; Protein: 15.5g; Fat: 5.9g; Sugar: 5g; Sodium: 401mg

---

286. Lemon Chicken Orzo

(Servings: 4, Cooking time: 30 minutes)

Ingredients:

- 1 tablespoon olive oil
- ¾ cup onion, diced
- 1 tablespoon garlic, minced
- ½ pound chicken, cut into small pieces
- ¾ cup celery, chopped
- Salt and pepper to taste
- ½ teaspoon thyme
- 1/3 cup orzo
- 2 cups chicken broth
- 1 tablespoon lemon juice
- ¼ cup heavy cream

Directions for Cooking:

1. Press the Sauté button on the Instant Pot and heat the oil. Stir in the onions and garlic until fragrant.
2. Stir in the chicken and celery. Season with salt and pepper to taste. Keep stirring for three minutes until the chicken becomes lightly golden.
3. Add in thyme, orzo, chicken broth and lemon juice.
4. Close Instant Pot, press the Manual button, choose high settings, and set time to 25 minutes.
5. Once done cooking, do a QPR.
6. Open the lid and press the Sauté button. Add in the heavy cream and allow to simmer.
7. Serve and enjoy.

Nutrition information:

Calories per serving: 282; Carbohydrates: 10g; Protein:15.8g; Fat: 8.7g; Sugar: 3.1g; Sodium: 768mg

---

287. Winter Melon and Tofu Soup

(Servings: 3, Cooking time: 1 hour and 5 minutes)

Ingredients:

- 1-pound pork bones,
- 5 cups water
- Salt and pepper to taste
- 3 slices of ginger
- 1 cup tofu, cubed
- 1 cup winter melon
- Green onions for garnish

Directions for Cooking:

1. Place the pork bones and water in the Instant Pot. Season with salt and pepper to taste.
2. Close Instant Pot, press the Manual button, choose high settings, and set time to 60 minutes.
3. Once done cooking, do a QPR.
4. Open the lid and take out the bones. Set aside for future use.
5. Press the Sauté button.
6. Stir in the ginger, tofu, and winter melon. Allow to simmer for 5 minutes.
7. Garnish with green onions on top.
8. Serve and enjoy.

Nutrition information:

Calories per serving: 404; Carbohydrates: 27.8g; Protein: 28.8g; Fat: 20.6g; Sugar: 2.9g; Sodium: 1743mg

---

288. Mexican Albondigas Soup

(Servings: 4, Cooking time: 25 minutes)

Ingredients:

- 1-pound packaged meatballs
- 2 cloves of garlic, minced
- 1 onion, chopped
- ½ green bell pepper, chopped
- 4 carrots, chopped
- 1 can diced tomatoes
- 3 cups chicken broth
- Salt and pepper to taste
- Chopped cilantro for garnish

Directions for Cooking:

1. Place the meatballs, garlic, and onions in the Instant Pot. Press the Sauté button and allow to sear on all sides for three minutes.
2. Stir in the rest of the ingredients except for the cilantro.
3. Close Instant Pot, press the Manual button, choose high settings, and set time to 20 minutes.
4. Once done cooking, do a QPR.
5. Open the lid and stir in the cilantro.
6. Serve and enjoy.

Nutrition information:

Calories per serving: 642; Carbohydrates: 22.6g; Protein: 74.4g; Fat: 27.2g; Sugar: 7.5g; Sodium: 1485mg

---

289. Butternut Squash and Cauliflower Soup

(Servings: 4, Cooking time: 12 minutes)

Ingredients:

- 2 tablespoons oil
- 1 onion, diced
- 3 cloves of garlic, minced
- 1-pound frozen cauliflower
- 1-pound frozen butternut squash
- 2 cups of vegetable broth
- 1 teaspoon paprika
- 1 teaspoon dried thyme
- Salt and pepper to taste
- ½ cup half-and-half

Directions for Cooking:

1. Press the Sauté button on the Instant Pot and heat oil.
2. Stir in the onions and garlic. Sauté until fragrant.
3. Add in the rest of the ingredients.
4. Close Instant Pot, press the button, choose high settings, and set time to 10 minutes.
5. Once done cooking, do a QPR.
6. Open the lid and transfer the contents into a blender. Pulse until smooth. Serve with cheese on top if desired.
7. Serve and enjoy.

Nutrition information:

Calories per serving: 98; Carbohydrates:15.2 g; Protein:1.9 g; Fat: 3.8g; Sugar: 3.8g; Sodium:168mg

---

290. Instant Pot Taco Soup

(Servings: 8, Cooking time: 30 minutes)

Ingredients:

- 2 pounds ground beef
- 1 onion, chopped
- 4 cloves of garlic, minced
- 2 tablespoons chili powder
- 2 teaspoons cumin
- 1 cup diced tomatoes
- 3 cups beef broth
- Salt and pepper to taste
- ½ cup cream cheese
- ½ cup heavy cream

Directions for Cooking:

1. Press the Sauté button on the Instant Pot and stir in the beef, onion, garlic, chili powder, and cumin.
2. Stir in the tomatoes and beef broth. Season with salt and pepper to taste.
3. Close Instant Pot, press the button, choose high settings, and set time to 20 minutes.
4. Once done cooking, do a QPR.
5. Open the lid and press the Sauté button. Stir in the cream cheese and heavy cream.
6. Serve and enjoy.

Nutrition information:

Calories per serving: 386; Carbohydrates: 8g; Protein: 27g; Fat: 28g; Sugar: 4g; Sodium: 831mg

---

291. En Caldo De Res Soup

(Servings: 6, Cooking time: 20 minutes)

Ingredients:

- 1 tablespoon oil
- 2 pounds beef shank, sliced thinly
- 1 onion, chopped
- 1 chayote, peeled and sliced
- 2 zucchinis, sliced
- 2 carrots, sliced
- 2 corn cut into 3 big pieces
- ½ head of cabbage, cut into wedges
- 1 bay leaf
- Salt and pepper to taste
- 6 cups water
- Lime wedges
- Cilantro for garnish

Directions for Cooking:

1. Press the Sauté button on the Instant Pot and heat oil.
2. Place the beef and onions in the Instant Pot and allow to brown on all sides.
3. Stir in the chayote, zucchini, carrots, corn, cabbage, and bay leaf. Season with salt and pepper to taste. Allow the vegetables to sweat before pouring in water.
4. Close Instant Pot, press the Manual button, choose high settings, and set time to 15 minutes.
5. Once done cooking, do a QPR.
6. Once the lid is open, garnish with lime wedges and cilantro on top.
7. Serve and enjoy.

Nutrition information:

Calories per serving: 171; Carbohydrates: 18g; Protein: 18g; Fat: 3g; Sugar: 4g; Sodium: 76mg

---

292. Cream of Asparagus Soup

(Servings: 4, Cooking time: 13 minutes)

Ingredients:

- 1 teaspoon coconut oil
- ½ stick butter
- 2 cloves of garlic, minced
- 1 onion, diced
- ½ cup chopped celery
- 1-pound asparagus, chopped
- 2 cups vegetable stock
- 1 cup heavy cream
- Salt to taste

Directions for Cooking:

1. Press the Sauté button on the Instant Pot and heat the oil and butter. Sauté the garlic, onion, and celery until fragrant.
2. Stir in the rest of the ingredients.
3. Close Instant Pot, press the Manual button, choose high settings, and set time to 10 minutes.
4. Once done cooking, do a QPR.
5. Open the lid and transfer into a blender. Pulse until smooth.
6. Serve and enjoy.

Nutrition information:

Calories per serving: 353; Carbohydrates: 20.6g; Protein: 7.1g; Fat: 27.9g; Sugar: 4.8g; Sodium: 183mg

---

293. Sweet Potato, Black Bean, And Quinoa Chili Soup

(Servings: 6, Cooking time: 30 minutes)

Ingredients:

- 1 bell pepper, diced
- 3 medium-sized sweet potatoes, peeled and diced
- 1 onion, diced
- 3 cloves of garlic, minced
- 3 stalks of celery, chopped
- 4 cups vegetable broth
- 2 tablespoons tomato paste
- 1 cup diced tomatoes
- 1 can black beans, rinsed and drained
- 2 teaspoons each of paprika and cumin
- Salt to taste
- ½ cup quinoa
- 5 cups vegetable broth

Directions for Cooking:

1. Place all ingredients in the Instant Pot. Give a good stir.
2. Close Instant Pot, press the Manual button, choose high settings, and set time to 30 minutes.
3. Once done cooking, do a QPR.
4. Serve and enjoy.

Nutrition information:

Calories per serving:375 ; Carbohydrates: 73.7g; Protein: 18.1g; Fat: g; Sugar: 4.8g; Sodium: 954mg

---

294. Ham and White Bean Soup

(Servings: 5, Cooking time: 45 minutes)

Ingredients:

- 1 tablespoon olive oil
- 3 cloves of garlic, minced
- 1 onion, chopped
- 1-pound ham, sliced
- 1 tomato, chopped
- 1-pound great northern beans, soaked overnight
- 4 cups vegetable stock
- 2 cups water
- Salt and pepper to taste
- 1 teaspoon dried mint
- 1 teaspoon dried paprika
- 1 teaspoon dried thyme

Directions for Cooking:

1. Press the Sauté button on the Instant Pot and heat the oil.
2. Sauté the garlic and onion until fragrant. Stir in the ham and allow to render its fat. Add in the rest of the ingredients.
3. Close Instant Pot, press the Manual button, choose high settings, and set time to 40 minutes.
4. Once done cooking, do a QPR.
5. Serve and enjoy.

Nutrition information:

Calories per serving: 240; Carbohydrates: 16g; Protein: 17g; Fat: 11g; Sugar: 2g; Sodium: 745mg

---

295. Easy Kimchi Soup

(Servings: 5, Cooking time: 35 minutes)

Ingredients:

- 2 tablespoons olive oil
- 2 cloves of garlic, minced
- 1-inch ginger
- 1 onion, chopped
- 2 pounds beef stew, cut into chunks
- Salt and pepper to taste
- 1 cup commercial kimchi
- 5 cups chicken broth
- 1 package firm tofu

Directions for cooking:

1. Press the Sauté button on the Instant Pot and heat the oil. Sauté the garlic, ginger, and onion. Stir in the beef and allow to brown on all sides.
2. Stir in salt and pepper to taste.
3. Add the kimchi and chicken broth.
4. Close Instant Pot, press the Manual button, choose high settings, and set time to 25 minutes.
5. Once done cooking, do a QPR.
6. Open the lid and stir in the tofu. Allow to simmer for at least 5 minutes.
7. Serve and enjoy.

Nutrition information:

Calories per serving:808 ; Carbohydrates: 10.5g; Protein:102.9g; Fat: 39.4g; Sugar: 1.6g; Sodium: 1148mg

---

296. Instant Pot Tortellini Soup

(Servings: 6, Cooking time: 25 minutes)

Ingredients:

- 1-pound Italian sausage
- 1 onion, diced
- 2 stalks of celery, diced
- 4 cloves of garlic, minced
- Salt and pepper to taste
- 1/3 cup sherry wine
- 2 carrots, diced
- 1 can diced tomatoes
- 1-pound fresh cheese tortellini
- 8 cups chicken stock
- 3 cups kale, chopped
- Grated parmesan cheese

Directions for Cooking:

1. Press the Sauté button on the Instant Pot and stir in the Italian sausage, onion, celery, and garlic. Season with salt and pepper to taste.
2. Add in the wine, carrots, tomatoes, tortellini, and chicken stock.
3. Close Instant Pot, press the Manual button, choose high settings, and set time to 20 minutes.
4. Once done cooking, do a QPR.
5. Open the lid and press the Sauté button and stir in the kale. Allow to simmer until the kale is cooked through.
6. Serve and enjoy.

Nutrition information:

Calories per serving: 711; Carbohydrates: 56.8g; Protein: 35.7g; Fat: 37.8g; Sugar: 9g; Sodium: 1124mg

---

297. Beef Stroganoff Soup

(Servings: 6, Cooking time: 25 minutes)

Ingredients:

- 1 ½ pounds stew meat
- 6 cups beef broth
- 4 tablespoons Worcestershire sauce
- ½ teaspoon Italian seasoning
- 1 ½ teaspoon onion powder
- 2 teaspoons garlic powder
- ½ cup sour cream
- 8 ounces mushrooms, sliced
- Salt and pepper to taste
- 8 ounces short noodles, blanched

Directions for Cooking:

1. Place the meat, broth, Worcestershire sauce, Italian seasoning, onion powder, garlic powder, sour cream, and mushrooms. Season with salt and pepper to taste.
2. Close Instant Pot, press the Manual button, choose high settings, and set time to 20 minutes.
3. Once done cooking, do a QPR.
4. Open the lid and press the Sauté button. Stir in the noodles and allow to simmer for 5 minutes.
5. Serve and enjoy.

Nutrition information:

Calories per serving:588 ; Carbohydrates: 65g; Protein: 39.6g; Fat: 20.1g; Sugar: 12.8g; Sodium: 639mg

---

Instant Pot Rice & Pasta Recipes

298. Shrimp, Mushrooms & Asparagus Risotto

(Servings: 4, Cooking Time: 20 minutes)

Ingredients:

- 2 tsp olive oil
- 1 small red or yellow onion, diced
- 1-1/2 cups Arborio rice
- 1 cup sliced cremini or white button mushrooms
- 1/2 cup dry white wine
- 3-1/2 cups chicken broth
- 1 Tbsp butter
- 1 cup chopped asparagus
- 3/4 lb large shrimp, defrosted if frozen, peeled and deveined
- Heaping 1/4 cup grated Parmigiano-Reggiano cheese
- 1/2 tsp fresh black pepper

Nutrition information:

Calories per serving: 454; Carbohydrates: 28.0g; Protein: 43.1g; Fat: 24.3g; Sugar: 2.1g; Sodium: 1055mg

Directions for Cooking:

1. Press browning button and heat oil. Sauté onions for 3 minutes.
2. Stir in mushrooms and rice. Cook for 5 minutes.
3. Add wine and deglaze pot for a minute.
4. Add chicken broth. Press cancel.
5. Close Instant Pot, press pressure cook button, choose high settings, and set time to 6 minutes.
6. Once done cooking, do a QPR.
7. Press cancel, press brown button, stir in asparagus and butter. Cook for a minute.
8. Add shrimps and stirring frequently, cook for 3 minutes.
9. Serve and enjoy.

---

299. Wild Rice Pilaf

(Servings: 8, Cooking Time: 50 minutes)

Ingredients:

- 2 tablespoons olive oil
- 2 brown onions chopped
- 2 cloves garlic minced
- 12 oz mushrooms sliced
- 1/4 cup white wine
- 1/2 teaspoon salt
- 5 sprigs fresh thyme (or 1/2 tsp dried thyme leaves)
- 2 cups wild rice brown basmati blend
- 2 cups stock
- 1/2 cup parsley chopped
- 1/2 cup pine nuts (or almond slices)

Directions for Cooking:

1. Press sauté and heat oil. Sauté onions for 5 minutes.
2. Add garlic and sauté for another minute.
3. Stir in white wine and deglaze pot for a minute. Press cancel.
4. Stir in salt, thyme, rice, and stock. Mix well.
5. Close Instant Pot, press pressure cook button, choose high settings, and set time to 28 minutes.
6. Once done cooking, do a QPR.
7. Stir in pine nuts and parsley. Serve and enjoy

Nutrition information:

Calories per serving: 263; Carbohydrates: 36.0g; Protein: 8.0g; Fat: 9.0g; Sugar: 3.0g; Sodium: 389mg

---

300. Pasta Puttanesca

(Servings: 4, Cooking Time: 5 minutes)

Ingredients:

- 3 cloves garlic minced
- 4 cups pasta sauce
- 3 cups water
- 4 cups pasta such as penne or fusilli
- 1/4 teaspoon crushed red pepper flakes
- 1 Tablespoon capers
- 1/2 cup Kalamata olives sliced
- salt to taste
- pepper to taste

Directions for Cooking:

1. Press sauté and add a splash of water. Add garlic and sauté for 30 seconds. Press cancel.
2. Stir in olives, capers, crushed red pepper flakes, pasta, water, and pasta sauce. Mix well.
3. Close Instant Pot, press pressure cook button, choose high settings, and set time to 5 minutes.
4. Once done cooking, do a QPR.
5. Mix well and adjust seasoning to taste
6. Serve and enjoy

Nutrition information:

Calories per serving: 504; Carbohydrates: 98.0g; Protein: 18.0g; Fat: 4.0g; Sugar: 13.0g; Sodium: 1620mg

---

301. Cheesy & Easy Beef Bowties

(Servings: 8, Cooking Time: 20 minutes)

Ingredients:

- 1-lb Farfalle pasta
- 1-lb ground beef
- 1 jar vodka sauce (24 ounce)
- 3 cups beef stock (unsalted)
- 1 tbsp Italian seasoning
- 1 tbsp dry minced onion
- 1 ½ tsp garlic powder
- 1 tsp salt
- ½ tsp pepper
- 1 ½ cups mozzarella (shredded)
- ½ cup parmesan (grated)

Nutrition information:

Calories per serving: 297; Carbohydrates: 24.3g; Protein: 27.2g; Fat: 10.1g; Sugar: 3.3g; Sodium: 1098mg

Directions for Cooking:

1. Press sauté button and once hot cook beef until browned, around 10 minutes.
2. Stir in pepper, salt, garlic powder, Italian seasoning, and minced onion. Cook for 2 minutes.
3. Add beef stock and deglaze pot. Press cancel.
4. Add pasta, pushing it down but not mixing it in.
5. Layer the vodka sauce on top.
6. Close Instant Pot, press pressure cook button, choose high settings, and set time to 5 minutes.
7. Once done cooking, do a 2-minute natural release and then a QPR.
8. Stir in mozzarella and parmesan. Mix well.
9. Serve and enjoy

---

302. Fettucine Alfredo

(Servings: 5, Cooking Time: 10 minutes)

Ingredients:

- 3 Tbsp Butter, cut in a few small pieces
- 4 cloves Garlic, pressed/minced
- 2 cups Chicken Broth
- 8 oz Fettuccine Noodles, broken in half
- 1-lb small Chicken Breasts, uncooked cut larger breasts in half
- 1 1/2 cups Heavy Cream
- 1 tsp Salt (or more to taste)
- 1/2 tsp Pepper
- 1 cup Parmesan Cheese, grated

Directions for Cooking:

1. Place the butter and garlic in the pot.
2. Pour in the chicken broth.
3. Sprinkle in the fettuccine noodles, in a random pattern, and gently press them down.
4. If Adding Chicken: Add the chicken breasts, and space evenly over the noodles. Pour the cream over them, then sprinkle with the salt and pepper..
5. Close Instant Pot, press pressure cook button, choose high settings, and set time to 5 minutes.
6. Once done cooking, do a QPR.
7. Stir in Parmesan and mix well. Let it rest for 5 minutes.
8. Serve and enjoy

Nutrition information:

Calories per serving: 469; Carbohydrates: 17.8g; Protein: 37.2g; Fat: 27.1g; Sugar: 1.5g; Sodium: 1405mg

---

303. Goulash

(Servings: 8, Cooking Time: 25minutes)

Ingredients:

- 1 lb ground turkey
- 1 tablespoon minced garlic
- 2 ½ tablespoons Italian seasoning
- 1 tablespoon minced onion
- 1 teaspoon salt
- 2 bay leaves
- 1 chopped zucchini
- 1 cup chopped red and green bell peppers
- 3 ounces whole wheat pasta
- 1 14-ounce can crushed tomatoes
- 1 can of water

Directions for Cooking:

1. Press sauté button and sauté ground turkey until browned, around 10 minutes.
2. Stir in bay leaves, salt, Italian seasoning, minced onions, and garlic. Mix well.
3. Stir in tomatoes, fill empty can of tomatoes with water and add to pot. Mix well. Stir in pasta.
4. Close Instant Pot, press pressure cook button, choose high settings, and set time to 10 minutes.
5. Once done cooking, do a QPR.
6. Stir in zucchini and bell peppers. Cover and let it sit for 5 minutes.
7. Serve and enjoy

Nutrition information:

Calories per serving: 204; Carbohydrates: 25.7g; Protein: 16.0g; Fat: 4.9g; Sugar: 1.9g; Sodium: 576mg

304. Shrimp-Clam Cocktail Risotto

(Servings: 4, Cooking Time: 30 minutes)

Ingredients:

- 4 cups of PC Bacon Flavour Tomato Clam Cocktail (half the bottle)
- 2 tbsp butter
- 1 chopped onion
- 1 tbsp smoked paprika
- 1 tsp dried oregano
- 1/2 tsp salt
- 1/2 tsp freshly ground black pepper
- 1 1/2 cup arborio rice
- 1 cup of raw deveined shrimp
- ¼ cup freshly grated Parmesan

Directions for Cooking:

1. Press sauté button and melt butter. Stir in onions and cook for 5 minutes.
2. Add paprika, oregano, salt, and pepper. Sauté for a minute.
3. Add rice and sauté for a minute.
4. Add clam cocktail and deglaze pot. Press cancel.
5. Close Instant Pot, press pressure cook button, choose high settings, and set time to 10 minutes.
6. Once done cooking, do a QPR.
7. Stir in shrimp, mix well, and let it rest for 5 minutes.
8. Add Parmesan and let it rest for 5 minutes more.
9. Serve and enjoy

Nutrition information:

Calories per serving: 398; Carbohydrates: 56.8g; Protein: 16.7g; Fat: 17.9g; Sugar: 12.7g; Sodium: 1612mg

---

305. Broccoli-Beef Rice

(Servings: 4, Cooking Time: 25 minutes)

Ingredients:

- 1 ½-lbs ground beef
- 3 ½ cups water
- 1 ½ cups rice
- 12-oz frozen chopped broccoli
- 1 jar double cheddar pasta sauce
- 1 tsp onion powder
- 1 tsp garlic powder

Directions for Cooking:

1. Press sauté button and brown beef for 10 minutes.
2. Stir in water and rice. Evenly spread rice. Press cancel.
3. Close Instant Pot, press pressure cook button, choose high settings, and set time to 7 minutes.
4. Once done cooking, do a QPR.
5. Stir in garlic powder, onion powder, and broccoli. Let it rest for 5 minutes while covered.
6. Serve and enjoy.

Nutrition information:

Calories per serving: 549; Carbohydrates: 34.1g; Protein: 53.0g; Fat: 28.1g; Sugar: 6.1g; Sodium: 730mg

---

306. Easy-Creamy Ziti

(Servings: 4, Cooking Time: 20 minutes)

Ingredients:

- 1 1/2 cup chicken broth
- 1 cup heavy cream
- 1 tsp minced garlic dried
- salt and pepper to taste
- 8 oz dry ziti pasta
- 1 cup red pasta sauce
- 1 cup parmesan cheese shredded
- 1/2 cup mozzarella cheese shredded

Nutrition information:

Calories per serving: 457; Carbohydrates: 54.6g; Protein: 17.4g; Fat: 19.8g; Sugar: 4.2g; Sodium: 1022mg

Directions for Cooking:

1. In pot, add broth, cream, garlic, salt, pepper, and noodles. Do not mix but ensure that noodles are covered. You can push pasta down.
2. Close Instant Pot, press pressure cook button, choose high settings, and set time to 6 minutes.
3. Once done cooking, do a 6-minute natural release and then do a QPR.
4. Stir in red pasta sauce. Slowly add the cheese while stirring. Let it rest for 5 minutes.
5. Serve and enjoy.

---

307. Chicken Noodle Casserole

(Servings: 4, Cooking Time: 20 minutes)

Ingredients:

- 1 ½-lbs of chicken, cut into 2" squares
- 3/4 of a bag of egg noodles
- 1 can of cream of chicken or mushroom
- 1/2 bag of peas and carrots frozen
- 1/2 cup of diced onion
- 2 cloves of garlic
- 1 stalk celery, diced
- Salt and pepper

Directions for Cooking:

1. Add noodles in pot and cover with water. Add another cup of water.
2. Place chicken on top of pasta.
3. Sprinkle carrots, peas, minced garlic, celery, and diced onion on top.
4. Season with pepper and salt. Mix well.
5. Close Instant Pot, press pressure cook button, choose high settings, and set time to 5 minutes.
6. Once done cooking, do a 10-minute natural release and then do a QPR.
7. Stir in cream of mushroom and mix well. Let it rest for 5 minutes covered.
8. Serve and enjoy.

Nutrition information:

Calories per serving: 451; Carbohydrates: 41.1g; Protein: 43.8g; Fat: 11.7g; Sugar: 6.2g; Sodium: 745mg

---

308. Saffron Rice

(Servings: 4, Cooking Time: minutes)

Ingredients:

- 1 cup basmati rice or Jasmine Rice
- 1 cup water
- 1/2 teaspoon salt
- 1 teaspoon ghee or oil
- 1/2 teaspoon saffron: soaked in 1 tablespoon hot water
- 2 tablespoon slivered almonds : optional
- Other optional ingredients
- 1 tablespoon cashews
- 1 tablespoons raisin

Directions for Cooking:

1. Rinse and drain rice in Instant Pot insert.
2. Add remaining ingredients.
3. Close Instant Pot, press pressure cook button, choose high settings, and set time to 6 minutes.
4. Once done cooking, do a 10-minute natural release and then do a QPR.
5. Serve and enjoy.

Nutrition information:
Calories per serving: 233; Carbohydrates: 41.0g; Protein: 4.0g; Fat: 5.0g; Sugar: 8.0g; Sodium: 297mg

---

309. Mac and Cheese

(Servings: 8, Cooking Time: 4 minutes)

Ingredients:

- 1 tbsp olive oil
- 12-oz bacon 1" pieces, diced
- 16-oz rigatoni pasta
- 4 cups water
- 2 cups cheddar cheese sharp or extra sharp and shredded
- 1 cup heavy cream
- 1 tbsp kosher salt
- 1 tbsp dry mustard
- 1 tbsp flour

Directions for Cooking:

1. Press sauté and heat oil. Add bacon and cook for 3 minutes per side until crisped.
2. Press cancel. Drain fat.
3. Place bacon on bottom of pot. Add pasta on top and pour in water.
4. Close Instant Pot, press pressure cook button, choose high settings, and set time to 4 minutes.
5. Once done cooking, do a QPR.
6. Press cancel, press sauté and stir in mustard, salt, cream, and cheese. Mix well.
7. Sprinkle flour, mix well, and cook for 5 minutes.
8. Serve and enjoy.

Nutrition information:
Calories per serving: 356; Carbohydrates: 21.2g; Protein: 14.1g; Fat: 25.3g; Sugar: 1.5g; Sodium: 1715mg

---

310. Creamy Chicken Pasta the Italian Way

(Servings: 4, Cooking Time: 15 minutes)

Ingredients:

- 1 chicken breast, cubed
- 16-ounces penne pasta
- 1 can diced tomatoes w/green chilies
- 1½ cans water
- ½ teaspoon sea salt
- 1 tablespoon basil
- ¼ teaspoon pepper
- 1 clove garlic, chopped
- ¼ teaspoon paprika
- 1 teaspoon oregano
- 4 ounces cream cheese
- 1 small onion
- ¼ cup Parmesan cheese

Directions for Cooking:

1. Add all ingredients except for cream cheese in Instant Pot. Mix well.
2. Close Instant Pot, press pressure cook button, choose high settings, and set time to 10 minutes.
3. Once done cooking, do a QPR.
4. Stir in cream cheese and let it rest for 5 minutes. Mix well.
5. Serve and enjoy

Nutrition information:
Calories per serving: 392; Carbohydrates: 37.0g; Protein: 22.4g; Fat: 17.5g; Sugar: 1.9g; Sodium: 688mg

---

311. Chili Mac n Cheese

(Servings: 6, Cooking Time: 11 minutes)

Ingredients:

- 1 ½-pounds lean ground beef
- 1 onion, diced
- ½ teaspoon salt
- ¼ teaspoon pepper
- ½ teaspoon dried thyme
- ¼ cup ketchup
- 3 cups elbow macaroni
- 3 cups beef broth
- 1 cup shredded cheddar cheese

Directions for Cooking:

1. Press sauté and cook ground beef and onions for 10 minutes.
2. Season with pepper and salt.
3. Add macaroni, ketchup, beef broth and dried thyme. Mix well. Press cancel.
4. Close Instant Pot, press pressure cook button, choose high settings, and set time to 6 minutes.
5. Once done cooking, do a QPR.
6. Stir in cheese and let it rest for 5 minutes. Mix well.
7. Serve and enjoy

Nutrition information:
Calories per serving: 519; Carbohydrates: 54.2g; Protein: 40.2g; Fat: 14.6g; Sugar: 4.4g; Sodium: 547mg

---

312. Cheesy-Tuna Pasta

(Servings: 6, Cooking Time: 10minutes)

Ingredients:

- 1 can tuna drained
- 16-oz egg noodles
- 1 cup frozen peas
- 28-oz can cream mushroom soup
- 4-oz cheddar cheese
- 3 cups water

Directions for Cooking:

1. Add pasta and water in pot.
2. Sprinkle peas, mushroom soup and tuna.
3. Close Instant Pot, press pressure cook button, choose high settings, and set time to 4 minutes.
4. Once done cooking, do a QPR.
5. Stir in cheese and mix well. Let it rest for 5 minutes.
6. Serve and enjoy

Nutrition information:

Calories per serving: 540; Carbohydrates: 67.0g; Protein: 31.0g; Fat: 15.0g; Sugar: 3.0g; Sodium: 1211mg

---

313. Beef Enchilada Pasta

(Servings: 4, Cooking Time: 25 minutes)

Ingredients:

- 8 oz elbow noodles
- 1-lb ground beef
- 1 cup shredded cheese
- 12-oz can enchilada sauce
- 2 cups beef broth (or 15 oz can)
- 2 Tbsp chili powder
- salt & pepper (to taste)

Directions for Cooking:

1. Press sauté and cook beef until browned, around 10 minutes. Drain fat.
2. Stir in chili powder and cook for a minute.
3. Add enchilada sauce, pasta, and broth. Press cancel.
4. Close Instant Pot, press pressure cook button, choose high settings, and set time to 4 minutes.
5. Once done cooking, do a 3-minute natural release and then do a QPR.
6. Stir in pepper, salt, and cheese. Let it rest for 5 minutes.
7. Serve and enjoy.

Nutrition information:

Calories per serving: 516; Carbohydrates: 22.5g; Protein: 39.5g; Fat: 29.4g; Sugar: 3.4g; Sodium: 1248mg

---

314. Easy Spaghetti

(Servings: 4, Cooking Time: 30 minutes)

Ingredients:

- 1-lb ground beef
- 1 Tbsp minced onion
- 1 tsp garlic powder
- 26 oz. jar marinara sauce
- 16 oz. spaghetti pasta
- 2 1/2 cups beef stock, chicken stock or water
- ¼ cup Parmesan cheese, as garnish

Directions for Cooking:

1. Press sauté and cook ground beef, onions, and garlic powder for 10 minutes or until beef us browned.
2. Break noodles in half and add to pot.
3. Stir in stock, marinara and spaghetti sauce. Mix well.
4. Close Instant Pot, press pressure cook button, choose high settings, and set time to 6 minutes.
5. Once done cooking, do a QPR.
6. Serve and enjoy with cheese.

Nutrition information:

Calories per serving: 446; Carbohydrates: 24.4g; Protein: 38.0g; Fat: 22.2g; Sugar: 14.4g; Sodium: 2261mg

---

315. Cajun Chicken and Rice

(Servings: 4, Cooking Time: 15 minutes)

Ingredients:

- 1 9 oz package VeeTee Brown Rice
- 1 lb. chicken breast cut thin
- 1 cup chicken broth
- 1 teaspoon Cajun seasoning
- 1 small onion diced
- 1 red bell pepper diced
- 3 cloves garlic minced
- 2 tablespoons tomato pasta
- salt and pepper to taste

Directions for Cooking:

1. Season chicken with Cajun spice.
2. Add all ingredients in pot except for rice
3. Close Instant Pot, press pressure cook button, choose high settings, and set time to 10 minutes.
4. Once done cooking, do a QPR.
5. Remove chicken and stir in rice. Shred chicken and return to pot.
6. Press brown button and cook for 5 minutes.
7. Serve and enjoy.

Nutrition information:

Calories per serving: 212; Carbohydrates: 24.5g; Protein: 22.4g; Fat: 2.9g; Sugar: 3.5g; Sodium: 1488mg

---

316. Rice Pudding

(Servings: 6, Cooking Time: 30 minutes)

Ingredients:

- 2 cups raw whole milk or dairy-free milk of choice
- 1 1/4 cups water
- 1 cup basmati rice
- 3/4 cup heavy cream OR coconut cream
- 1/4 cup maple syrup
- 1/8 teaspoon sea salt
- inside scrapings from 1 vanilla bean OR 1 teaspoon vanilla extract

Directions for Cooking:

1. Place rice in fine mesh colander. Rinse well in several changes of water.
2. Then, place rice in Instant Pot. Add water, milk, maple syrup, and sea salt. Stir briefly.
3. Close Instant Pot, press porridge button.
4. Once done cooking, do a 10-minute natural release and then do a QPR.
5. Serve and enjoy.

Nutrition information:

Calories per serving: 198; Carbohydrates: 22.8g; Protein: 5.8g; Fat: 12.3g; Sugar: 12.3g; Sodium: 99mg

---

317. Cinnamon-Raisin Rice Pudding

(Servings: 4, Cooking Time: 35 minutes)

Ingredients:

- 1 Cup Short Grain Brown Rice
- 1 1/2 Cups Water 1 tbsp Vanilla Extract
- 1 tbsp Vanilla Extract
- 1 Cinnamon Stick
- 1 tbsp butter
- 1 Cup Raisins
- 3 tbsp Honey
- 1/2 Cup Heavy Cream

Directions for Cooking:

1. Add rice, water, vanilla, cinnamon stick, and butter into Instant Pot.
2. Close Instant Pot, press pressure cook button, choose high settings, and set time to 20 minutes.
3. Once done cooking, do a 15-minute natural release and then do a QPR.
4. Discard cinnamon stick.
5. Stir in cream, honey and raisins. Let it rest for 5 minutes.
6. Serve and enjoy.

Nutrition information:

Calories per serving: 414; Carbohydrates: 35.0g; Protein: 1.7g; Fat: 8.9g; Sugar: 23.9g; Sodium: 39mg

---

318. Red Beans and Rice

(Servings: 10, Cooking Time: 30 minutes)

Ingredients:

- 1 package (16 ounces) dried kidney beans (about 2-1/2 cups)
- 2 cups cubed ham (about 1 pound)
- 1 package (12 ounces) andouille chicken sausage, sliced
- 1 medium green pepper, chopped
- 1 medium onion, chopped
- 2 celery ribs, chopped
- 1 tablespoon hot pepper sauce
- 2 garlic cloves, minced
- 1 teaspoon salt
- Hot cooked rice

Nutrition information:

Calories per serving: 249; Carbohydrates: 31.0g; Protein: 23.0g; Fat: 5.0g; Sugar: 2.0g; Sodium: 788mg

Directions for Cooking:

1. Rinse beans and soak overnight in water. Discard water the next day.
2. Press sauté button and cook chicken sausage links for 5 minutes.
3. Stir in ham and cook for 2 minutes.
4. Stir in salt, garlic, pepper sauce, vegetables, beans, and about 4 cups of water. Mix well. Press cancel.
5. Close Instant Pot, press pressure cook button, choose high settings, and set time to 30 minutes.
6. Once done cooking, do a QPR.
7. Serve and enjoy with hot cooked rice.

---

319. Spicy Mushroom Fried Rice

(Servings: 6, Cooking Time: 25minutes)

Ingredients:

- 2 cups jasmine rice
- 1 tbsp oil
- 1 12-oz jar of sliced mushrooms
- 1/2 cup of diced onion
- 1 jalapeno sliced
- 2 cups chicken broth
- 2 tablespoons soy sauce
- salt and pepper to taste

Directions for Cooking:

1. Press sauté and heat oil.
2. Stir in onion, jalapeno, and mushrooms. Cook for 3 minutes.
3. Stir in rice and sauté for 2 minutes.
4. Add soy sauce, chicken broth, salt and pepper to taste. Mix well. Press cancel.
5. Close Instant Pot, press rice button.
6. Once done cooking, do a QPR.
7. Fluff rice, serve and enjoy

Nutrition information:

Calories per serving: 187; Carbohydrates: 25.5g; Protein: 8.0g; Fat: 11.9g; Sugar: 4.1g; Sodium: 409mg

---

320. Spicy Mexican Chicken and Rice

(Servings: 6, Cooking Time: 15 minutes)

Ingredients:

- 1 10 oz package VeeTee Spanish Style Rice
- 2 boneless skinless chicken breasts
- 2 tablespoons olive oil
- 1 cup onion chopped
- 1 green bell pepper chopped
- 1 1 oz packet Chicken Taco Seasoning
- 1 10 oz can red enchilada sauce
- 1 10 oz can diced tomatoes and chilies
- 1 cup shredded Mexican blended cheese
- 1 15 oz can black beans, drained and rinsed
- 1 cup frozen corn
- salt and pepper to taste

Directions for Cooking:

1. Press sauté and heat oil.
2. Stir in chicken. Season with pepper and salt. Cook for 6 minutes.
3. Stir in bell peppers and onions. Cook for 3 minutes.
4. Add enchilada sauce, corn, black beans, chilies, diced tomatoes, taco seasoning, and rice. Mix well. Press cancel.
5. Close Instant Pot, press pressure cook button, choose high settings, and set time to 5 minutes.
6. Once done cooking, do a QPR.
7. Stir in cheese, mix well and let it rest for 5 minutes.
8. Serve and enjoy.

Nutrition information:

Calories per serving: 438; Carbohydrates: 38.4g; Protein: 37.1g; Fat: 16.2g; Sugar: 3.8g; Sodium: 675mg

---

321. Cooking a Simple Rice in Instant Pot

(Servings: 4, Cooking Time: 22 minutes)

Ingredients:

- 1 cup Long Grain White Rice,
- 1 1/2 cups Water
- 1 teaspoon Olive Oil
- Pinch of Salt
- Pinch Ground Pepper

Directions for Cooking:

1. Place rice in a strainer and rinse well. Set aside in strainer and drain well.
2. In Instant pot, add oil and coat well sides and bottom of pot.
3. Add rice water, salt and pepper in pot.
4. Close Instant Pot, press rice button.
5. Once done cooking, do a QPR.
6. Serve and enjoy.

Nutrition information:

Calories per serving: 63; Carbohydrates: 11.6g; Protein: 1.1g; Fat: 1.3g; Sugar: 6.1g; Sodium: 585mg

---

322. Shrimp Scampi Paella

(Servings: 4, Cooking Time: 5 minutes)

Ingredients:

- 1pound frozen wild caught shrimp, 16-20 count shell & tail on
- 1 cup Jasmine Rice
- 1/4cup butter
- 1/4cup chopped fresh Parsley
- 1teaspoon sea salt
- 1/4teaspoon black pepper
- 1pinch crushed red pepper or to taste
- 1medium lemon, juiced
- 1pinch saffron
- 1 1/2cups filtered water or chicken broth
- 4 cloves garlic minced or pressed

Directions for Cooking:

1. Add all ingredients in pot and mix well.
2. Close Instant Pot, press pressure cook button, choose high settings, and set time to 5 minutes.
3. Once done cooking, do a QPR.
4. Serve and enjoy.

Nutrition information:

Calories per serving: 299; Carbohydrates: 16.1g; Protein: 27.3g; Fat: 18.5g; Sugar: 0.9g; Sodium: 1174mg

---

323. Coconut Rice

(Servings: 4, Cooking Time: 10 minutes)

Ingredients:

- 1 1/2 cups Jasmine Rice
- 1 can (14 ounces) Coconut Milk
- 1/2 cup water
- 1 teaspoon sugar
- 1/4 teaspoon salt
- 2 tbsp Toasted coconut, optional

Directions for Cooking:

1. Rinse rice and drain well. Transfer to pot.
2. Stir in all ingredients in pot except for toasted coconut.
3. Close Instant Pot, press pressure cook button, choose high settings, and set time to 3 minutes.
4. Once done cooking, do a 7-minute natural release and then do a QPR.
5. Fluff rice, serve and enjoy with toasted coconut garnish.

Nutrition information:

Calories per serving: 372; Carbohydrates: 28.4g; Protein: 8.2g; Fat: 32.9g; Sugar: 4.5g; Sodium: 171mg

---

324. Mexican Rice

(Servings: 6, Cooking Time: 30 minutes)

Ingredients:

- 2 cups long-grain rice (such as Lundberg Farms Brown Basmati)
- 1/2 white onion (chopped)
- 1/2 cup tomato paste
- 3 cloves garlic (minced)
- 1 small jalapeño (optional)
- 2 teaspoons salt
- 2 cups water

Directions for Cooking:

1. Press sauté and heat oil.
2. Stir in salt, garlic, onion, and rice. Sauté for 4 minutes.
3. Add tomato paste and water. Mix well. Add jalapeno. Press cancel.
4. Close Instant Pot, press pressure cook button, choose high settings, and set time to 3 minutes.
5. Once done cooking, do a 15-minute natural release and then do a QPR.
6. Serve and enjoy.

Nutrition information:

Calories per serving: 253; Carbohydrates: 53.1g; Protein: 5.9g; Fat: 2.1g; Sugar: 3.8g; Sodium: 759.2mg

---

325. Mexican Beefy Rice

(Servings: 4, Cooking Time: 16 minutes)

Ingredients:

- 1 tablespoon olive oil
- 1-pound lean ground beef
- 1 cup diced red onion
- 1 teaspoon chili powder Hatch chile powder
- 1/2 teaspoon ground cumin
- 1/2 teaspoon salt
- 1 cup long grain white rice rinsed well and drained
- 2 cups water
- 2 cups chunky salsa
- 15 ounces black beans rinsed and drained
- 1 cup cooked corn kernels
- 2 tablespoons chopped fresh cilantro
- 1 cup shredded cheese 4 Cheese Mexican blend

Directions for Cooking:

1. Press sauté and sauté salt, cumin, chili powder, onion, and beef for 8 minutes until beef is browned and cooked.
2. Stir in salsa, water, and rice. Deglaze pot. Press cancel.
3. Close Instant Pot, press pressure cook button, choose high settings, and set time to 8 minutes.
4. Once done cooking, do a QPR.
5. Press cancel and press brown button.
6. Stir in cilantro, corn, and black beans. Cook for 3 minutes while stirring frequently.
7. Stir in cheese.
8. Serve and enjoy.

Nutrition information:

Calories per serving: 622; Carbohydrates: 48.7g; Protein: 48.2g; Fat: 26.0g; Sugar: 9.9g; Sodium: 1999mg

---

326. Cajun Red Beans & Rice

(Servings: 10, Cook ng Time: minutes)

Ingredients:

- 1 medium onion diced
- 1 bell pepper diced
- 3 celery stalks diced
- 3 cloves garlic minced
- 1-pound dry red kidney beans
- 1 tsp salt or more to taste
- 1/2 tsp black pepper
- 1/4 tsp white pepper (optional)
- 1 tsp hot sauce
- 1 tsp fresh thyme or ½ tsp dried thyme
- 2 leaves bay
- 7 cups water
- 1-pound chicken andouille sausage cut into thin slices
- 10 cups cooked rice

Directions for Cooking:

1. Except for rice and sausage, mix all ingredients in Instant Pot.
2. Close Instant Pot, press pressure cook button, choose high settings, and set time to 28 minutes.
3. Once done cooking, do a QPR.
4. Add sausage. Press cancel, close pot, press manual, choose high pressure, cook for 15 minutes.
5. Do a full natural release.
6. Serve and enjoy on top of rice.

Nutrition information:

Calories per serving: 461; Carbohydrates: 77.0g; Protein: 21.0g; Fat: 7.0g; Sugar: 2.0g; Sodium: 735mg

---

327. Chai Spiced Rice Pudding

(Servings: 4, Cooking Time: 15 minutes)

Ingredients:

- 1 cup short grain rice (also sold as pudding rice)
- 1 cup almond milk (unsweetened)
- 1 cup coconut milk
- 1 + ½ cups water
- 2 tablespoons brown sugar
- 6 Medjool dates, sliced (peeps out)
- 1 teaspoon cinnamon powder
- 1 teaspoon ground ginger powder
- ¼ teaspoon ground nutmeg
- 5 cardamom pods
- 2 cloves or ¼ teaspoon Allspice powder
- 1 teaspoon vanilla extract
- Pinch of salt
- garnish: berries, nuts, chopped dates or other dried fruit

Directions for Cooking:

1. Combine all ingredients in Instant Pot except for garnish ingredients.
2. Close Instant Pot, press pressure cook button, choose high settings, and set time to 10 minutes.
3. Once done cooking, do a 5-minute natural release and then do a QPR.
4. Serve and enjoy with desired garnish.

Nutrition information:

Calories per serving: 535; Carbohydrates: 81.5g; Protein: 8.4g; Fat: 21.7g; Sugar: 32.2g; Sodium: 56mg

---

328. Chinese Sausage on Brown Rice

(Servings: 4, Cooking Time: 30 minutes)

Ingredients:

- 1/2 cup dried shrimp
- 4 Chinese dried mushrooms
- 3 Chinese sausage (lap cheung), diced
- 2 tablespoons cooking oil
- 1 shallot, minced
- 2 1/4 cups brown rice, rinsed and drained
- 3 cups chicken or vegetable broth
- 1/4 cup chopped cilantro

Directions for Cooking:

1. Soak the dried ingredients: In a small bowl, add the dried shrimp and cover with just-boiled hot water. Let soak up for 10 minutes and drain, discarding water.
2. In a separate small bowl, add the dried mushrooms and cover with just-boiled hot water. Let soak up for 30 minutes, and drain, discarding water. Chop/dice the shrimp and the mushrooms.
3. Press sauté and heat oil. Sauté shallot for 30 seconds.
4. Add shrimp and cook for 2 minutes.
5. Add Chinese sausage and mushrooms cook for a minute.
6. Add rice and chicken broth. Deglaze pot. Press cancel.
7. Close Instant Pot, press pressure cook button, choose high settings, and set time to 5 minutes.
8. Once done cooking, do a 15-minute natural release and then do a QPR.
9. Serve and enjoy with cilantro as garnish.

Nutrition information:

Calories per serving: 473; Carbohydrates: 58.9g; Protein: 18.6g; Fat: 17.9g; Sugar: 2.9g; Sodium: 1056mg

Instant Pot Dessert Recipes

329. Curried Tahini Carrots

(Servings: 6, Cooking Time: 10 minutes)

Ingredients:

- 2 carrots, peeled and julienned
- 1 cup organic raisins
- ¼ cup pumpkin seeds, roasted
- 1/3 cup tahini
- 2 tablespoons curry powder
- ¼ cup lemon juice
- 2 tablespoons maple syrup
- ¼ teaspoon ground black pepper

Directions for Cooking:

1. Mix all ingredients in pot.
2. Close Instant Pot, press pressure cook button, choose high settings, and set time to 10 minutes.
3. Once done cooking, do a full natural release.
4. Serve and enjoy.

Nutrition information:

Calories per serving: 142; Carbohydrates: 12.1g; Protein: 4.3g; Fat: 9.8g; Sugar: 0g; Sodium: 44mg

---

330. Zucchini & Walnut Bread

(Servings: 6, Cooking Time: 6 hours)

Ingredients:

- 1 ¾ cups brown rice flour
- ½ teaspoon baking soda
- ¼ teaspoon baking powder
- 2 eggs
- 2 cups grated zucchini
- ¾ cup dates, pitted and chopped
- ¾ cup walnuts, chopped

Nutrition information:

Calories per serving: 329; Carbohydrates: 50.9g; Protein: 8.3g; Fat: 11.1g; Sugar: 5.8g; Sodium: 144mg

Directions for Cooking:

1. Grease the inner pot with olive oil.
2. In a mixing bowl, combine all ingredients to create a dough.
3. Place the dough in the greased inner pot.
4. Close Instant Pot, press slow cook button, choose low settings, set vent to venting, and set time to 6 hours.
5. Serve and enjoy

---

331. Nuts & Cherry Delight

(Servings: 4, Cooking Time: 4 hours)

Ingredients:

- ¼ cup walnuts
- ½ cup chopped dates
- ¼ cup chopped figs
- ½ cup coconut flakes
- 1 organic egg
- 1 teaspoon vanilla extract
- 2 cups chopped cherries

Directions for Cooking:

1. Add all ingredients in Instant Pot.
2. Close Instant Pot, press slow cook button, choose low settings, set vent to venting and set time to 4 hours.
3. Once done cooking, serve and enjoy

Nutrition information:

Calories per serving: 236; Carbohydrates: 37.2g; Protein: 5.1g; Fat: 8.9g; Sugar: 2.1g; Sodium: 66mg

---

332. Cranberry Nut Bread

(Servings: 12, Cooking Time: 6 hours)

Ingredients:

- 2 cups brown rice flour
- ¼ cup chopped dates
- ¼ cup chopped figs
- ¾ teaspoon salt
- 1 ½ teaspoon baking powder
- ½ teaspoon baking soda
- 1 cup chopped cranberries
- ½ cup chopped almonds
- 1 tablespoon orange zest
- 1 egg, beaten
- 1 cup orange juice, freshly squeezed
- ½ cup coconut milk

Directions for Cooking:

1. In a mixing bowl, combine all ingredients until you form a batter.
2. Grease the inner pot of the Instant Pot or place a parchment paper at the bottom.
3. Pour the batter into the pot.
4. Close Instant Pot, press slow cook button, choose low settings, set vent to venting and set time to 6 hours.
5. Once done cooking, serve and enjoy

Nutrition information:

Calories per serving: 169; Carbohydrates: 30.7g; Protein: 3.2g; Fat: 4.1g; Sugar: 1.3g; Sodium: 212mg

---

333. Nuts & Dates Bar

(Servings: 12, Cooking Time: 6 hours)

Ingredients:

- 2 cups dates, chopped
- 1 cup maple syrup
- 1/8 teaspoon ground cinnamon
- ¾ teaspoon salt
- 1/8 teaspoon ground nutmeg
- 1 cup brown rice flour
- 1 cup coconut milk
- ½ cup walnuts, chopped
- ½ cup cashews, chopped

Directions for Cooking:

1. Combine all ingredients in Instant Pot.
2. Close Instant Pot, press slow cook button, choose low settings, set vent to venting and set time to 6 hours.
3. Once done cooking, do a let it cool.
4. Serve and enjoy

Nutrition information:

Calories per serving: 318; Carbohydrates: 50.8g; Protein: 3.8g; Fat: 13.1g; Sugar: 0g; Sodium: 185mg

---

334. Dark Chocolate Glaze

(Servings: 4, Cooking Time: 10minutes)

Ingredients:

- 3 tablespoons coconut oil
- 8 ounces dark chocolate
- ¼ cup coconut sugar
- 1/3 cup coconut milk

Nutrition information:

Calories per serving: 177; Carbohydrates: 18.1g; Protein:1.6g; Fat:18.1g; Sugar: 3.4g; Sodium: 8mg

Directions for Cooking:

1. Place in the Instant Pot and press the Sauté button.
2. Allow to simmer until all ingredients are well incorporated.
3. Drizzle glaze over your favorite dessert or store in an airtight container in the fridge.

---

335. Cherry-Chocolate Pudding

(Servings: 8, Cooking Time: 6 hours)

Ingredients:

- 1 ½ cup coconut milk
- ¼ cup chia seeds
- 3 tablespoons raw cacao powder
- 3 tablespoons maple syrup
- ½ cup brown rice flour
- ½ cup cherries, pitted and chopped

Directions for Cooking:

1. Grease Instant Pot.
2. In a bowl, whisk well ingredients. Pour into pot.
3. Close Instant Pot, press slow cook button, choose low settings, set vent to venting and set time to 6 hours.
4. Once done cooking, refrigerate until cool.
5. Serve and enjoy

Nutrition information:

Calories per serving: 195; Carbohydrates: 19.1g; Protein: 2.9g; Fat: 12.9g; Sugar: 0g; Sodium: 11mg

---

336. Choco-Dipped Frozen Bananas

(Servings: 6, Cooking Time: 10 minutes)

Ingredients:

- 3 large bananas, cut into thirds
- 12 ounces dark chocolate
- 1 cup salted pistachios
- ½ cup cocoa nibs

Directions for Cooking:

1. Insert popsicles on the banana slices.
2. Place the bananas in the fridge for 4 hours to freeze them.
3. Mix together the pistachios and cocoa nibs in a glass and mix until well combined. Set aside.
4. Meanwhile, put the chocolate in the instant Pot and press the Sauté button.
5. Heat to melt the chocolate. Place in a deep glass.
6. Dip the frozen bananas in the melted chocolate before dredging into the pistachio mixture.
7. Place in the fridge to harden.

Nutrition information:

Calories per serving:531; Carbohydrates: 51.6g; Protein: 10.1g; Fat: 34.5g; Sugar: 2.7g; Sodium: 101mg

---

337. Choco-Coco Macaroons

(Servings: 15, Cooking Time: 10 minutes)

Ingredients:

- 3 cups coconut flakes
- ¼ cup coconut oil
- 3 eggs, beaten
- 1/3 cup cocoa powder
- 1 tablespoon liquid stevia

Directions for Cooking:

1. Press the "Sauté" button on the Instant Pot.
2. Add all ingredients and pour ¼ cup water.
3. Stir constantly for 10 minutes.
4. Turn off the Instant Pot and scoop small balls from the mixture.
5. Allow to set in the fridge for 1 hour.

Nutrition information:

Calories per serving:141; Carbohydrates:8.1 g; Protein: 2.6g; Fat: 15.2g; Sugar: 0g; Sodium: 69mg

---

338. Dark Chocolate Hot Cocoa

(Servings: 1, Cooking Time: 15 minutes)

Ingredients:

- 1 cup coconut milk
- 1 ½ teaspoon coconut sugar
- 2 ounces dark chocolate
- A dash of cinnamon

Directions for Cooking:

1. Place the coconut milk, coconut sugar, and dark chocolate in the Instant Pot.
2. Close the lid and make sure that the steam release valve is set to "Sealing."
3. Press the Manual button and adjust the cooking time to 15 minutes.
4. Do quick pressure release.
5. Garnish with a dash of cinnamon before serving.

Nutrition information:

Calories per serving: 906; Carbohydrates: 43.1g; Protein: 9.9g; Fat: 81.3g; Sugar: -5.7g; Sodium: 47mg

---

339. Lemon Blueberry Cake

(Servings: 5, Cooking Time: 10 minutes)

Ingredients:

- ½ cups coconut flour
- 4 large eggs
- 1 teaspoon baking soda
- ½ cup coconut milk
- ½ teaspoon lemon zest

Directions for Cooking:

1. Combine all ingredients in a mixing bowl.
2. Pour into a mug.
3. Place a steam rack in the Instant Pot and pour a cup of water.
4. Place the mug on the steam rack.
5. Close the lid and make sure that the vent points to "Sealing."
6. Press the "Steam" button and adjust the time to 10 minutes.
7. Do natural pressure release.

Nutrition information:

Calories per serving: 259; Carbohydrates: 10.3g; Protein: 7.2g; Fat: 20.9g; Sugar: 0g; Sodium: 34mg

---

340. Brownie Fudge

(Servings: 10, Cooking Time: 6 hours)

Ingredients:

- ¾ cup coconut milk
- 2 tablespoons butter, melted
- 4 egg yolks, beaten
- 5 tablespoons cacao powder
- 1 teaspoon erythritol

Directions for Cooking:

1. Place all ingredients in the Instant Pot and mix until well combined.
2. Pour the batter into the greased inner pot.
3. Close the lid and make sure that the vent points to "Venting."
4. Press the "Slow Cook" button and adjust the time to 6 hours.

Nutrition information:

Calories per serving: 84; Carbohydrates: 1.2g; Protein: 1.5g; Fat: 8.4g; Sugar: 0g; Sodium: 25mg

---

341. Berry Compote

(Servings: 10, Cooking Time: 6 hours)

Ingredients:

- 1 cup raspberries
- 1 cup full fat coconut milk

Directions for Cooking:

1. Place the raspberries in the Instant Pot.
2. Add 1/8 cup of water.
3. Close the lid and make sure that the vent points to "Venting."
4. Press the "Slow Cook" button and adjust the time to 6 hours.
5. While the berry compote is cooking, make the coconut cream.
6. In a bowl, place the coconut milk.
7. Use a hand mixer and whisk until it becomes thick and foamy.
8. Place on a bowl and top with the berry compote.

Nutrition information:

Calories per serving: 78; Carbohydrates: 7.3g; Protein:0.8 g; Fat: 8.1g; Sugar: 2.4g; Sodium: 4mg

---

342. Creamy Choco Mousse

(Servings: 4, Cooking Time: 10 minutes)

Ingredients:

- 2 cups coconut milk, freshly squeezed
- 2 teaspoons vanilla extract
- 2 tablespoons erythritol
- 2 tablespoons cocoa powder, sifted
- Cocoa nibs for garnish

Directions for Cooking:

1. Place the coconut milk, vanilla extract, sweetener, and cocoa powder in the Instant Pot.
2. Press the "Sauté" button and allow to simmer for 10 minutes.
3. Pour into the ramekins and allow to set in the fridge for an hour.
4. Garnish with cacao nibs before serving.

Nutrition information:

Calories per serving:291; Carbohydrates: 9.2g; Protein: 3.5g; Fat: 29.5g; Sugar: 0g; Sodium: 19mg

---

343. Vanilla Jello

(Servings: 6, Cooking Time: 6 minutes)

Ingredients:

- 1 cup boiling water
- 2 tablespoons gelatin powder, unsweetened
- 3 tablespoons erythritol
- 1 cup heavy cream
- 1 teaspoon vanilla extract

Nutrition information:

Calories per serving: 105; Carbohydrates: 5.2g; Protein: 3.3; Fat: 7.9g; Sugar: 0g; Sodium: 31mg

Directions for Cooking:

1. Place the boiling water in the Instant Pot.
2. Press the "Sauté" button on the Instant Pot and allow the water to simmer.
3. Add the gelatin powder and allow to dissolve.
4. Stir in the rest of the ingredients.
5. Pour the mixture into jello molds.
6. Place in the fridge to set for 2 hours.

---

344. Salted Caramel Icing on Apple Bread

(Servings: 12, Cooking Time: 35 minutes)

Ingredients:

- 2 eggs
- 2 sticks butter
- 3 cup sugar
- 1 tablespoon apple pie spice
- 3 cups apples, peeled and cubed
- 2 cups flour
- 1 tablespoon baking powder
- 1 tablespoon vanilla
- 1 cup heavy cream
- 2 cups powdered sugar

Directions for Cooking:

1. In a mixing bowl, combine the eggs, 1 stick butter, 1 cup sugar, and apple pie spice. Mix until creamy and smooth. Add in the apples and mix well.
2. In another bowl, mix together flour and baking powder. Add this mixture to the apple mixture. Stir and pour the batter into a greased spring form pan.
3. Place a steamer rack in the Instant Pot and pour 1 ½ cup water. Place the pan on the trivet.
4. Close the lid and press the manual button. Cook on high for 35 minutes.
5. Do a natural pressure release.
6. Meanwhile, make the icing by mixing 1 stick butter, 2 cups sugar, heavy cream and powdered sugar. Heat over medium low flame.
7. Pour the icing on top of the apple bread.

Nutrition information:

Calories per serving: 494; Carbohydrates: 87.7g; Protein: 4.0g; Fat: 15.0g; Sugar: 69.6g; Sodium: 101mg

---

345. Mini Lava Cake

(Servings: 3, Cooking Time: 6 minutes)

Ingredients:

- 1 egg
- 4 tablespoon sugar
- 2 tablespoon olive oil
- 4 tablespoon milk
- 4 tablespoon all-purpose flour
- 1 tablespoon cacao powder
- ½ teaspoon baking powder
- Pinch of salt
- Powdered sugar for dusting

Nutrition information:

Calories per serving: 193; Carbohydrates: 20.0g; Protein: 3.5g; Fat: 11.1g; Sugar: 11.5g; Sodium: 31.0mg

Directions for Cooking:

1. Grease the ramekins with butter or oil. Set aside
2. Pour 1 cup of water in the Instant Pot and place the steamer rack.
3. In a medium bowl, mix all the ingredients except the powdered sugar. Blend until well combined.
4. Pour in the ramekins.
5. Place the ramekins in the Instant Pot and close the lid.
6. Press the manual button and cook on high for 6 minutes.
7. Once the Instant Pot beeps, remove the ramekin and sprinkle powdered sugar.
8. Serve and enjoy.

---

346. Apple Crisp

(Servings: 4, Cooking Time: 25 minutes)

Ingredients:

- 5 medium apples, peeled and chopped
- ½ teaspoon nutmeg
- 2 teaspoon cinnamon
- 1 tablespoon maple syrup
- ½ cup water
- 4 tablespoon butter
- ¾ cup old fashioned rolled oats
- ¼ cup brown sugar
- ¼ cup flour
- ½ teaspoon salt

Directions for Cooking:

1. Place the apples in the Instant Pot and sprinkle with nutmeg and cinnamon. Pour in maple syrup and water.
2. In a small bowl, melt the butter in the microwave oven. Add to the melted butter oats, brown sugar, flour and salt.
3. Drop a spoonful of mixture on the apples.
4. Close the lid on the Instant Pot. Press the manual setting and cook on high for 8 minutes.
5. Use natural pressure release.
6. Serve warm and topped with vanilla ice cream.

Nutrition information:
Calories per serving: 362; Carbohydrates: 67.1g; Protein: 4.7g; Fat: 13.3g; Sugar: 40.3g; Sodium: 390mg

---

347. Thai Coconut Rice

(Servings: 4,Cooking Time: 20 minutes)

Ingredients:

- 1 cup Thai sweet rice
- 1 ½ cups water
- 1 can full fat coconut milk
- A pinch of salt
- 4 tablespoon pure sugar
- ½ teaspoon cornstarch + 2 tablespoon water
- 1 large mango, sliced
- Sesame seeds for garnish

Directions for Cooking:

1. Place rice and water in the Instant Pot.
2. Close the lid and press the manual button. Cook on high for 5 minutes.
3. Turn off the Instant Pot and do natural pressure release for 10 minutes.
4. While the rice is cooking, place the coconut milk, salt, and sugar in a saucepan. Heat over medium heat for 10 minutes while stirring constantly.
5. Once the Instant Pot lid can be open, add the coconut milk mixture. Stir well. Place a clean kitchen towel over the opening of the lid and let it rest for 10 minutes.
6. Meanwhile, mix cornstarch with water and add to the rice. Press the sauté button and mix until the rice becomes creamy and thick.
7. Serve with mango slices and sesame seeds.

Nutrition information:
Calories per serving: 301; Carbohydrates: 36.5g; Protein: 3.5g; Fat: 17.5g; Sugar: 21.6g; Sodium: 163mg

---

348. Apple sauce

(Servings: 8, Cooking Time: 8 minutes)

Ingredients:

- 8 medium apples, peeled and cored
- 1 cup water
- 2 teaspoon cinnamon, ground

Directions for Cooking:

1. Place the apples in the Instant Pot. Pour in the water.
2. Close the lid and press the manual button. Cook on high for 8 minutes.
3. Do natural pressure release and open the lid.
4. Remove the excess water.
5. Place the apples in a blender and process until smooth.
6. Add the rest of the ingredients.
7. Serve chilled.

Nutrition information:

Calories per serving: 96; Carbohydrates: 25.7g; Protein: 0.5g; Fat: 0.3g; Sugar: 18.9g; Sodium: 2mg

---

349. Custard Cheesecake

(Servings: 6, Cooking Time: 25 minutes)

Ingredients:

- 1 ½ cup custard cream biscuits
- ¼ cup melted butter
- 2 cup full fat cream cheese
- ½ cup caster sugar
- 2 large eggs
- 1 teaspoon vanilla
- 2 drops of almond extract
- ¾ cup double cream

Directions for Cooking:

1. Place the custard cream biscuits and butter in the food processor and pulse until a fine crumb is formed. This will be the dough
2. Press the dough in ramekins or small spring form pans.
3. Clean the food processor and pour in the cream cheese, caster sugar, eggs, vanilla extract, almond extract, and double cream. Process until well combined.
4. Pour the mixture to the ramekins or cake pan. Place a kitchen towel on top of the ramekin to absorb the excess liquid from forming on the cheesecake
5. Pour 1 ½ cup of water to the Instant Pot and place a trivet. Place the ramekins or cake pan on the trivet.
6. Close the lid and select the manual button. Cook on high for 25 minutes.
7. Do natural pressure release then remove the lid. Remove the kitchen towel.
8. Refrigerate.

Nutrition information:

Calories per serving: 459; Carbohydrates: 18.5g; Protein: 9.8g; Fat: 39.0g; Sugar: 16.2g; Sodium: 387mg

---

350. Deliciously Good Peach Dessert

(Servings: 8, Cooking Time: 15 minutes)

Ingredients:

- 8 cups peaches, thinly sliced
- ¼ cup brown sugar
- 1 teaspoon cinnamon
- 1/8 teaspoon salt
- ¼ cup butter

Directions for Cooking:

1. Place the peaches in a mixing bowl and add brown sugar, cinnamon and salt. Toss to combine everything. Add butter and mix again.
2. Place the peaches inside ramekins.
3. Place a steamer rack in the Instant Pot.
4. Arrange the ramekins on the steamer rack.
5. Close the lid and press the manual button. Cook on high for 15 minutes.
6. Do natural pressure release.
7. Serve and enjoy warm or cold.

Nutrition information:
Calories per serving: 272; Carbohydrates: 59.2g; Protein: 1.3g; Fat: 6.0g; Sugar: 55.5g; Sodium: 102mg

---

351. Berry Cobbler

(Servings: 4, Cooking Time: 10 minutes)

Ingredients:

- 30 ounces frozen mixed berries
- ½ cup granulated white sugar, divided
- 2 ½ cup commercial baking mix
- ½ cup light vanilla soy milk
- 3 tablespoon whipped butter
- 2 teaspoon cinnamon

Directions for Cooking:

1. Prepare the filling by mixing berries with ¼ cup white sugar and ½ cup commercial baking mix.
2. In another bowl, prepare the topping by combining 2 cups commercial baking mix, soy milk, ¼ cup white sugar, butter and cinnamon.
3. Place the filling in ramekins. Add the topping mixture.
4. Place a trivet or steam rack at the bottom of the Instant Pot and pour 1 cup water.
5. Place the ramekins on the rack.
6. Close the lid and press the manual button. Cook on high for 10 minutes.
7. Do natural pressure release for 10-minutes.
8. Serve and enjoy.

Nutrition information:
Calories per serving: 243; Carbohydrates: 30.1g; Protein: 1.8g; Fat: 14.8g; Sugar: 20.5g; Sodium: 72mg

---

352. Mini Peanut Butter Choco Cakes

(Servings: 4, Cooking Time: 15 minutes)

Ingredients:

- 1 can black beans, drained and rinsed
- ½ cup cocoa powder, unsweetened
- ½ cup egg whites
- 1/3 cup canned pumpkin
- 1/3 cup unsweetened applesauce
- ¼ cup brown sugar
- 1 teaspoon vanilla extract
- 1 ½ teaspoon baking powder
- ¼ teaspoon salt
- 3 tablespoon peanut butter baking chips

Directions for Cooking:

1. Place all the ingredients except the peanut butter chips inside a food processor. Process until smooth.
2. Add the peanut butter chips and fold until evenly distributed within the batter.
3. Place the batter in a ramekin sprayed with cooking oil.
4. Place a steam rack in the Instant Pot and add 1 ½ cup water.
5. Place the ramekins with the batter onto the steamer rack.
6. Close the lid and press the manual button. Cook on high for 10 minutes.
7. Do natural pressure release.
8. Insert a toothpick in the middle of the cakes and check if it comes out clean.
9. Serve chilled.

Nutrition information:
Calories per serving: 218; Carbohydrates: 34.9g; Protein: 12.0g; Fat: 6.5g; Sugar: 15.9g; Sodium: 229mg

---

353. Choco Fudge

(Servings: 24, Cooking Time: 25 minutes)

Ingredients:

- 3 ¼-ounces dark chocolate with a minimum of 70% cocoa, chopped
- 3 ¼-ounces butter
- 1 teaspoon vanilla extract
- 2 cups heavy whipping cream

Directions for Cooking:

1. Press sauté button on Instant Pot.
2. Add vanilla and heavy cream and bring to a simmer.
3. Continue simmering for 20 minutes or until mixture is reduced to 50% its original amount. Stir frequently to prevent burning.
4. Press cancel button and stir in butter.
5. Mix well until butter is melted and thoroughly incorporated.
6. Add chocolate and mix until thoroughly melted and combined.
7. In a square baking dish, grease bottom and sides with cooking spray, pour in chocolate mixture.
8. Stick into the fridge for at least 4 hours.
9. Slice into 24 equal pieces and enjoy.
10. Refrigerate at all times.

Nutrition information:
Calories per serving: 83; Carbohydrates: 2.3g; Protein: 0.6g; Fat: 8.1g; Sugar: 2.0g; Sodium: 31.0mg

---

354. Mocha Pudding Cake

(Servings: 6, Cooking Time: 25 minutes)

Ingredients:

- 2/3 cup granulated sweetener
- 5 large eggs
- 1/8 teaspoon salt
- 1/3 cup almond flour
- 4 tablespoons unsweetened cocoa powder
- 1 teaspoon vanilla extract
- 2 tablespoons instant coffee crystals
- ½ cup heavy cream
- 2-ounces unsweetened chocolate
- ¾ cup butter
- Coconut oil spray

Directions for Cooking:

1. Grease sides and bottom of Instant Pot with cooking spray.
2. Press sauté button.
3. Add butter and chocolate. Mix well. Make sure to mix constantly so as the bottom doesn't burn. Once fully incorporated, press cancel to keep warm.
4. Meanwhile, in a small bowl whisk well vanilla, coffee crystals, and heavy cream.
5. In another bowl, mix well salt, almond flour, and cocoa powder.
6. In a mixing bowl, beat eggs until thick and pale, around 5 minutes while slowly stirring in sweetener.
7. While beating, slowly drizzle and mix in melted butter mixture.
8. Mix in the almond flour mixture and mix well.
9. Add the coffee mixture and beat until fully incorporated.
10. Pour batter into Instant Pot.
11. Place a paper towel on top of pot this will absorb condensation.
12. Cover pot, press slow cooker button, and adjust to 2-hour cooking time.

Nutrition information:
Calories per serving: 397; Carbohydrates: 27.9g; Protein: 3.6g; Fat: 31.2g; Sugar: 21.9g; Sodium: 253mg

---

355. Salted Choco Treat

(Servings: 10, Cooking Time: 15 minutes)

Ingredients:

- Sea salt
- 1 tablespoon pumpkin seeds
- 2 tablespoons roasted unsweetened coconut chips
- 10 hazelnuts or pecan/walnuts
- 3 ½-ounces dark chocolate (minimum of 70% cocoa solids)

Directions for Cooking:

1. On Instant Pot, add 1/2 cup of water and press sauté button.
2. On a heat proof bowl, place chocolate and slowly lower into Instant Pot.
3. Continue heating bowl until chocolate is melted. If needed you can add more water into Instant Pot.
4. Once chocolate is melted, stir in salt, pumpkin seeds, coconut chips, and walnuts.
5. Refrigerate for at least two hours, cut into strips and enjoy.

Nutrition information:
Calories per serving: 83; Carbohydrates: 8.1g; Protein: 1.3g; Fat: 5.1g; Sugar: 5.1g; Sodium: 13.0mg

---

356. Tapioca Pudding

(Servings: 4, Cooking Time: 20 minutes)

Ingredients:

- ½ lemon, zested
- ½ cup sugar
- ½ cup water
- 1 ¼ cups whole milk
- 1/3 cup seed tapioca pearls

Directions for Cooking:

1. Prepare the Instant Pot by placing the inner pot inside.
2. Add steamer basket and a cup of water.
3. In fine mesh strainer, rinse tapioca pearls and pour into heat proof bowl. Mix in sugar, zest, water, and milk.
4. Place bowl in steamer basket.
5. Cover and lock lid. Close the pressure release valve and press soup/stew button. Set the timer to 20 minutes.
6. Once done cooking, press cancel, and do the natural release method.
7. Serve while warm or place in the fridge to cool and enjoy.

Nutrition information:

Calories per serving: 164; Carbohydrates: 33.9g; Protein: 2.3g; Fat: 2.4g; Sugar: 22.6g; Sodium: 35.0mg

---

357. Cherry Compote

(Servings: 8, Cooking Time: 10 minutes)

Ingredients:

- 1 package frozen cherries
- 2 tablespoon lemon juice
- ¾ cup sugar
- 2 tablespoon cornstarch
- 2 tablespoon water
- ¼ teaspoon almond extract

Directions for Cooking:

1. Place the cherries, lemon juice and sugar in the Instant Pot. Stir to mix everything.
2. Close the lid and press the Fish/Veg/Steam button. Adjust the cooking time to 5 minutes.
3. Do natural pressure release.
4. Meanwhile, mix the cornstarch, water and almond extract.
5. Once the lid is open, pour the slurry over the cherries. Press the same button and cook until the sauce thickens.
6. Once done cooking, refrigerate until cool.
7. Serve and enjoy.

Nutrition information:

Calories per serving: 46; Carbohydrates: 11.6g; Protein: 0g; Fat: 0g; Sugar: 9.4g; Sodium: 0mg

---

358. Hazelnut Flan

(Servings: 4, Cooking Time: 50 minutes)

Ingredients:

- ¾ + 1/3 cup granulated sugar
- ¼ cup water
- 3 eggs
- 2 egg yolks
- A pinch of salt
- 2 cups milk
- ½ cup whipping cream
- 1 teaspoon vanilla extract
- 2 tablespoon hazelnut syrup

Directions for Cooking:

1. Prepare the caramel base by heating the ¾ cup sugar and ¼ cup water. Bring to a boil and place on ramekins before it hardens. Set aside.
2. Place a trivet or steamer basket in the Instant Pot and add 1 ½ cups of water.
3. In a mixing bowl, beat the eggs, yolks and 1/3 cup of sugar. Add a pinch of salt.
4. Heat milk in a saucepan over medium heat until it bubbles. Add milk to eggs to temper the eggs.
5. Stir in the cream, vanilla and Hazelnut syrup.
6. Pour mixture on ramekins and cover with tin foil.
7. Place inside on the steamer basket and close the lid.
8. Press the Fish/Veg/ Steam button and adjust the cooking time to 50 minutes.
9. Do natural pressure release.

Nutrition information:

Calories per serving: 325; Carbohydrates:35.12g; Protein: 12.16g; Fat: 15.16g; Sugar:34.21g; Sodium: 141mg

---

359. Chickpea Hummus

(Servings: 8, Cooking Time: 18 minutes)

Ingredients:

- 1 cup chickpeas
- 4 cloves of garlic
- 1 bay leaf
- 2 tablespoon tahini
- 1juice of lemon
- ¼ teaspoon cumin
- ½ teaspoon salt
- A dash of paprika
- ½ teaspoon parsley
- A dash of extra virgin olive oil

Directions for Cooking:

1. Place the chickpeas in the Instant Pot and add 6 cups of water. Add two cloves of garlic and bay leaf in the pot.
2. Close the lid of the Instant Pot and press the Beans/Lentils button and adjust the cooking time for 18 minutes.
3. Do natural pressure release.
4. Transfer the chickpeas in a food processor and add the remaining garlic, tahini, lemon, cumin, and salt.
5. Pulse until smooth.
6. Transfer to a bowl and garnish with paprika, parsley and olive oil.

Nutrition information:

Calories per serving: 109.1; Carbohydrates: 0.2g; Protein: 4.1g; Fat: 3.8g; Sugar:0.2g; Sodium: 332.9mg

---

360. Keto Ranch Dip

(Serves: 8, Cooking Time: 2 minutes)

Ingredients:

- 1 cup egg white, beaten
- 1 lemon juice, freshly squeezed
- Salt and pepper to taste
- 1 teaspoon mustard paste
- 1 cup olive oil

Nutrition information:

Calories per serving: 258; Carbohydrates: 1.2g; Protein: 3.4g; Fat: 27.1g; Sugar: 0g; Sodium: 58mg

Directions for Cooking:

1. Place all ingredients in the Instant Pot and whisk vigorously.
2. Press the "Sauté" button and allow to heat up for 2 minutes while stirring.
3. Do not allow to simmer.
4. Pour into container and store in the fridge for 2 weeks.

---

361. A l-Around Gravy

(Serves: 6, Preparation Time: 5 minutes, Cooking Time: 10 minutes)

Ingredients:

- 2 tablespoons butter
- 1 white onion, chopped
- ¼ cup coconut milk
- 2 cups bone broth
- 1 tablespoon balsamic vinegar

Nutrition information:

Calories per serving: 59; Carbohydrates: 1.1g; Protein: 0.2g; Fat: 6.3g; Sugar: 0g; Sodium: 33mg

Directions for Cooking:

1. Press the "Sauté" button on the Instant Pot.Melt the butter and sauté the onions for 2 minutes.
2. Add the rest of the ingredients.
3. Stir constantly for 5 minutes or until slightly thickened.

---

362. Béarnaise Sauce

(Serves: 4, Cooking Time: 3 minutes)

Ingredients

- 2/3 pounds butter
- 4 egg yolks, beaten
- 2 teaspoons lemon juice, freshly squeezed
- ¼ teaspoon onion powder
- 2 tablespoon fresh tarragon

Directions for Cooking:

1. Press the "Sauté" button on the Instant Pot.
2. Melt the butter for 3 minutes.
3. Transfer into a mixing bowl.
4. While whisking the melted hot butter, slowly add the egg yolks.
5. Continue stirring so that no lumps form.
6. Add the lemon juice, onion powder, and fresh tarragon.
7. Store in the fridge for up to 2 weeks.

Nutrition information:

Calories per serving: 603; Carbohydrates: 1.4g; Protein: 3.5g; Fat: 66.2g; Sugar: 0g; Sodium:497 mg

---

363. Caesar Salad Dressing

(Serves: 6, Cooking Time: 3 hours)

Ingredients:

- ½ cup olive oil
- 1 tablespoon Dijon mustard
- ½ cup parmesan cheese, grated
- 2/3-ounce anchovies, chopped
- ½ lemon juice, freshly squeezed

Directions for Cooking:

1. Place all ingredients in the Instant Pot.
2. Add ¼ cup of water and season with salt and pepper to taste.
3. Close the lid and make sure that the vent points to "Venting."
4. Press the "Slow Cook" button and adjust the time to 3 hours.

Nutrition information:

Calories per serving:203; Carbohydrates: 1.5g; Protein: 3.4g; Fat: 20.7g; Sugar: 0g; Sodium: 296mg

---

364. Cranberry Sauce

(Servings: 8, Cooking Time: 6 hours)

Ingredients:

- 1-pound cranberries
- ½ cup water
- 1 stick butter
- 1 lemon, juice and zest

Directions for Cooking:

1. Place all ingredients in the Instant Pot.
2. Close the lid and make sure that the vent points to "Venting."
3. Press the "Slow Cook" button and adjust the time to 6 hours.
4. Open the lid and strain the cranberry sauce.
5. Discard the strained solid.

Nutrition information:

Calories per serving:174; Carbohydrates: 8.1g; Protein: 0.9g; Fat: 15.5g; Sugar: 1.2g; Sodium: 127mg

---

365. Chia-Blackberry Jam

(Servings: 6, Cooking Time: 6 hours)

Ingredients:

- 3 cups blackberries, fresh
- 4 tablespoons lemon juice, freshly squeezed
- ¼ cup erythritol
- 4 tablespoons chia seeds
- 5 tablespoons butter

Nutrition information:

Calories per serving:236; Carbohydrates: 33g; Protein: 2.9g; Fat: 11.8g; Sugar: 0g; Sodium: 81mg

Directions for Cooking:

1. Place all ingredients in the Instant Pot.
2. Close the lid and make sure that the vent points to "Venting."
3. Press the "Slow Cook" button and adjust the time to 6 hours.

---

366. Caramel Sauce

(Servings: 9, Cooking Time: 6 hours)

Ingredients:

- ¼ cup butter
- ½ cup coconut milk
- ¼ teaspoon xanthan gum
- 2 tablespoons water
- ½ cup erythritol

Directions for Cooking:

1. Place all ingredients in the Instant Pot.
2. Close the lid and make sure that the vent points to "Venting."
3. Press the "Slow Cook" button and adjust the time to 6 hours.

Nutrition information:

Calories per serving: 76; Carbohydrates: 0.7g; Protein: 0.4g; Fat: 8.3g; Sugar: 0g; Sodium: 43mg;

---

367. Hot Fudge Sauce

(Servings: 9, Cooking Time: 5 hours)

Ingredients:

- 1 cup whipping cream
- 1/3 cup powdered Swerve sweetener
- 2 ½ ounces chocolate, unsweetened
- ½ teaspoon vanilla extract

Directions for Cooking:

1. Place all ingredients in the Instant Pot.
2. Close the lid and make sure that the vent points to "Venting."
3. Press the "Slow Cook" button and adjust the time to 5 hours.
4. Mix before serving.

Nutrition information:

Calories per serving: 126; Carbohydrates: 3.7g; Protein: 1.7g; Fat: 14.8g; Sugar: 0g; Sodium: 19mg

---

368. Artichoke-Spinach Dip

(Servings: 10, Cooking Time: 4 minutes)

Ingredients:

- 8-oz cream cheese
- 10-oz box Frozen spinach
- 16-oz Shredded Parmesan cheese
- 8-oz Shredded mozzarella
- 1/2 cup chicken broth
- 14-oz can artichoke hearts
- 1/2 cup sour cream
- 1/2 cup mayo
- 3 cloves garlic
- 1 tsp onion powder

Directions for Cooking:

1. Squeeze out excess water from spinach.
2. Add all ingredients in Instant pot except for cheese. Mix well.
3. Close Instant Pot, press the Manual button, choose high settings, and set time to 4 minutes.
4. Once done cooking, do a QPR.
5. Stir in cheese.
6. Serve and enjoy.

Nutrition information:

Calories per serving: 330; Carbohydrates: 6.0g; Protein: 15.0g; Fat: 26.0g; Sugar:1.0g; Sodium: 844mg

---

369. Creamy Artichoke Dip

(Servings: 8, Cooking Time: 15 minutes)

Ingredients:

- ½ cup dry cannellini beans, soaked overnight
- 8 medium-sized artichokes, cleaned and trimmed
- 1 cup water
- ½ lemon, juiced
- 2 cloves of garlic, minced
- ¾ cup plain non-fat yogurt
- 1 teaspoon salt
- ¼ teaspoon pepper
- ¾ cup grated parmigiana cheese

Directions for Cooking:

1. Place the beans, artichokes and water in the Instant Pot.
2. Close the lid and press the Fish/Veg/Steam button. Set the cooking time to 15 minutes.
3. Do quick pressure release and drain the water.
4. In a food processor, place the beans and artichokes.
5. Season with lemon juice, garlic, yogurt, salt and pepper.
6. Pulse until fine.
7. Add the grated parmigiana cheese.

Nutrition information:

Calories per serving: 134; Carbohydrates: 20.95g; Protein: 9.36g; Fat:3.27g; Sugar: 3.46g; Sodium: 629mg

---

370. Colorful Peperonata Sauce

(Servings: 6, Cooking Time: 6 minutes)

Ingredients:

- 1 tablespoon olive oil
- 1 red onion, sliced into strips
- 2 cloves of garlic
- 2 red peppers, sliced into thick strips
- 2 yellow peppers, sliced into thick strips
- 1 green pepper, thinly sliced
- 2 medium tomatoes, sliced
- 1 bunch of basil
- Salt and pepper

Directions for Cooking:

1. Without the lid on, press the sauté button and heat the oil.
2. Sauté the onion and garlic for 3 minutes.
3. Add the peppers and tomatoes.
4. Stir in basil and season with salt and pepper to taste.
5. Close the lid, press cancel, press manual, and adjust the cooking time to 3 minutes.
6. Do a QPR.
7. Adjust seasoning to taste and enjoy.

Nutrition information:

Calories per serving: 36; Carbohydrates: 3.55g; Protein: 0.68g; Fat: 2.38g; Sugar:1.92g; Sodium: 31mg

---

371. Creamy Chicken Liver Pate

(Servings: 8, Cooking Time: 15 minutes)

Ingredients:

- 1 tablespoon butter
- ¾ pounds chicken liver
- 1 onion, chopped
- 1 bay leaf
- ¼ cup red wine
- 2 anchovies in oil
- 1 tablespoon capers
- 1 teaspoon rum
- Salt and pepper to taste

Directions for Cooking:

1. Without the lid on, place butter in the Instant Pot and press the Meat button.
2. Add the chicken livers, onions and bay leaves. Stir to combine everything.
3. Close the lid and adjust the cooking time to 15 minutes.
4. Once the Instant Pot is done, do natural pressure release.
5. Remove the bay leaves and transfer the contents in a food processor or blender.
6. Add the red wine, anchovies, capers, and rum.
7. Season with salt and pepper.
8. Pulse until smooth.

Nutrition information:
Calories per serving: 111; Carbohydrates:4.68g; Protein: 6.32g; Fat: 7.1g; Sugar: 0.88g; Sodium:239mg

---

372. Olive Oil & Eggplant Dip

(Servings: 6, Cooking Time: 5 minutes)

Ingredients:

- 4 tablespoon olive oil
- 2-pounds eggplant, sliced
- 4 garlic cloves
- 1 teaspoon salt
- 1 lemon, juiced
- 1 tablespoon tahini
- ⅓ cup black olives, pitted and sliced
- A few sprigs of thyme
- A dash of extra virgin oil

Directions for Cooking:

1. Press the Fish/Veg/Steam button on the Instant Pot.
2. Heat the oil and add the eggplants. Fry the eggplants for 3 minutes on each side. Stir in the garlic.
3. Add 1 cup of water and close the lid. Press the Fish/Veg/Steam and cook for 5 minutes.
4. Do natural pressure release and take the eggplants out and transfer to a food processor.
5. Add in salt, lemon juice and tahini.
6. Pulse until smooth.
7. Place in a bowl and garnish with olives, thyme and a dash of extra virgin olive oil.

Nutrition information:
Calories per serving: 155; Carbohydrates: 16.8g; Protein: 2g; Fat:11.7g; Sugar: 5.6g; Sodium: 820.9mg

---

373. Buffalo Chicken Dip

(Servings: 15, Cooking Time: 20 minutes)

Ingredients:

- 2 chicken breasts
- 2 (8-ounce) packages of cream cheese (I used low-fat)
- 1 cup ranch dressing or you can use blue cheese dressing if you want
- 3/4 cup Louisiana hot sauce
- 2 cups shredded cheddar cheese
- 3 Tbs. butter
- 2 green onions, chopped
- 2-3 packages of Crunch master Crackers

Directions for Cooking:

1. Mix in ranch, hot sauce, butter, cream cheese, and chicken in instant Pot.
2. Close Instant Pot, press the Manual button, choose high settings, and set time to 20 minutes.
3. Once done cooking, do a QPR.
4. Remove chicken and mix in cheese.
5. Shred chicken and return to pot. Mix well.
6. Sprinkle with green onions.
7. Serve and enjoy with crackers.

Nutrition information:
Calories per serving: 270; Carbohydrates: 6.1g; Protein: 20.6g; Fat: 18.0g; Sugar:1.9g; Sodium: 607mg

---

374. Huge Vat of Tomato Sauce

(Servings: 8, Cooking Time: 25 minutes)

Ingredients:

- 4 tablespoons olive oil
- 2-3 medium yellow onions, sliced into rings
- 2 large carrots, roughly chopped
- 1 celery stalk, roughly chopped
- 6 pounds (3k) plum tomatoes, quartered
- 6-8 fresh basil leaves

Directions for Cooking:

1. Press sauté and heat oil.
2. Sauté onions for 5 minutes.
3. Add celery and carrots, sauté for 5 minutes.
4. Add tomatoes and mix well. Mash tomatoes with a potato masher. Cook until it begins to boil.
5. Close Instant Pot, press the Manual button, choose high settings, and set time to 5 minutes.
6. Once done cooking, do a QPR.
7. Mix contents well. With an immersion blender, puree tomatoes.
8. Transfer to jars for storage and use when ready.

Nutrition information:
Calories per serving: 171.6; Carbohydrates: 0.4g; Protein: 4.0g; Fat: 8.4g; Sugar:0.4g; Sodium: 48mg

---

375. Strawberry Jam

(Servings: 20, Cooking Time: 26 minutes)

Ingredients:

- 2 pounds fresh strawberries , hulled and halved
- 1 cup granulated sugar
- 2 Tablespoons lemon juice
- 3 Tablespoons cornstarch
- 1 1/2 Tablespoons water

Directions for Cooking:

1. Mix in lemon juice, sugar, and strawberries in Instant Pot. Let it stand for 10 minutes.
2. Close Instant Pot, press the Manual button, choose high settings, and set time to 1 minutes.
3. Once done cooking, do a 15-minute natural release and then a QPR.
4. Mix water and cornstarch in a small bowl. Stir in pot and stir until thickened.
5. Let jam cool completely and transfer to a lidded jar.

Nutrition information:
Calories per serving: 58; Carbohydrates: 14.7g; Protein: 0.3g; Fat: 0.1g; Sugar:12.2g; Sodium: 1.0mg

---

1000 Days Instant pot meal plan

Instant Pot Meal Plan	The meal plan for 1st month			
	Week 1	Week 2	Week 3	Week 4
SUN	1.Wild West Style Omelet Quiche	2.Mini Frittata from Leftover Meat	3.No-Crust Quiche with Spinach & Tomato	4.Breakfast Egg Casserole Mexican Style
MON	52.Instant Pot Pork Carnitas	54.Pork Tenderloin in Garlic Herb Rub	56.Instant Pot Gumbo	55.Hearty Pork Black Bean Nachos
TUE	106.Chinese Take-out General Tso's Chicken	107.Best Instant Pot Chicken Breast	108.Hawaiian Chicken Instant Pot	109.Honey Bourbon Chicken
WED	168.Miso &BokChoy on Sesame-Ginger Salmon	170.Easy Shrimp Pasta	171.Salmon Quickie	169.Alaskan Crab Legs in Instant Pot
THUS	200.Instant Pot Black Bean Chili	201Vegetarian Mushroom Bourguignon	202.Vegetarian Fajita Pasta	203.Instant Pot Tomato Soup
FRI	258.Singaporean Prawn and Pork Ribs Noodle Soup	259.Chicken Wonton Soup	260.Instant Pot Mexican Chicken Tomato Soup	261.Instant Pot Chicken Rice Porridge
SAT	298.Shrimp, Mushrooms & Asparagus Risotto	299.Wild Rice Pilaf	300.Pasta Puttanesca	301.Cheesy & Easy Beef Bowties

Instant Pot Meal Plan	The meal plan for 2nd month			
	Week 1	Week 2	Week 3	Week 4
SUN	5.Peppers, Cheese & Sausage Frittata	6.Decadent Eggs in Ramekins	7.Hash Brown and Egg Casserole	8.Walnut-Banana Oats
MON	53.Instant Korean Ribs	57.Barbecue Pulled Pork	58.Spare Ribs and Black Bean Sauce	59.Instant Pot Mesquite Ribs
TUE	106.Chinese Take-out General Tso's Chicken	107.Best Instant Pot Chicken Breast	108.Hawaiian Chicken Instant Pot	109.Honey Bourbon Chicken
WED	172.Creamy Parmesan-Herb Sauce Over Salmon	173.Easy Steamed Mussels	174.Easy Fish Tacos	175.Mascarpone-Salmon Risotto
THUS	204.One-Pot Refried Black Beans	205.Pasta Mediterranean	206.Cilantro Lime Quinoa Salad	207.Mashed Cauliflower Casserole

FRI	262.New England clam chowder	263.Vegan Ginger Noodle Soup	264.Instant Pot Salmon Tortellini Soup	265.Instant Pot Chicken Ramen
SAT	302.Fettucine Alfredo	303.Goulash	304Shrimp-Clam Cocktail Risotto	305.Broccoli-Beef Rice

Instant Pot Meal Plan	The meal plan for 3rd month			
	Week 1	Week 2	Week 3	Week 4
SUN	9.Creamy Oats with Peaches	10.Eggs & Ham Brekky Casserole	11.Smoked Salmon & Eggs in Ramekins	12.Nutty-Strawberry Oatmeal
MON	60.Ginger Pork Shogayaki	61.Instant Pot Hoisin Meatballs	62.Beer-Braised Pulled Ham	64.Chinese Pork Bone Soup
TUE	110.Creamy Tuscan Garlic Chicken	111.Chili Lime Chicken Thighs	112.One Pot Peruvian Chicken	113.Chicken Cacciatore
WED	176.Shrimp Scampi in Instant Pot	177.Salmon with Pepper-Lemon	178.Feta & Tomatoes on Shrimp	179.Salmon on Rice Pilaf
THUS	208.Instant Pot Creamy Garlic and Veggies Pasta	209.Instant Pot Black Bean Soup	210.Cauliflower and Pasta Alfredo	211.Instant Pot Mushroom Risotto
FRI	266.Instant Pot Summer Soup	267.Lebanese Chicken Soup	268.Fish and Potato Chowder	269.Zuppa Toscana
SAT	306.Easy-Creamy Ziti	307.Chicken Noodle Casserole	308.Saffron Rice	309.Mac and Cheese

Instant Pot Meal Plan	The meal plan for 4th month			
	Week 1	Week 2	Week 3	Week 4
SUN	13.Vanilla-Latte Oatmeal	14.Egg & Bacon Breakfast Risotto	15.Breakfast Quinoa with Cinnamon-Apple	16.Strawberry-Cheesecake Flavored Breakfast Quinoa
MON	65.Shrimp Pork Dumplings (Humai)	63.Sweet Balsamic Pork	66.Instant Pot Korean Beef	68.Instant Pot Mongolian Beef
TUE	114.Instant Pot Chicken and Dumplings	115.Instant Pot Mississippi Chicken	116.Instant Pot Butter Chicken	117.Chinese Takeout Sweet and Sour Chicken
WED	180.Lemon-Tahini Sauce over Salmon	182.Crab Quiche without Crust	183.Ginger-Orange Sauce over Salmon	184.Salmon with Shoyu-Pineapple Sauce
THUS	212.Instant Pot Pulled BBQ Jackfruit	213.Easy Autumn Soup	214.Veggie Spanish rice	215.Instant Pot Steamed Cauliflower

FRI	270.Seattle Seafood Chowder	271.Chicken and Corn Chowder	272.Butternut Squash Apple Soup	273.Spicy Tomato Chicken Soup
SAT	310.Creamy Chicken Pasta the Italian Way	311.Chili Mac n Cheese	312.Cheesy-Tuna Pasta	313.Beef Enchilada Pasta

Instant Pot Meal Plan	**The meal plan for 5th month**			
	Week 1	**Week 2**	**Week 3**	**Week 4**
SUN	17.Cornmeal-Porridge Jamaican Style Brekky	18.Traditional Pancake in Instant Pot	19.Oat, Millet & Apple Porridge	20.Hashed Sweet Potato
MON	69.Instant Pot Barbacoa Beef	70.Instant Pot Beef Tips	71.Sesame Beef Asparagus Salad	72.Persian Beef Stew
TUE	118.Instant Pot Honey Garlic Chicken	119.Instant Pot Orange Chicken	120.One Pot Chicken Curry	121.Instant Pot Ranch Chicken
WED	181.Salmon Over Potatoes & Broccoli	185.Clams in Pale Ale	186.Shrimps with Spiced Pineapples	187.Citrusy Salmon en Papilote
THUS	216.Lemon Butter Broccoli	217.Sweet Potato Hash	218.Indian Green Bean Curried Potatoes	219.Easy Rustic Lentil Soup
FRI	274.Buffalo Chicken Soup	275.Broccoli Cheese Soup	276.Instant Pot Vegetable Beef Soup	277.Peasant Chicken and Veggie Soup
SAT	314.Easy Spaghetti	315.Cajun Chicken and Rice	316.Rice Pudding	317.Cinnamon-Raisin Rice Pudding

Instant Pot Meal Plan	**The meal plan for 6th month**			
	Week 1	**Week 2**	**Week 3**	**Week 4**
SUN	21.Cheesy Eggs in Instant Pot	22.Simple Breakfast Hash	23.Spinach, Sausage & Sweet Potato Hash	24.Potato Hash with Spanish Chorizo
MON	73.Instant Pot Beef Curry	74.Instant Pot Beef Stew Bourguignon	78.Instant Pot Meatloaf	75.Instant Pot Shredded Beef
TUE	122.Instant Pot Gingered Orange Chicken	123.Instant Pot Cashew Chicken	124.Taiwanese Chicken San Bei Ji	125.Instant Pot Teriyaki Chicken
WED	188.Easy Sweet-Soy Salmon	189.Asparagus & Salmon with Buttered Garlic Sauce	190.Olive & Tuna Rigatoni	191.Orange-Ginger Sauce over Fish

THUS	220.Organic Spinach Pasta	221.Vegan Pasta Puttanesca	222.Broccoli Macaroni and Cheese	223.Instant Pot Garlic Hummus
FRI	278.Cabbage Soup with Ground Beef	279 Instant Pot French Onion Soup	280.Vegan Red Lentil Soup	281.Cream of Celery Soup
SAT	318.Red Beans and Rice	319.Spicy Mushroom Fried Rice	320.Spicy Mexican Chicken and Rice	321.Cooking a Simple Rice in Instant Pot

Instant Pot Meal Plan	The meal plan for 7th month			
	Week 1	Week 2	Week 3	Week 4
SUN	25.French Toast Casserole	26.Ranch Dressed Bacon-Potato Brekky	27.Banana Bread for Breakfast	28.Slow Cooked Cinnamon-Oats
MON	77.Chili Lime Steak Bowl	79.Simple Instant Pot Beef Stew	80.Instant Pot Beef Burritos	81.Instant Pot Picadillo
TUE	125. Instant Pot Teriyaki Chicken	126.Spicy Chicken Rice Meal	127.Instant Pot Chicken and Corn Soup	128.Instant Pot Hawaiian Chicken
WED	192.Salmon Croquette	193.Dill & Lemon Salmon	194.Asian Style Salmon Soy-Free	195.Easy Tuna Pasta Casserole
THUS	224.Cauliflower and Potato Soup	225.One-Pot Vegetarian Lentil Tortilla Soup	226.Vegan BBQ Meatballs	227.Simple Garden Pasta
FRI	282.Instant Pot Pork Shank Carrots Soup	283.Instant Pot Beef and Vegetable Soup	284.Unstuffed Cabbage Roll Soup	285.Instant Pot Beef Borscht
SAT	322.Shrimp Scampi Paella	323.Coconut Rice	324.Mexican Rice	325.Mexican Beefy Rice

Instant Pot Meal Plan	The meal plan for 8th month			
	Week 1	Week 2	Week 3	Week 4
SUN	29.Another Breakfast Burrito Recipe	30.Easy-Cheesy Breakfast Egg Casserole	31.Broccoli and Egg Casserole	32.Scotch Eggs in Pressure Cooke
MON	82.Tex Mex Beef Stew	83.Instant Pot Beef Tips	79.Simple Instant Pot Beef Stew	84.Instant Pot Mediterranean Beef
TUE	129.Greek Chicken Rice	130.Instant Pot Butter Chicken	131.Honey Mustard Curry Chicken	132.Instant Pot Simple Chicken Dinner

WED	196.Mahi-Mahi in Sweet Spicy sauce	197.Caramel Salmon Vietnamese Style	198.Tilapia with Basil-Tomato Dressing	199.Cod the Mediterranean Way
THUS	228.Vegan Lasagna Soup	229.Vegan "Buttered" Chicken	230.One-Pot Cauliflower Cheddar Pasta	231.Instant Pot Tempeh Tajine
FRI	286.Lemon Chicken Orzo	287.Winter Melon and Tofu Soup	288.Mexican Albondigas Soup	289.Butternut Squash and Cauliflower Soup
SAT	326.Cajun Red Beans & Rice	327.Chai Spiced Rice Pudding	328.Chinese Sausage on Brown Rice	329.Curried Tahini Carrots

Instant Pot Meal Plan	**The meal plan for 9th month**			
	Week 1	**Week 2**	**Week 3**	**Week 4**
SUN	33.Buckwheat Porridge in Instant Pot	34.Maple-Cranberry Oatmeal	35.Pepper, Ham & Broccoli Frittata	36.Carrot Cake Flavored Oatmeal
MON	85.Instant Pot Taco Meat	86.Beef Cheesy Potatoes	87.Sweet Potato Chili Recipe	88.Instant Pot Stuffed Peppers
TUE	133.Instant Pot Chicken Pot Pie	134.Creamy Salsa Chicken	135.Balsamic Ginger Chicken	136.Buffalo Chicken Wings
WED	168.Miso & BokChoy on Sesame-Ginger Salmon	Cherry-Chocolate Pudding	170.Easy Shrimp Pasta	171.Salmon Quickie
THUS	232.Veggie Shepherd's Pie	233.Vegan Baked Beans	234.One-Pot Vegetable Barley Soup	235.Creamy Tomato Soup
FRI	290.Instant Pot Taco Soup	291.En Caldo De Res Soup	292.Cream of Asparagus Soup	293.Sweet Potato, Black Bean, And Quinoa Chili Soup
SAT	330.Zucchini & Walnut Bread	298.Shrimp, Mushrooms & Asparagus Risotto	299.Wild Rice Pilaf	300.Pasta Puttanesca

Instant Pot Meal Plan	**The meal plan for 10th month**			
	Week 1	**Week 2**	**Week 3**	**Week 4**
SUN	37.Cheese and Bacon Quiche	38.6-Ingredient Breakfast Granola	39.Simple Cinnamon French Toast	40.Coconut-Rice Pudding in Instant Pot
MON	89.Braised Brisket	90.Instant Pot Corned Beef and Cabbages	91.Instant Pot Guinness Beef Stew Recipe	92.Easy Instant Pot Beef
TUE	137.Instant Pot Korean Chicken	C138.hipotle Chicken Tacos	139.BBQ Pulled Chicken Sliders	140.Instant Pot Salsa Verde Chicken

WED	169.Alaskan Crab Legs in Instant Pot	172.Creamy Parmesan-Herb Sauce Over Salmon	173.Easy Steamed Mussels	331.Nuts & Cherry Delight
THUS	236.One-Pot Veggie Curry Dish	237.Vegan Carrot Ginger Soup	238.Split Pea Soup	239.Three Cheese Mushroom and Tortellini
FRI	294.Ham and White Bean Soup	295.Easy Kimchi Soup	296.Instant Pot Tortellini Soup	297.Beef Stroganoff Soup
SAT	332.Cranberry Nut Bread	301.Cheesy & Easy Beef Bowties	302.Fettucine Alfredo	303.Goulash

Instant Pot Meal Plan	**The meal plan for 11th month**			
	Week 1	**Week 2**	**Week 3**	**Week 4**
SUN	41.An Extra-Ordinary Breakfast Casserole	42.Cornbread for Breakfast	43.Delicata and Apple Porridge	44.Ham, Tomatoes, and Spinach Frittata
MON	93.Instant Pot Ghormeh Sabzi	94.BBQ Instant Pot Ribs	95.Instant Pot Adovado	96.Asian Pot Roast
TUE	141.Instant Pot Ginger Garlic Drumsticks	142.Instant Pot Whole Chicken	143.Instant Pot Chicken Adobo	144.Instant Pot Kung Pao Chicken
WED	174.Easy Fish Tacos	175.Mascarpone-Salmon Risotto	176.Shrimp Scampi in Instant Pot	Choco-Dipped Frozen Bananas
THUS	240.Curried Black Eyed Peas	241.Quinoa Burrito Bowls	242.Instant Pot Veggie Clear Soup	243.Cheesy Lentils and Brown Rice
FRI	334.Dark Chocolate Glaze	259.Chicken Wonton Soup	258.Singaporean Prawn and Pork Ribs Noodle Soup	260.Instant Pot Mexican Chicken Tomato Soup
SAT	304.Shrimp-Clam Cocktail Risotto	305.Broccoli-Beef Rice	306.Easy-Creamy Ziti	307.Chicken Noodle Casserole

Instant Pot Meal Plan	**The meal plan for 12th month**			
	Week 1	**Week 2**	**Week 3**	**Week 4**
SUN	45.Breakfast Fajita Casserole	46.Slow Cooked Oats the Irish Way	47.Meat Lovers No-Crust Quiche	48.Quiche the Mexican Way
MON	97.Apple Bacon BBQ Pulled Pork	98.Balsamic-Honey Pork Roast	99.Apple Barbecue Ribs	100.Pork Tenderloin Green Chili
TUE	145.Instant Pot Shredded Buffalo Chicken	146.Instant Pot Chicken Saag	147.Instant Pot Chicken Tacos	148.Coconut Chicken Curry

WED	177.Salmon with Pepper-Lemon	178.Feta & Tomatoes on Shrimp	179.Salmon on Rice Pilaf	180.Lemon-Tahini Sauce over Salmon
THUS	244.Spicy Chili and Beer Macaroni	245.Vegetarian Quinoa Chili	246.Instant Pot Acorn Squash	247.Instant Pot Chickpea Gumbo
FRI	260.Instant Pot Chicken Rice Porridge	262.New England clam chowder	338.Dark Chocolate Hot Cocoa	263.Vegan Ginger Noodle Soup
SAT	308.Saffron Rice	309.Mac and Cheese	310.Creamy Chicken Pasta the Italian Way	339.Lemon Blueberry Cake

Instant Pot Meal Plan	**The meal plan for 13th month**			
	Week 1	**Week 2**	**Week 3**	**Week 4**
SUN	49.Zucchini-Choco Breakfast Cake	50.Creamy potato Hash Breakfast Casserole	51.Nutella-Raspberry Breakfast Porridge	337.Choco-Coco Macaroons
MON	101.Teriyaki Pork Tenderloin	102.Southwestern Pork Chops	103.Tropical Beef with Peppers and Pineapple	104.Herb-Crusted Beef
TUE	149.One-Pot Thai Red Curry	150.Jamaican Chicken Curry	151.Instant Pot Chicken Tetrazzini	152.Instant Pot Chicken Shawarma
WED	182.Crab Quiche without Crust	183.Ginger-Orange Sauce over Salmon	184.Salmon with Shoyu-Pineapple Sauce	181Salmon Over Potatoes & Broccoli
THUS	248.Instant Pot Pinto Beans	249.Instant Pot Hearty Vegetable and Brown Rice Soup	250.Portobello Pot Roast	251.Creamy Parsnips and Chive Soup
FRI	264.Instant Pot Salmon Tortellini Soup	265.Instant Pot Chicken Ramen	266.Instant Pot Summer Soup	267.Lebanese Chicken Soup
SAT	311.Chili Mac n Cheese	340.Brownie Fudge	312.Cheesy-Tuna Pasta	313.Beef Enchilada Pasta

Instant Pot Meal Plan	**The meal plan for 14th month**			
	Week 1	**Week 2**	**Week 3**	**Week 4**
SUN	1.Wild West Style Omelet Quiche	2.Mini Frittata from Leftover Meat	3.No-Crust Quiche with Spinach & Tomato	4.Breakfast Egg Casserole Mexican Style
MON	105.Caribbean Pineapple Filet Mignon	52.Instant Pot Pork Carnitas	54.Pork Tenderloin in Garlic Herb Rub	56.Instant Pot Gumbo

TUE	153.One-Pot Mediterranean Chicken Paste	154.Creamy Garlic Tuscan Chicken Pasta	155.Instant Pot Chicken Soup	156.Instant Pot Chicken Chowder
WED	185.Clams in Pale Ale	341.Berry Compote	186.Shrimps with Spiced Pineapples	187.Citrusy Salmon en Papilote
THUS	252.Vegan Potato Corn Chowder	253.Smoky Pecan Brussels sprouts	254.Maple Bourbon Sweet Potato Chili	255.Cauliflower Tikka Masala
FRI	268.Fish and Potato Chowder	269.Zuppa Toscana	270.Seattle Seafood Chowder	342.Creamy Choco Mousse
SAT	314.Easy Spaghetti	315.Cajun Chicken and Rice	316.Rice Pudding	317.Cinnamon-Raisin Rice Pudding

Instant Pot Meal Plan	**The meal plan for 15th month**			
	Week 1	**Week 2**	**Week 3**	**Week 4**
SUN	343.Vanilla Jello	5.Peppers, Cheese & Sausage Frittata	6.Decadent Eggs in Ramekins	7.Hash Brown and Egg Casserole
MON	55.Hearty Pork Black Bean Nachos	53.Instant Korean Ribs	57.Barbecue Pulled Pork	Salted Caramel Icing on Apple Bread
TUE	157.Instant Pot Chicken and Rice Soup	158.Instant Pot Chicken Fajita Soup	159.Instant Pot Chicken Stock	160.White Bean Chicken Chili
WED	188.Easy Sweet-Soy Salmon	189.Asparagus & Salmon with Buttered Garlic Sauce	190.Olive & Tuna Rigatoni	191.Orange-Ginger Sauce over Fish
THUS	256.Vegan Udon Noodles Bowl	257.Basmati Rice Pilaf	200.Instant Pot Black Bean Chili	201.Vegetarian Mushroom Bourguignon
FRI	271.Chicken and Corn Chowder	272.Butternut Squash Apple Soup	273.Spicy Tomato Chicken Soup	274.Buffalo Chicken Soup
SAT	318.Red Beans and Rice	319.Spicy Mushroom Fried Rice	320.Spicy Mexican Chicken and Rice	321.Cooking a Simple Rice in Instant Pot

Instant Pot Meal Plan	**The meal plan for 16th month**			
	Week 1	**Week 2**	**Week 3**	**Week 4**
SUN	8.Walnut-Banana Oats	9.Creamy Oats with Peaches	10.Eggs & Ham Brekky Casserole	345.Mini Lava Cake
MON	58.Spare Ribs and Black Bean Sauce	59.Instant Pot Mesquite Ribs	60.Ginger Pork Shogayaki	61.Instant Pot Hoisin Meatballs

TUE	346.Apple Crisp	161.Low Carb Poblano Chicken Soup	162.Instant Pot Chicken Curry Soup	163.Instant Pot Chicken Taco Soup
WED	192.Salmon Croquette	193.Dill & Lemon Salmon	194.Asian Style Salmon Soy-Free	195.Easy Tuna Pasta Casserole
THUS	202.Vegetarian Fajita Pasta	203.Instant Pot Tomato Soup	204.One-Pot Refried Black Beans	205.Pasta Mediterranean
FRI	275.Broccoli Cheese Soup	276.Instant Pot Vegetable Beef Soup	347.Thai Coconut Rice	277.Peasant Chicken and Veggie Soup
SAT	322.Shrimp Scampi Paella	323.Coconut Rice	324.Mexican Rice	325.Mexican Beefy Rice

Instant Pot Meal Plan	**The meal plan for 17th month**			
	Week 1	**Week 2**	**Week 3**	**Week 4**
SUN	11.Smoked Salmon & Eggs in Ramekins	12.Nutty-Strawberry Oatmeal	13.Vanilla-Latte Oatmeal	14.Egg & Bacon Breakfast Risotto
MON	62.Beer-Braised Pulled Ham	348.Apple sauce	64.Chinese Pork Bone Soup	65.Shrimp Pork Dumplings (Humai)
TUE	164.Healthy Chicken Stew	165.Paleo Buffalo Chicken Chili	166.Buffalo Chicken Meatballs	350.Deliciously Good Peach Dessert
WED	349.Custard Cheesecake	196.Mahi-Mahi in Sweet Spicy sauce	197.Caramel Salmon Vietnamese Style	198.Tilapia with Basil-Tomato Dressing
THUS	206.Cilantro Lime Quinoa Salad	207.Mashed Cauliflower Casserole	208.Instant Pot Creamy Garlic and Veggies Pasta	209.Instant Pot Black Bean Soup
FRI	278.Cabbage Soup with Ground Beef	279.Instant Pot French Onion Soup	280.Vegan Red Lentil Soup	281.Cream of Celery Soup
SAT	326.Cajun Red Beans & Rice	327.Chai Spiced Rice Pudding	328.Chinese Sausage on Brown Rice	298.Shrimp, Mushrooms & Asparagus Risotto

Instant Pot Meal Plan	**The meal plan for 18th month**			
	Week 1	**Week 2**	**Week 3**	**Week 4**
SUN	351.Berry Cobbler	15.Breakfast Quinoa with Cinnamon-Apple	16.Strawberry-Cheesecake Flavored Breakfast Quinoa	17.Cornmeal-Porridge Jamaican Style Brekky

MON	63.Sweet Balsamic Pork	66.Instant Pot Korean Beef	68.Instant Pot Mongolian Beef	69.Instant Pot Barbacoa Beef
TUE	167.Instant Pot Frozen Chicken	106.Chinese Take-out General Tso's Chicken	107.Best Instant Pot Chicken Breast	352.Mini Peanut Butter Choco Cakes
WED	199.Cod the Mediterranean Way	168.Miso & Bok Choy on Sesame-Ginger Salmon	170.Easy Shrimp Pasta	171.Salmon Quickie
THUS	210.Cauliflower and Pasta Alfredo	211.Instant Pot Mushroom Risotto	212.Instant Pot Pulled BBQ Jackfruit	213.Easy Autumn Soup
FRI	282.Instant Pot Pork Shank Carrots Soup	354.Mocha Pudding Cake	283.Instant Pot Beef and Vegetable Soup	284.Unstuffed Cabbage Roll Soup
SAT	299.Wild Rice Pilaf	300.Pasta Puttanesca	301.Cheesy & Easy Beef Bowties	302.Fettucine Alfredo

Instant Pot Meal Plan	**The meal plan for 19th month**			
	Week 1	**Week 2**	**Week 3**	**Week 4**
SUN	18.Traditional Pancake in Instant Pot	19.Oat, Millet & Apple Porridge	20.Hashed Sweet Potato	21.Cheesy Eggs in Instant Pot
MON	353.Choco Fudge	70.Instant Pot Beef Tips	71.Sesame Beef Asparagus Salad	72.Persian Beef Stew
TUE	108.Hawaiian Chicken Instant Pot	109.Honey Bourbon Chicken	110.Creamy Tuscan Garlic Chicken	111.Chili Lime Chicken Thighs
WED	169.Alaskan Crab Legs in Instant Pot	172.Creamy Parmesan-Herb Sauce Over Salmon	173.Easy Steamed Mussels	355.Salted Choco Treat
THUS	214.Veggie Spanish rice	215.Instant Pot Steamed Cauliflower	216.Lemon Butter Broccoli	217.Sweet Potato Hash
FRI	285.Instant Pot Beef Borscht	286.Lemon Chicken Orzo	287.Winter Melon and Tofu Soup	288.Mexican Albondigas Soup
SAT	303.Goulash	304.Shrimp-Clam Cocktail Risotto	305.Broccoli-Beef Rice	306.Easy-Creamy Ziti

Instant Pot Meal Plan	**The meal plan for 20th month**			
	Week 1	**Week 2**	**Week 3**	**Week 4**
SUN	22.Simple Breakfast Hash	356.Tapioca Pudding	23.Spinach, Sausage & Sweet Potato Hash	24.Potato Hash with Spanish Chorizo

1000 DAYS MEAL PLAN

MON	73.Instant Pot Beef Curry	74.Instant Pot Beef Stew Bourguignon	78.Instant Pot Meatloaf	75.Instant Pot Shredded Beef
TUE	112.One Pot Peruvian Chicken	113. Chicken Cacciatore	114.Instant Pot Chicken and Dumplings	115.Instant Pot Mississippi Chicken
WED	174.Easy Fish Tacos	175.Mascarpone-Salmon Risotto	357.Cherry Compote	176.Shrimp Scampi in Instant Pot
THUS	218.Indian Green Bean Curried Potatoes	219.Easy Rustic Lentil Soup	220.Organic Spinach Pasta	221.Vegan Pasta Puttanesca
FRI	289.Butternut Squash and Cauliflower Soup	290.Instant Pot Taco Soup	291.En Caldo De Res Soup	292.Cream of Asparagus Soup
SAT	358.Hazelnut Flan	307.Chicken Noodle Casserole	308.Saffron Rice	309.Mac and Cheese

Instant Pot Meal Plan	**The meal plan for 21st month**			
	Week 1	**Week 2**	**Week 3**	**Week 4**
SUN	26.Ranch Dressed Bacon-Potato Brekky	25.French Toast Casserole	27.Banana Bread for Breakfast	28.Slow Cooked Cinnamon-Oats
MON	360.Keto Ranch Dip	77.Chili Lime Steak Bowl	67.Italian Beef Dinner	80.Instant Pot Beef Burritos
TUE	116.Instant Pot Butter Chicken	117.Chinese Takeout Sweet and Sour Chicken	118.Instant Pot Honey Garlic Chicken	119.Instant Pot Orange Chicken
WED	177.Salmon with Pepper-Lemon	178.Feta & Tomatoes on Shrimp	179.Salmon on Rice Pilaf	361.All-Around Gravy
THUS	222.Broccoli Macaroni and Cheese	223.Instant Pot Garlic Hummus	224.Cauliflower and Potato Soup	225.One-Pot Vegetarian Lentil Tortilla Soup
FRI	293.Sweet Potato, Black Bean, And Quinoa Chili Soup	294.Ham and White Bean Soup	295.Easy Kimchi Soup	296.Instant Pot Tortellini Soup
SAT	310.Creamy Chicken Pasta the Italian Way	311.Chili Mac n Cheese	312.Cheesy-Tuna Pasta	313.Beef Enchilada Pasta

Instant Pot Meal Plan	**The meal plan for 22nd month**			
	Week 1	**Week 2**	**Week 3**	**Week 4**
SUN	29.Another Breakfast Burrito Recipe	30.Easy-Cheesy Breakfast Egg Casserole	362.Béarnaise Sauce	31.Broccoli and Egg Casserole

1000 DAYS MEAL PLAN

MON	80.Instant Pot Picadillo	82.Tex Mex Beef Stew	83.Instant Pot Beef Tips	79 . Simple Instant Pot Beef Stew
TUE	120.One Pot Chicken Curry	121.Instant Pot Ranch Chicken	122.Instant Pot Gingered Orange Chicken	123.Instant Pot Cashew Chicken
WED	363.Caesar Salad Dressing	180.Lemon-Tahini Sauce over Salmon	182.Crab Quiche without Crust	183.Ginger-Orange Sauce over Salmon
THUS	226.Vegan BBQ Meatballs	227.Simple Garden Pasta	228.Vegan Lasagna Soup	229.Vegan "Buttered" Chicken
FRI	297.Beef Stroganoff Soup	258.Singaporean Prawn and Pork Ribs Noodle Soup	259.Chicken Wonton Soup	364.Cranberry Sauce
SAT	314Easy Spaghetti	315.Cajun Chicken and Rice	316.Rice Pudding	317.Cinnamon-Raisin Rice Pudding

Instant Pot Meal Plan	**The meal plan for 23rd month**			
	Week 1	**Week 2**	**Week 3**	**Week 4**
SUN	32.Scotch Eggs in Pressure Cooker	33.Buckwheat Porridge in Instant Pot	34.Maple-Cranberry Oatmeal	35.Pepper, Ham & Broccoli Frittata
MON	365.Chia-Blackberry Jam	84.Instant Pot Mediterranean Beef	85.Instant Pot Taco Meat	86.Beef Cheesy Potatoes
TUE	124.Taiwanese Chicken San Bei Ji	125.Instant Pot Teriyaki Chicken	339. Lemon Blueberry Cake	126.Spicy Chicken Rice Meal
WED	184.Salmon with Shoyu-Pineapple Sauce	181.Salmon Over Potatoes & Broccoli	185.Clams in Pale Ale	366.Caramel Sauce
THUS	230.One-Pot Cauliflower Cheddar Pasta	231.Instant Pot Tempeh Tajine	232.Veggie Shepherd's Pie	233.Vegan Baked Beans
FRI	367.Hot Fudge Sauce	260.Instant Pot Mexican Chicken Tomato Soup	261.Instant Pot Chicken Rice Porridge	262.New England clam chowder
SAT	318.Red Beans and Rice	319.Spicy Mushroom Fried Rice	320.Spicy Mexican Chicken and Rice	278.Cabbage Soup with Ground Beef

1000 DAYS MEAL PLAN

Instant Pot Meal Plan	The meal plan for 24th month			
	Week 1	Week 2	Week 3	Week 4
SUN	36.Carrot Cake Flavored Oatmeal	37.Cheese and Bacon Quiche	38.6-Ingredient Breakfast Granola	39.Simple Cinnamon French Toast
MON	87.Sweet Potato Chili Recipe	88.Instant Pot Stuffed Peppers	89.Braised Brisket	369.Creamy Artichoke Dip
TUE	370.Colorful Peperonata Sauce	127.Instant Pot Chicken and Corn Soup	128.Instant Pot Hawaiian Chicken	129.Greek Chicken Rice
WED	186.Shrimps with Spiced Pineapples	187.Citrusy Salmon en Papilote	371.Creamy Chicken Liver Pate	188.Easy Sweet-Soy Salmon
THUS	234.One-Pot Vegetable Barley Soup	235.Creamy Tomato Soup	236.One-Pot Veggie Curry Dish	237.Vegan Carrot Ginger Soup
FRI	263.Vegan Ginger Noodle Soup	264.Instant Pot Salmon Tortellini Soup	265.Instant Pot Chicken Ramen	372.Olive Oil & Eggplant Dip
SAT	321.Cooking a Simple Rice in Instant Pot	322.Shrimp Scampi Paella	323.Coconut Rice	324.Mexican Rice
Instant Pot Meal Plan	**The meal plan for 25th month**			
	Week 1	**Week 2**	**Week 3**	**Week 4**
SUN	40.Coconut-Rice Pudding in Instant Pot	41.An Extra-Ordinary Breakfast Casserole	42.Cornbread for Breakfast	359.Chickpea Hummus
MON	90.Instant Pot Corned Beef and Cabbages	91.Instant Pot Guinness Beef Stew Recipe	92.Easy Instant Pot Beef	93.Instant Pot Ghormeh Sabzi
TUE	130.Instant Pot Butter Chicken	131.Honey Mustard Curry Chicken	132.Instant Pot Simple Chicken Dinner	133.Instant Pot Chicken Pot Pie
WED	189.Asparagus & Salmon with Buttered Garlic Sauce	373.Buffalo Chicken Dip	190.Olive & Tuna Rigatoni	191.Orange-Ginger Sauce over Fish
THUS	238.Split Pea Soup	239.Three Cheese Mushroom and Tortellini	240.Curried Black Eyed Peas	241.Quinoa Burrito Bowls
FRI	266.Instant Pot Summer Soup	267.Lebanese Chicken Soup	268.Fish and Potato Chowder	269.Zuppa Toscana
SAT	325.Mexican Beefy Rice	326.Cajun Red Beans & Rice	327.Chai Spiced Rice Pudding	328.Chinese Sausage on Brown Rice

1000 DAYS MEAL PLAN

Instant Pot Meal Plan	The meal plan for 26th month			
	Week 1	**Week 2**	**Week 3**	**Week 4**
SUN	43.Delicata and Apple Porridge	44.Ham, Tomatoes, and Spinach Frittata	45.Breakfast Fajita Casserole	46.Slow Cooked Oats the Irish Way
MON	94.BBQ Instant Pot Ribs	95.Instant Pot Adovado	374.Huge Vat of Tomato Sauce	96.Asian Pot Roast
TUE	134.Creamy Salsa Chicken	135.Balsamic Ginger Chicken	136.Buffalo Chicken Wings	137.Instant Pot Korean Chicken
WED	368.Artichoke-Spinach Dip	192.Salmon Croquette	193.Dill & Lemon Salmon	194.Asian Style Salmon Soy-Free
THUS	242.Instant Pot Veggie Clear Soup	243.Cheesy Lentils and Brown Rice	244.Spicy Chili and Beer Macaroni	245.Vegetarian Quinoa Chili
FRI	270.Seattle Seafood Chowder	271.Chicken and Corn Chowder	375.Strawberry Jam	272.Butternut Squash Apple Soup
SAT	298.Shrimp, Mushrooms & Asparagus Risotto	299.Wild Rice Pilaf	300.Pasta Puttanesca	301.Cheesy & Easy Beef Bowties

Instant Pot Meal Plan	The meal plan for 27th month			
	Week 1	**Week 2**	**Week 3**	**Week 4**
SUN	Curried Tahini Carrots	47.Meat Lovers No-Crust Quiche	48.Quiche the Mexican Way	49.Zucchini-Choco Breakfast Cake
MON	97.Apple Bacon BBQ Pulled Pork	98.Balsamic-Honey Pork Roast	99.Apple Barbecue Ribs	100.Pork Tenderloin Green Chili
TUE	138.Chipotle Chicken Tacos	139.BBQ Pulled Chicken Sliders	330.Zucchini & Walnut Bread	140.Instant Pot Salsa Verde Chicken
WED	332.Cranberry Nut Bread	195.Easy Tuna Pasta Casserole	196.Mahi-Mahi in Sweet Spicy sauce	197.Caramel Salmon Vietnamese Style
THUS	246.Instant Pot Acorn Squash	247.Instant Pot Chickpea Gumbo	248.Instant Pot Pinto Beans	249.Instant Pot Hearty Vegetable and Brown Rice Soup
FRI	273.Spicy Tomato Chicken Soup	274.Buffalo Chicken Soup	275.Broccoli Cheese Soup	276.Instant Pot Vegetable Beef Soup
SAT	302.Fettucine Alfredo	303.Goulash	304.Shrimp-Clam Cocktail Risotto	333.Nuts & Dates Bar

1000 DAYS MEAL PLAN

Instant Pot Meal Plan	The meal plan for 28th month			
	Week 1	**Week 2**	**Week 3**	**Week 4**
SUN	50.Creamy potato Hash Breakfast Casserole	51.Nutella-Raspberry Breakfast Porridge	1.Wild West Style Omelet Quiche	2.Mini Frittata from Leftover Meat
MON	101.Teriyaki Pork Tenderloin	331.Nuts & Cherry Delight	102.Southwestern Pork Chops	103.Tropical Beef with Peppers and Pineapple
TUE	141.Instant Pot Ginger Garlic Drumsticks	142.Instant Pot Whole Chicken	143.Instant Pot Chicken Adobo	144.Instant Pot Kung Pao Chicken
WED	335.Cherry-Chocolate Pudding	198.Tilapia with Basil-Tomato Dressing	199.Cod the Mediterranean Way	168.Miso & BokChoy on Sesame-Ginger Salmon
THUS	250.Portobello Pot Roast	251.Creamy Parsnips and Chive Soup	252.Vegan Potato Corn Chowder	253.Smoky Pecan Brussels sprouts
FRI	277.Peasant Chicken and Veggie Soup	278.Cabbage Soup with Ground Beef	279.Instant Pot French Onion Soup	336.Choco-Dipped Frozen Bananas
SAT	305.Broccoli-Beef Rice	E306.asy-Creamy Ziti	307.Chicken Noodle Casserole	308.Saffron Rice

Instant Pot Meal Plan	The meal plan for 29th month			
	Week 1	**Week 2**	**Week 3**	**Week 4**
SUN	3.No-Crust Quiche with Spinach & Tomato	4.Breakfast Egg Casserole Mexican Style	5.Peppers, Cheese & Sausage Frittata	6.Decadent Eggs in Ramekins
MON	334.Dark Chocolate Glaze	104.Herb-Crusted Beef	105.Caribbean Pineapple Filet Mignon	52.Instant Pot Pork Carnitas
TUE	145.Instant Pot Shredded Buffalo Chicken	146.Instant Pot Chicken Saag	147.Instant Pot Chicken Tacos	338.Dark Chocolate Hot Cocoa
WED	170.Easy Shrimp Pasta	339.Lemon Blueberry Cake	171.Salmon Quickie	169.Alaskan Crab Legs in Instant Pot
THUS	254.Maple Bourbon Sweet Potato Chili	255.Cauliflower Tikka Masala	256.Vegan Udon Noodles Bowl	257.Basmati Rice Pilaf
FRI	280.Vegan Red Lentil Soup	281.Cream of Celery Soup	282.Instant Pot Pork Shank Carrots Soup	283.Instant Pot Beef and Vegetable Soup

SAT	337.Choco-Coco Macaroons	309.Mac and Cheese	310.Creamy Chicken Pasta the Italian Way	311.Chili Mac n Cheese

Instant Pot Meal Plan	The meal plan for 30th month			
	Week 1	Week 2	Week 3	Week 4
SUN	7.Hash Brown and Egg Casserole	8.Walnut-Banana Oats	9.Creamy Oats with Peaches	10.Eggs & Ham Brekky Casserole
MON	340.Brownie Fudge	54.Pork Tenderloin in Garlic Herb Rub	56.Instant Pot Gumbo	55.Hearty Pork Black Bean Nachos
TUE	148.Coconut Chicken Curry	149.One-Pot Thai Red Curry	150.Jamaican Chicken Curry	151.Instant Pot Chicken Tetrazzini
WED	172.Creamy Parmesan-Herb Sauce Over Salmon	173.Easy Steamed Mussels	341.Berry Compote	174.Easy Fish Tacos
THUS	200.Instant Pot Black Bean Chili	201.Vegetarian Mushroom Bourguignon	202.Vegetarian Fajita Pasta	203.Instant Pot Tomato Soup
FRI	284.Unstuffed Cabbage Roll Soup	285.Instant Pot Beef Borscht	286.Lemon Chicken Orzo	342.Creamy Choco Mousse
SAT	312.Cheesy-Tuna Pasta	313.Beef Enchilada Pasta	314.Easy Spaghetti	315.Cajun Chicken and Rice

Instant Pot Meal Plan	The meal plan for 31st month			
	Week 1	Week 2	Week 3	Week 4
SUN	11.Smoked Salmon & Eggs in Ramekins	12.Nutty-Strawberry Oatmeal	13.Vanilla-Latte Oatmeal	14.Egg & Bacon Breakfast Risotto
MON	53.Instant Korean Ribs	57.Barbecue Pulled Pork	343.Vanilla Jello	58.Spare Ribs and Black Bean Sauce
TUE	152.Instant Pot Chicken Shawarma	153.One-Pot Mediterranean Chicken Paste	154.Creamy Garlic Tuscan Chicken Pasta	155.Instant Pot Chicken Soup
WED	344.Salted Caramel Icing on Apple Bread	175.Mascarpone-Salmon Risotto	176.Shrimp Scampi in Instant Pot	177.Salmon with Pepper-Lemon
THUS	204.One-Pot Refried Black Beans	205.Pasta Mediterranean	206.Cilantro Lime Quinoa Salad	207.Mashed Cauliflower Casserole
FRI	287.Winter Melon and Tofu Soup	288.Mexican Albondigas Soup	289.Butternut Squash and Cauliflower Soup	345.Mini Lava Cake

SAT	316.Rice Pudding	317.Cinnamon-Raisin Rice Pudding	318.Red Beans and Rice	319.Spicy Mushroom Fried Rice

Instant Pot Meal Plan	The meal plan for 32nd month			
	Week 1	Week 2	Week 3	Week 4
SUN	346.Apple Crisp	15.Breakfast Quinoa with Cinnamon-Apple	16.Strawberry-Cheesecake Flavored Breakfast Quinoa	17.Cornmeal-Porridge Jamaican Style Brekky
MON	59.Instant Pot Mesquite Ribs	60.Ginger Pork Shogayaki	61.Instant Pot Hoisin Meatballs	62.Beer-Braised Pulled Ham
TUE	156.Instant Pot Chicken Chowder	157.Instant Pot Chicken and Rice Soup	158.Instant Pot Chicken Fajita Soup	347.Thai Coconut Rice
WED	178.Feta & Tomatoes on Shrimp	179.Salmon on Rice Pilaf	180.Lemon-Tahini Sauce over Salmon	182.Crab Quiche without Crust
THUS	208.Instant Pot Creamy Garlic and Veggies Pasta	348.Apple sauce	209.Instant Pot Black Bean Soup	210.Cauliflower and Pasta Alfredo
FRI	290.Instant Pot Taco Soup	291.En Caldo De Res Soup	292.Cream of Asparagus Soup	293.Sweet Potato, Black Bean, And Quinoa Chili Soup
SAT	320.Spicy Mexican Chicken and Rice	321.Cooking a Simple Rice in Instant Pot	322.Shrimp Scampi Paella	323.Coconut Rice
Instant Pot Meal Plan	The meal plan for 33rd month			
	Week 1	Week 2	Week 3	Week 4
SUN	18.Traditional Pancake in Instant Pot	19.Oat, Millet & Apple Porridge	20.Hashed Sweet Potato	21.Cheesy Eggs in Instant Pot
MON	64.Chinese Pork Bone Soup	65.Shrimp Pork Dumplings (Humai)	63.Sweet Balsamic Pork	66.Instant Pot Korean Beef
TUE	349.Custard Cheese cake	159.Instant Pot Chicken Stock	160.White Bean Chicken Chili	161.Low Carb Poblano Chicken Soup
WED	183.Ginger-Orange Sauce over Salmon	184.Salmon with Shoyu-Pineapple Sauce	181.Salmon Over Potatoes & Broccoli	350.Deliciously Good Peach Dessert
THUS	211.Instant Pot Mushroom Risotto	212.Instant Pot Pulled BBQ Jackfruit	213.Easy Autumn Soup	214.Veggie Spanish rice

FRI	294.Ham and White Bean Soup	295.Easy Kimchi Soup	296.Instant Pot Tortellini Soup	297.Beef Stroganoff Soup
SAT	324.Mexican Rice	351.Berry Cobbler	325.Mexican Beefy Rice	326.Cajun Red Beans & Rice

Instant Pot Meal Plan	The meal plan for 34th month			
	Week 1	Week 2	Week 3	Week 4
SUN	22.Simple Breakfast Hash	23.Spinach, Sausage & Sweet Potato Hash	24.Potato Hash with Spanish Chorizo	25.French Toast Casserole
MON	68.Instant Pot Mongolian Beef	69.Instant Pot Barbacoa Beef	70.Instant PotBeef Tips	71.Sesame Beef Asparagus Salad
TUE	162.Instant Pot Chicken Curry Soup	352.Mini Peanut Butter Choco Cakes	163.Instant Pot Chicken Taco Soup	164.Healthy Chicken Stew
WED	185.Clams in Pale Ale	186.Shrimps with Spiced Pineapples	187.Citrusy Salmon en Papilote	188.Easy Sweet-Soy Salmon
THUS	215.Instant Pot Steamed Cauliflower	216.Lemon Butter Broccoli	217.Sweet Potato Hash	354.Mocha Pudding Cake
FRI	258.Singaporean Prawn and Pork Ribs Noodle Soup	259.Chicken Wonton Soup	260.Instant Pot Mexican Chicken Tomato Soup	261.Instant Pot Chicken Rice Porridge
SAT	327.Chai Spiced Rice Pudding	328.Chinese Sausage on Brown Rice	298.Shrimp, Mushrooms & Asparagus Risotto	299.Wild Rice Pilaf

Instant Pot Meal Plan	The meal plan for 35th month			
	Week 1	Week 2	Week 3	Week 4
SUN	26.Ranch Dressed Bacon-Potato Brekky	27.Banana Bread for Breakfast	28.Slow Cooked Cinnamon-Oats	29.Another Breakfast Burrito Recipe
MON	72.PersianBeef Stew	73.Instant Pot Beef Curry	74.Instant Pot Beef Stew Bourguignon	353.Choco Fudge
TUE	355.Salted Choco Treat	165.Paleo Buffalo Chicken Chili	166.Buffalo Chicken Meatballs	167.Instant Pot Frozen Chicken
WED	189.Asparagus & Salmon with Buttered Garlic Sauce	190.Olive & Tuna Rigatoni	191.Orange-Ginger Sauce over Fish	192.Salmon Croquette

THUS	218.Indian Green Bean Curried Potatoes	219.Easy Rustic Lentil Soup	220.Organic Spinach Pasta	221.Vegan Pasta Puttanesca
FRI	262.New England clam chowder	263.Vegan Ginger Noodle Soup	356.Tapioca Pudding	264.Instant Pot Salmon Tortellini Soup
SAT	300.Pasta Puttanesca	301.Cheesy & Easy Beef Bowties	302.Fettucine Alfredo	303.Goulash

Instant Pot Meal Plan	The meal plan for 36th month			
	Week 1	Week 2	Week 3	Week 4
SUN	30.Easy-Cheesy Breakfast Egg Casserole	31.Broccoli and Egg Casserole	32.Scotch Eggs in Pressure Cooker	33.Buckwheat Porridge in Instant Pot
MON	78.Instant Pot Meatloaf	75.Instant Pot Shredded Beef	77.Chili Lime Steak Bowl	67.Italian Beef Dinner
TUE	106.Chinese Take-out General Tso's Chicken	107.Best Instant Pot Chicken Breast	108.Hawaiian Chicken Instant Pot	109.Honey Bourbon Chicken
WED	193.Dill & Lemon Salmon	194.Asian Style Salmon Soy-Free	195.Easy Tuna Pasta Casserole	196.Mahi-Mahi in Sweet Spicy sauce
THUS	222.Broccoli Macaroni and Cheese	223.Instant Pot Garlic Hummus	224.Cauliflower and Potato Soup	225.One-Pot Vegetarian Lentil Tortilla Soup
FRI	290.Instant Pot Taco Soup	291.En Caldo De Res Soup	292.Cream of Asparagus Soup	293.Sweet Potato, Black Bean, And Quinoa Chili Soup
SAT	332.Cranberry Nut Bread	301.Cheesy & Easy Beef Bowties	302.Fettucine Alfredo	303.Goulash

Measurement Conversion Charts

Volume Equivalents(Liquid)

US Standard	US Standard(Ounces)	Metric(Approximate)
2 tablespoons	**1 fl.oz.**	**30 mL**
1/4 cup	**2 fl.oz.**	**60 mL**
1/2 cup	**4 fl.oz.**	**120 mL**
1 cup	**8 fl.oz.**	**240 mL**
1 1/2 cup	**12 fl.oz.**	**355 mL**
2 cups or 1 pint	**16 fl.oz.**	**475 mL**
4 cups or 1 quart	**32 fl.oz.**	**1 L**
1 gallon	**128 fl.oz.**	**4 L**

Volume Equivalents (DRY)

US standard	Metric (Approximate)
1/8 teaspoon	**0.5 mL**
1/4 teaspoon	**1 mL**
1/2 teaspoon	**2 mL**
3/4 teaspoon	**4 mL**
1 teaspoon	**5 mL**
1 tablespoon	**15 mL**
1/4 cup	**59 mL**
1/2 cup	**118 mL**
3/4 cup	**177 mL**
1 cup	**235 mL**
2 cups	**475 mL**
3 cups	**700 mL**
4 cups	**1 L**

Weight Equivalents

US Standard	Metric (Approximate)
1/2 ounce	**15g**
1 ounce	**30g**
2 ounce	**60g**
4 ounce	**115g**
8 ounce	**225g**
12 ounce	**340g**
16 ounces or 1 pound	**455g**

Oven Temperatures

Fahrenheit (F)	Celsius(C) (Approximate)
250	**121**
300	**149**
325	**163**
350	**177**
375	**190**
400	**205**
425	**218**
450	**232**

Made in the USA
Middletown, DE
05 July 2019